The Notorious Luke Short

The Notorious Luke Short

Sporting Man of the Wild West

by
Jack DeMattos
and
Chuck Parsons

With a Foreword by Rick Miller

Number 16 in the A. C. Greene Series

Denton, Texas

Printed in the United States of America.

10 9 8 7 6 5 4 3 2 1

Permissions:

University of North Texas Press

1155 Union Circle #311336

Denton, TX 76203-5017

The paper used in this book meets the minimum requirements of the American National Standard for Permanence of Paper for Printed Library Materials, z39.48.1984. Binding materials have been chosen for durability.

Library of Congress Cataloging-in-Publication Data

DeMattos, Jack, 1944- author.

The notorious Luke Short : sporting man of the Wild West / by Jack DeMattos and Chuck Parsons ; with a foreword by Rick Miller. -- Edition: first.

pages cm. -- (Number 16 in the A.C. Greene series)

Includes bibliographical references and index.

ISBN 978-1-57441-594-0 (cloth : alk. paper) --

1. Short, Luke L., 1854-1893. 2. Gamblers--West (U.S.)--Biography. 3. Cowboys--West (U.S.)--Biography. 4. Frontier and pioneer life--West (U.S.) 5. West (U.S.)--Biography. I. Parsons, Chuck, author. II. Title. III. Series: A.C. Greene series ; no. 16.

F594.S565D46 2015

795.092--dc23

[B]

2015003807

978-1-57441-602-2 (ebook)

The Notorious Luke Short: Sporting Man of the Wild West is Number 16 in the A. C. Greene Series

The electronic edition of this book was made possible by the support of the Vick Family Foundation.

This biography is dedicated to Michael Wayne Short (November 30, 1957–August 1, 2010), the great-grandnephew of Luke Short and to his "soul mate" Judy Ohmer. The story of Michael and Judy began with their childhood in the Territory of Alaska and evolved into a special love relationship when they became adults. According to Judy: "Michael and I were never really sure when we became life partners or very significant others. We probably always were, but didn't know it until we were older." Judy has generously agreed to share Michael's collection of Short family photos with the authors, as well as Luke's marriage record, which she tracked down. Thanks to Judy and Michael, this biography will provide the first detailed account of an earlier romance between two people named Luke Short and Hattie Buck who also "became life partners or very significant others."

- *Jack DeMattos*
- *Chuck Parsons*

Table of Contents

List of Illustrations

FOREWORD

It's an iconic photograph—a group of stone-faced men, sitting and standing, staring stolidly back at the camera. There's no way to detect that it was a celebratory pose, an image of the "Dodge City Peace Commission" taken to celebrate the victory of one group of gamblers and hard cases over another, a competing group of similar ilk. At least two men in the group—Wyatt Earp and Bat Masterson—went on to achieve a singular notoriety and fame of their own, helped along by a healthy dose of fictional television exploitation in the 1960s. The rest, for the most part, became mere footnotes in the history of the gunfighter west.

Standing in the rear, the men to either side of him standing much taller, is the diminutive Luke Short. It was for his sake that the so-called "Dodge City War" occurred in the first place, but, for some reason he never quite achieved the prominence of Earp and Masterson. He had been a cowboy, scouted during the Indian wars, and evolved into a well-known gambler, or "sporting man," and was the survivor in two well-publicized gunfights. Like Earp and Masterson, he survived to die with "his boots off." Yet he is not placed in the pantheon of famous gunfighters, such as Earp, John Wesley Hardin, Ben Thompson, and others. He has remained one of those characters in the shadow of others, familiar only to the aficionados of the Old West.

Two primary biographies were previously published about Short, one in 1961 by William Cox, and another in 1996 by Wayne Short, the grandson of Luke's brother, Henry Jenkins Short. Unfortunately, there was no effort at legitimate research in the former and a high degree of fictionalizing in the latter. Neither is a reliable source on which to base an understanding of the life of Luke Short.

The "wild west" is a uniquely American institution, including not just gunfighters and gamblers, but cowboys, ranchers, farmers, railroaders, Indians, and the many thousands of individuals and families who trekked westward, encountering all of the obstacles that nature and man could throw in their path. The era of the men we call "gunfighters" was brief, probably less than twenty years or so, personified by such figures as James Butler "Wild Bill" Hickok, Henry McCarty alias "Billy the Kid," Wyatt Earp and his brothers, and perhaps even extending to Luke Short's dispatching of the deadly Jim Courtright.

Early on, the American public was fascinated by these larger-than-life men, that fascination fueled by a flood of many fictional accounts of their exploits. Hickok was lionized and credited with larger-than-life feats as early as 1867 in a popular national publication. In the 1880s and 1890s, cheaply printed pulp paper books perpetuated the myth of the Old West, enlarging on the legend and mythology of noted lawmen and outlaws. Jesse James killed seven or eight men with one bullet, as the story was told. Billy the Kid killed twenty-one men, one for every year of his life. Unfortunately those myths took on a life of their own, and were repeated in so-called legitimate accounts of these characters. Legend became fact, and the true nature of these men remained obscured. Even today, the general public is victimized by the output of so-called historians who pass their works off as credible, yet have not done the digging into primary sources necessary to support their conclusions. Such was the fate of Luke Short.

Enter Jack DeMattos and Chuck Parsons, two highly respected historians of the American gunfighter west. Jack is the author of six previous books on the subject of the Wild West, including a biography of the enigmatic gunfighter, David Allen "Mysterious Dave" Mather. He was also Historical Consultant for *Real West* magazine, for which he wrote (and illustrated) a series of fifty articles called "Gunfighters of the Real West" that ran from January 1978 until December 1985. Each article profiled a different gunfighter—both the well-known and the not-so-familiar, ranging alphabetically from Clay Allison to John Joshua Webb.

Chuck Parsons, also well-known to readers of the gunfighter west, left a career as a high school principal in Wisconsin to follow his passion for the Old West to the much sunnier climes of Texas. He has since established his credentials as a first-rate researcher, and has published well over a dozen books on the subject. He was the long-time editor of the *Quarterly* for the National Association for Outlaw and Lawman History, and also served as the "Answer Man" for *True West* magazine.

Most of these Old West figures did not leave a paper trail that would allow a historian a century later to simply tell their story. There are gaps, and even the recorded accounts may have been written incorrectly. Thus, there is a temptation for the would-be historian to fabricate something, even if mere speculation, to fill the gaps. Likewise, there is a tendency to take secondary sources at face value and repeat them as accurate. That has happened to Luke Short.

The reader of this book will quickly note that the authors have thoroughly sourced their information, and the reliability of the information can be evaluated readily. Where there are conflicts in the facts, those are laid out. A major effort was made to explore all available repositories relating to Short, many of which could not be accessed as recently as a decade ago. If there is any subjectivity or speculation as to what was happening, it is based on reasonable conclusions from the information provided. The authors provide a fine account of a man who, though small in stature, had the grit expected of a frontiersman, and who, though with flaws, stood up for his principles. In his major physical encounters, in which his life was on the line, he was defending himself and was not the aggressor.

However, unlike past accounts of Luke Short, the authors have gone beyond the violent episodes in which Short was involved and explored all of the facets of his existence. He was not just a gunfighter. Beyond handiness with a six-shooter, Luke Short more correctly was a prominent "sporting man," ultimately earning wealth through legitimate gambling activities, an avocation that was really frowned on in the 1800s by only the more moral minority in the community. The authors track his confrontations with those moral authorities as well as his gambling competitors in Fort Worth, which is included for the first time in any account of Short's life. But beyond gambling as traditionally thought of in the Old West—poker, roulette, faro, etc.—as well as running a prosperous saloon, Short also became a noted turfman in legitimate racing circles on the east coast with his own stable of horses, as well as prominently involved in promotion of prizefights, all of which is ably chronicled by the authors. When looking at Luke Short, the whole man, one gets a sense of respectability and gentility, not the tawdriness or pathological tendencies generally ascribed to the traditional "gunfighter."

This biography gives Luke Short the complete, definitive inspection as a whole man that he deserves and finally sets the record straight.

Rick Miller, Harker Heights, Texas

Acknowledgments

Bob Boze Bell, Cave Creek, AZ; Kathie Bell, Curator of Collections and Education, Boot Hill Museum, Dodge City, KS; John Boessenecker, San Francisco, CA; Robert K. DeArment,Sylvania, OH; Charles David Grear, New Braunfels, TX; Kathleen Holt, owner of the Cimarron Hotel where Luke Short and his wife stayed one night, Cimarron, KS; Robert G. McCubbin,Santa Fe, NM; Mike Meiers, Cimarron, KS; Leon C. Metz, El Paso, TX; Rick Miller, Harker Heights, TX; Judy Ohmer, Hereford, AZ; Bob Palmquist,Tucson, AZ; Chris Penn, Marsham, England; Gary L. Roberts, Tifton, GA; William B. Secrest, Fresno, CA; Rick Selcer, Fort Worth, TX; Nancy Sosa, Tombstone, AZ; Tom Todd, Show Low, AZ; Bob Wood, Hugo, MN; David Wright, Leadville, CO; and Roy B. Young, Apache, OK. And four who have gone on: Nyle H. Miller (1907-1988); Joseph G. Rosa (1932-2015); Dale T. Schoenberger (1939-1993); Joseph W. Snell (1928-2011).

Of course the staff at the University of North Texas Press are invaluable for trusting our work as adequate to preserve in book form: Ron Chrisman, Director of the UNT Press; Karen DeVinney, key editor; and the recently retired "girl Friday" for lack of a more professional sounding title, Paula Oates. Thank you for so much.

We would be negligent indeed if we did not thank our wives at this point, Sandi DeMattos and Pat Parsons, who may have often wondered what there was about a little gambler of the 19th century which could hold our fascination for such a long time. Thank you our dears for your patience and understanding. We're sure this won't happen again.

These are, with few exceptions, all people we've known for years; a few became new friends while researching this book. Each played an important role in preserving our history—that of the Wild West as well as of America—that Luke Short was part of. If we have overlooked someone, our apologies. Thank you one and all.

Jack DeMattos
Chuck Parsons

The Notorious Luke Short

Introduction

> "In no outward particular did this man indicate the cowboy by birth and training, the gambler by choice and the slayer of men by force of circumstances. And yet Luke Short did all that."
>
> —*Omaha Daily Bee*, September 12, 1893.

Luke Short was all those and more. He personified, as much as anyone could, the portion of our history that we call the "Wild West." By the age of nineteen this "cowboy by birth" had made several cattle drives from Texas to the Kansas railheads. Toward the end of the Indian wars he also served as a dispatch rider and civilian scout. There is no doubt that Luke Short was a "gambler by choice," since his choice was between the hard life of a cowboy, as opposed to the easier life of a "sporting man." A successful gambler could make more money in one lucky day than a cowboy would see in a lifetime.

Leadville, Tombstone, Dodge City, and Fort Worth are usually the first places that come to mind when Luke Short's career as a gambler is considered. In reality, the various kinds of gambling that Short pursued went far beyond the games played on green cloth in the cow-towns and the mining camps. He was considered an authority on horse racing and became a familiar figure at tracks in Chicago, Memphis, Louisville, and Saratoga Springs.

Finally, as the "slayer of men by force of circumstances," Short had survived Indian fights, in which some Indians didn't, and was also the last man standing in two of the most celebrated encounters in gunfighter history. Bat Masterson, one of those gunfighters *cum* lawmen *cum* journalist, whose fame also came from being a "slayer of men by force of circumstances" recalled, years later, that Luke was "a little fellow . . . about five feet, six inches in height, and weighing in the neighborhood of one hundred and forty pounds." Masterson admitted Short was "a small package, but one with great dynamic force."[1]

Rarely have two men had as much in common as Luke Short and Bat Masterson. Bat, like Luke, was an autodidact who came from a large family. Both had fought Indians, served as civilian scouts, and would become two of the best known sporting men in the United States. Both have been described as "gunfighters" —but both were bibliophiles who reached for a book far more often than they reached for their pistols.

Bat always had Luke's back. When Short was kicked out of Dodge City it was Bat who recruited Wyatt Earp, and several others, to get Luke reinstated. Once successful, Short, Masterson, Earp, and five others celebrated by posing for what has become one of the most reproduced of all historic Wild West photographs.

It was Bat who got Luke interested in the sport of boxing. Initially indifferent to the sport, Luke soon found himself being the referee of at least one match. Once hooked, he decided to become a boxing promoter. His offers to stage championship fights were taken very seriously by newspapers across the country and the fighters themselves. Short offered fantastic prize money and had the funds to back his offers up. When Bat was put in charge of a group of men to maintain order at the Sullivan-Kilrain Heavyweight Championship fight in 1889, he made Luke his second in command. Luke and Bat were also together, at ringside, for the championship fight between John L. Sullivan and "Gentleman Jim" Corbett in 1892.

Gunfighter, gambler, fisticuff referee—Luke Short was all, but he also had a romantic side, as witnessed by A. G. Arkwright in July of 1897. Arkwright wrote a memoir which was printed in the *New York Sun*, recalling that during a vacation he was taking at the Arkansas Hot Springs, "Luke Short came there, to the hotel where I was staying, with his wife, the beautiful and accomplished daughter of an Emporia [Kansas] banker, whom he married under romantic circumstances."[2]

She was indeed beautiful, as the two known photographs of her illustrate. The family did reside in Emporia when she met Luke Short—although her father was not a banker.[3] She was Hattie Beatrice Buck and she was the love of Luke Short's life. Hattie would accompany Luke in his travels all over the country. Together they were guests at some of the nation's most opulent hotels—establishments as far removed from the rude frontier lodgings of Luke's cowboy days as it was possible to get. Hattie was "Mrs. Luke Short" for the last seven years of Luke's life. She shared all of the good times and, to her credit, refused to leave his side when everything came crashing down.

"I wish they would find somebody else to write about," Short was quoted as saying to a Dallas newspaper man. "The only thing that consoles me is that the poor fellow who wrote it probably made a dollar or two."[4] At times Luke Short did provide good copy for the press.

Luke Short has been the subject of two books published in 1961 and 1996. Both books used the word "biography" in part of their titles. When confronted with an absence of facts, each of the biographers not only elected to "print the legend," but decided to improve upon it by adding wrinkles of their own. Within these pages, Luke Short will be presented as he really was, using documentation that appeared during his lifetime. Whenever possible, Luke will be allowed to speak for himself thanks to surviving letters, newspaper reports, and court documents.

"The notorious Luke Short" was a phrase newspapers frequently used to describe the man while he was alive. This is the story of the "little fellow" who inspired all that notoriety.

Chapter 1

The Cowboy by Birth

> "[Abilene] was a paradise of variety shows and gambling establishments.
> Every thing was wide open and every thing went."
> —*Dallas Morning News*, September 9, 1893.

The well-dressed man relaxed as the boot black polished his shoes at the White Elephant, the most elegant saloon-gambling house in Fort Worth. He always made it a point when at work to dress immaculately, to set the tone for others to follow. This night, February 8, 1887, was no exception. Luke Short was known by nearly everyone in that section of the Lone Star State as a polished but dangerous gambler who seemed to always be in control of his emotions and environment.

Now a friend approached and asked, "Luke, anything between you and Jim Courtright?" Short, never loquacious, simply thought a moment and answered, "Nothing." The matter was forgotten.

With shoes polished Short approached the bar to converse with a couple of friends. Then someone called out to him, a note of concern in his voice, "Oh, Luke." This was no doubt the typical annoyance that frequently plagued important people, someone always disturbing your quiet time.

Out into the vestibule Luke Short walked, calmly, then noticed Jim Courtright and Jake Johnson conversing, the former an acquaintance who had a reputation as a dangerous man with a gun, the latter among Luke's closest friends. What could the matter be now?

Short joined Johnson and Courtright on the sidewalk in front of the White Elephant. During their conversation Luke hooked his thumbs in the armholes of his vest, then dropped them to adjust his clothing. One always had to appear neatly dressed, no matter the occasion. Then Courtright said, "Well, you needn't reach for your gun" and immediately reached for his own revolver. When Short saw that movement, he knew the calm verbal exchange was over and it now was a matter of life and death. Luke pulled his pistol and began shooting—once, twice, three times, and then a fourth time. Courtright, for all his reputation as a deadly gunfighter and having initiated the gun play, failed to fire a single shot, yet he had anticipated the gunfight! How could he be not ready? Courtright fell at the first fire, his torso in the entrance to Ella Blackwell's shooting gallery. His feet were on the sidewalk. How ironic.

Jim Courtright, the notorious two gun gambler-gunfighter with a reputation of having killed several men, now lay dying. Luke Short, who also had a reputation as a gunfighter-gambler, stood over the dying man, pondering why he couldn't be left alone.

* * * * *

There is seemingly no end to the long trail of erroneous information concerning Luke L. Short. Rather appropriately, it starts with controversy over the actual date and place of his birth. In 1961 William R. Cox published his biography of Short, claiming that Luke had been born in Mississippi.[1] After the publication of the Cox book nearly every historian writing on Luke L. Short gave Luke's birthplace as Mississippi.[2]

The Mississippi connection was amplified in 1980 with the appearance of a then seventy-one-year-old man who claimed that Luke L. Short was his grandfather. According to that man, who called himself "Luke Lamar Short II," the original "Luke Lamar Short" was born on February

19, 1854, near Laurel, Mississippi. None of this turned out to be true. The man calling himself Luke L. Short's grandson was an imposter. The real Luke L. Short was not born anywhere in Mississippi. He was not born on February 19, 1854, and there is absolutely no proof, beyond the claims of a bogus grandson, that Luke L. Short's middle name was Lamar.[3]

In 1996 a second biography of Luke L. Short appeared.[4] It was written by Wayne Short, the grandson of Henry Jenkins Short (1859–1917), Luke's younger brother. The book reads more like a novel than a biography. Wayne Short readily admitted on his opening page that he had "recreated dialogue in places in the interest of the story." Wayne Short does give the correct state where Luke was born. This is ironic, considering that he was the man supposedly responsible for the Mississippi information contained in the William R. Cox biography.[5]

According to his own testimony, Luke L. Short was born in Polk County, Arkansas, on January 22, 1854.[6] His parents, Josiah Washington Short and Hetty Brumley, were both born in Tennessee.[7] They were married in Arkansas City, Arkansas, during 1846. As it happens, Arkansas City is located near the border of Mississippi. This would be as close to Mississippi came to playing any role in the story of Luke L. Short's birth.

Soon after their wedding Josiah and Hetty Short moved to Polk County, Arkansas. Polk County is located on the western side of Arkansas, on the border of present-day Oklahoma. Josiah and Hetty's first child, Martha Francis Short, was born in Polk County April 10, 1847. She was followed by John Pleasant Short, born there in Polk County on September 5, 1848. The four members of the Short family that then existed were recorded on the 1850 United States Federal Census.[8]

The next child to arrive was Josiah Short, born in Polk County on May 30, 1851. He was followed by Young P. Short, born during November of 1852. Luke L. Short was next in line, born there on January 22, 1854. Catherine came next on February 19, 1856, followed by Henry Jenkins on February 15, 1859. He was the last of the Short children born in Polk County. Shortly after his birth the Short family, now consisting of nine members, moved to Montague County, Texas, two counties north of Tarrant County, where Luke Short would gain fame as a sporting man in county seat Fort Worth. The family was recorded there on the 1860 Federal Census.[9]

The final three Short children were all born in Texas: George Washington, born March 8, 1863; Belle Nannie, born March 24, 1864; and William B., born October 21, 1867. Two family members were unaccounted for when the 1870 census was taken. The family then consisted of ten members living at home.[10] It is noteworthy that the 1850, 1860, and 1870 Federal Census records support the Short family residence in Arkansas. There is no mention of the family living in Mississippi in any of those official records. In addition the 1860 and 1870 census records clearly state that Luke L. Short was born in Arkansas.

Luke Short never wrote an autobiography—but he did sit for two separate interviews in which he provided biographical sketches of his early life. The first occasion was on March 19, 1886, when he gave six pages of dictation to George H. Morrison, a researcher employed by historian Hubert Howe Bancroft (see appendix A).[11] The second occasion came when Short agreed to provide information for an article to be published in the March 15, 1890, issue of the *National Police Gazette.* When published, it profiled "Luke L. Short, the Famed Indian Fighter and Sporting Man," and offered "A History of His Life" (see appendix C). These remain especially valuable documents as they present the earliest known accounts of Luke's boyhood years in Texas, 1855–1869, and are probably more accurate than any written after his death.

Luke told the reporter that he had gone to Texas in 1858 at the age of four years, and gave his birth date as January 22, 1854. Curiously, the interview appeared in the third person, as if perhaps the *National Police Gazette* reporter took notes during the conversation and later presented it as such rather than providing it verbatim. "His parents settled in Gainesville, in Cooke County, then a small trading post" one learns, when the "country was full of Indians" including Apache, Kiowa, and

Comanche, "all of the most warlike character." Due to living in these surroundings young Luke Short "was very early inured to hardships and twice, when a mere boy, saw his father severely wounded by marauding Indians." J. W. Short, Luke's father, "purchased a large block of land lying on Elm Fork of the Trinity River . . . and went into the cattle business. Soon after he moved to the adjoining county of Montague." Only two years after the Civil War ended a greater fear covered the lands where white settlers intended to make their homes. In 1867 a raid resulted in many atrocities, which had a deep effect on young Luke Short.[12] A family, "consisting of a mother and four girls was captured, and the mother and the three older girls [were] parceled out to three other tribes. The baby girl was brained in sight of a few settlers, who were intrenched [*sic*] within a stockade." It is not clear if Luke Short witnessed this atrocity or if he merely learned of it later.

If he had not witnessed any of this slaughter he certainly recalled the one he did witness, which was in 1862. Luke's first encounter with Indians, according to the interview, "never left his mind. His father had gone out some distance from the house, when he was attacked by Indians." An elder brother, whether it was John, Josiah, or Young P. Short was not made clear to the *Gazette* reporter, went to his father's assistance, "but found that the bullets in the pouch which he carried did not fit the rifle. The father had been wounded twice in the head with arrows and severely lanced in the back." When young Short reached his father with the rifle he had to explain that the bullets did not fit. The father, thinking fast, took the rifle and told his son to go back to the house for the other gun; then "[f]einting at the savages with the useless rifle, the father stood them off." While this action took place Luke was in the yard and saw his brother come up, yelling for the rifle. But the "nervy little fellow ran into the house and finding he could not lift the rifle dragged it out and got it to his brother. His father came up about this time bleeding of wounds and Luke was so horrified that he started to run into the house, but seeing his mother run to his father's assistance he went also." The elder brother and his father then managed to drive the Indians away. It was in 1869 when Luke was old enough to take part in his first Indian fight, "when the red skins burned houses, killed women and children and devastated the country. After that he was in over thirty Indian engagements and became noted as a splendid shot, cool and nervy man, and brave to a fault."[13]

Luke, in 1869, was fifteen and began work as a cowboy as so many young men did in Texas at that time. It was the most logical start for a "cool and nervy man, and brave to a fault" as any individual who knew him would verify. In addition to beginning his working experience as a cowboy he began to deal in and speculate in livestock and cotton. This would not be unusual for a young ambitious man in his mid-teens like Luke Short in 1869.[14] Indeed, from 1869 to 1875 Luke was engaged in the cattle business and made several drives to Kansas. In those days being a drover was quite a desperate undertaking, with "both Indians and cowboys being pretty wild."[15]

One of the cowboys who could be "pretty wild" —if not the wildest of them all—was John Wesley Hardin. Both the eighteen-year-old "Wes" Hardin and the seventeen-year-old Luke Short were cowboys on cattle drives from Texas to Abilene, Kansas, in 1871. They rode with different outfits, and while one is tempted to consider them at least acquaintances, there is no proof that they ever met. A person Hardin and Short both knew, however, was Jacob Christopher "Jake" Johnson, a twenty-three-year-old cattleman in 1871, who was Hardin's boss. Fifteen years later Jake Johnson was one of Fort Worth's wealthiest citizens and a business partner of Luke Short; Hardin then was a prisoner in Huntsville penitentiary.

The earliest known account of Luke Short's activities in Abilene appeared in one of his obituaries, which offered this description of the town. "Abilene . . . was a great town not so many years ago" the account began. "It was the cattle outfitting station for the panhandle and the Indian Territory. Thither went the cowboy of the early times to blow in his wages and blow up the town. It was a paradise of variety shows and gambling establishments. Everything was wide open and everything went."[16] In the 1890s John Wesley Hardin recorded his memoirs of the cowboy days and his description of Abilene was similar. "I have seen many fast towns," Hardin recalled, "but I think Abilene beat them all. The town was filled with sporting men and women, gamblers, cowboys, desperadoes, and the like. It was well supplied with bar rooms, hotels, barber shops, and gambling houses, and every thing was open."[17]

Like Wes Hardin, Luke Short was, "scarcely more than a boy, took his chances with the rest" in the wild town of Abilene. Short, assured the reporter, "was known even then as a daring gambler who would stake his last cent on the turn of a card. He was a man of unquestioned courage, capable of holding his own with the wild spirits who resorted there." Short had a "quiet, easy manner [which] made him friends. He never sought a quarrel, but he never allowed anybody to tread on his toes, and once the fighting spirit was aroused there was nothing more to be dreaded than Luke Short." With a hint of regret, the reporter concluded his obituary stating that there was no record of Short getting into any serious trouble in Abilene, but possibly a few shooting scrapes "such as were common in those days is all. Nobody was killed."[18] Apparently, in this reporter's mind, if there was not a corpse following a gunfight it did not amount to "serious trouble."

It is impossible to accurately chart Luke Short's youthful travels during his cowboy period. He moved around a lot, as he would throughout his life, and often turned up in unlikely places. One incident that attracted attention took place in New Mexico when he was still a teenager. The exact date cannot be determined, but the incident in question most likely happened sometime in 1872. Years afterward a Chicago newspaper reporter recalled the event, which unfortunately leaves numerous questions that cannot be answered.

"It was in New Mexico that Luke Short first attracted public attention by a cool display of bravery" the *Inter Ocean* reporter began his tale.[19] The first United States Court in New Mexico was established at Socorro, located in Socorro County. "In this border town and the surrounding country" he wrote, setting the stage, "were hundreds of rough men who had lived so long outside the pale of civilization that they were almost as savage as the Apache and Comanche Indians who inhabited that part of the country." If the reader did not yet appreciate the conditions, the reporter made it clear that those characters "had been in the habit of making and enforcing their own laws." Finally the court was organized, which consisted of a judge from Arkansas, a young lawyer from Kansas, who was to act as the U.S. attorney, and a deputy marshal from an unidentified New Mexico mining camp. The first case was speedily concluded. After several days of additional court matters running "smoothly," a case was called which, if testimony was presented honestly and accurately, would "result in the punishment of a prominent citizen for murder." The case supposedly hinged on the testimony of one man who was friendly to the prosecution, and of course when called to the stand great excitement was evident in the rude courtroom. Tension filled the air. When a question of "vital importance" was posed the witness "hesitated, and seemed not fully to understand what had been asked of him." The judge ordered the attorney to ask the question again and make it "more explicit."

Then a voice came from "a miner of powerful build" who was among friends in the crowd, only a few feet from the prosecutor. The miner stated firmly: "If you ask that question again you will not live to hear the answer." As this miner spoke, a half-dozen men drew their revolvers, cocking them, which seemingly gave great emphasis to the words he had uttered. Then there was silence in the courtroom. The young attorney slowly turned. He now faced the uncouth audience, thought a few moments before speaking and said: "When I came here, I fully realized the danger that strict fidelity to duty would bring upon me. I left at home a young wife, whom I had hoped to see again, but if there is a man here who will tell her that I died doing my duty, I will repeat the question." Did any man in that courtroom realize the significance of those brave words?

At least one individual did. He had heard the brave words and arose in the center of the hall. He was "a young man, smooth of face, with a slim figure and in fact the general appearance of a boy just from school." But the onlookers could see that "in the pale face and sharp eyes of the young man" they could read the "decision and fearlessness" in his demeanor. He spoke with a calm and steady voice: "I am a stranger here, but if you ask that question and die, and I live, I will tell your wife that you died doing your duty; more I will tell her that you did not die alone." As Luke Short finished his brief statement, "he drew from his belt that every man in that country wore, a brace of revolvers which he held ready for use." The clicking of his weapons was the only sound heard in the courtroom. That same question was repeated without hesitation by the attorney and the witness answered. The guilt of the prisoner was established, he was convicted, and began to serve his life sentence in a Western United States penitentiary.

The young prosecutor was William Patrick Hackney,[20] who became one of the leading attorneys of the west. The young man "who supported justice in so fearless a manner" was Luke Short, who had "since gained a reputation throughout the West as a man to whom fear is unknown."[21]

In his 1886 dictation Luke said that he went to Kansas in 1873 and remained there about a year. He claimed he spent the year in Coffeyville where the "general condition of affairs to be found in frontier communities" included "some lawlessness."[22] Whether Luke contributed to any of that lawlessness he declined to say. After leaving Coffeyville Luke returned to Texas. From Texas he moved on to the Black Hills in 1876.

Chapter 2

Tall Tales and Short Facts

> "[Luke Short] could ride a broncho and throw a lariat; he could shoot both fast and straight, and was not afraid."
>
> W. B. "Bat" Masterson in *Human Life*, April 1907.

Luke Short told researcher George H. Morrison that he went "to the Black Hills in 1876" but remained there only a short time. The "state of society" in the Hills was anything but good, at least as perceived by Short who certainly was capable of making such judgment calls. Horse thieves and reckless characters abounded. In 1877 he left the Black Hills to go to Ogallala, Nebraska, which was then considered one of the largest shipping points in the west. The "state of society" there was also in a "rude state." Luke described it as being "infested with a reckless class of society."[1] There would be those who claimed that Luke Short himself was part of that "reckless class of society" in Nebraska. Perhaps he was; if so he was comfortable in that element of society.

The stories that were told vary widely and were written years after the period that Luke was in Nebraska. The one thing that these tales have in common is that they usually involve either a train or a railroad station. The earliest known version appeared in a long article published in the

Portland Oregonian on November 23, 1884. That article was devoted to the career of William Henry Harrison Llewellyn and was mainly concerned with his role in the capture of James M. "Doc" Middleton, a notorious horse-thief. W. H. H. Llewellyn had had considerable good fortune in his career fighting desperadoes. According to the article, Llewellyn had "arrested single-handed, Luke Short, the man who lately inaugurated a reign of terror at Dodge City, Kansas."[2]

Superintendent J. T. Clark of the Union Pacific had ordered M. F. Leech, a capable detective, to trail Short. Leech had been doing so for some time. One day he received word that his quarry was to reach North Platte on a certain train to meet "some of his confederates." Leech described Short as the toughest kind of tough man, and advised Clark "to have a small army on hand to arrest him." Thirty men were sent to North Platte to achieve that goal, and among them was Llewellyn. The day was cold and the train was very late. Because of these factors the "small army" found warmth and comfort in their bottles, and soon became drowsy. Llewellyn, apparently not a drinking man in this situation, told them to "catch a little sleep and he would awaken them when the train arrived." But, after thinking the matter over he changed his mind and decided to arrest Short alone. When the train did arrive, Short—"the desperado"—stepped off and started across the tracks to warm up in a saloon. Llewellyn, "then a beardless stripling"[3] followed Short, "and as Short turned to see who was behind him, covered him with his revolver, made him throw up his hands and marched him off to jail." Several hours later, when Llewellyn's assistants woke up intending now to hunt and capture the notorious Short, they were "chagrined" to find that Llewellyn "had stolen a march on them and arrested the terror of the plains alone."[4]

The next known account moved the action from North Platte to Ogallala, Nebraska. Once again a train was involved. Millard Fillmore Leech moved to the lead role in this version.[5] Leech recalled the incident took place in July of 1876 when Jay Gould came to Ogallala in his private car to inspect the cattle of Keith and Barton. With Gould were Sydney

Dillon, Guy C. Barton, M. C. Keith, and Supt. J. T. Clark of the Union Pacific.

> About an hour before the Gould train arrived I was informed by a little fellow named Frenchy, who stood in with the toughs, that a band of men had organized for the purpose of kidnapping Jay Gould on his arrival. In the gang were George Crandall, who acted as leader, Luke Short, William Phoebus, William Harris, alias Missouri Bill and Sam Brown.
>
> I got together a posse and locked the gang up and kept them locked up until after Mr. Gould had left. He was in Ogallala about four hours. At the request of Supt. Clark we kept the matter quiet, as he was afraid if Gould heard of it he would be backward about continuing his journey.

Leech added further interest to the tale explaining that about three weeks after this incident the gang went to his house in Ogallala, threatening to kill him. "I was away," he explained, "but they got my old father and mother out of bed and made my father dance for them while they shot around his feet." [6]

To accept this yarn, one has to believe that five men were arrested and imprisoned for a crime they *might* commit. Since they hadn't been charged with a crime, and apparently had no outstanding warrants against them, they were released as soon as Gould left town. It is no surprise that Leech claimed that "we kept the matter quiet." One is left to wonder why it took three weeks for the five "toughs" to go to the Leech house in Ogallala. The folks back in Nebraska didn't have to wonder. Two days after the article appeared in the *New York World*, the *Omaha World Herald* of February 25, 1895, offered a response, headlining its report a "fairy tale" by Leech. "M. F. Leech, formerly an operator and detective of the Union Pacific, was interviewed by a *New York World* reporter a few days ago" began the report intended to belittle Leech's veracity. It explained that Leech had "frustrated" a plan to abduct Joy Gould when he arrived in Ogallala. Supposedly Leech heard of the scheme and "arrested the entire gang and kept them in jail until Mr. Gould had departed." This was supposed to have occurred in July of 1876, and was accepted as a "fairy yarn" around Union Pacific headquarters, told "just to be entertaining." The Omaha newspaper continued, pointing out to its readers that Leech would be remembered "as the hero of the Big Spring[s] train robbery of twenty years ago." After trailing the robbers and then secreting himself in their camp he was able to provide information which led to the eradication of the notorious Sam Bass and his gang.[7]

The most famous account of Luke Short's Nebraska years was written in 1907 by Bat Masterson in one of a series of articles he wrote for the periodical, *Human Life*.[8] The events Bat described would have been nearly thirty years in the past, assuming they had happened the way Bat described them. The real question is whether they happened at all. Bat described how Luke had "no sooner reached the northern boundary line of Nebraska hard by the Sioux Indian reservation, than he established what he was pleased to call a 'trading ranch.'" Luke's intent of course was to trade with the Sioux Indians, whose reservation was "just across the line in North Dakota."[9] Wrote Bat, obviously forgetting that between Nebraska and North Dakota was a large amount of acreage known as South Dakota, that "[i]nstinctively he [Short] knew that the Indians loved whiskey, and as even in those days he carried on his shoulders something of a commercial head, he conceived the idea that a gallon of whiskey worth ninety cents was not a bad thing to trade an Indian for a buffalo robe worth ten dollars. Accordingly Luke proceeded to lay in a goodly supply of 'Pine Top,' by which the whiskey traded to the Indians in exchange for their robes was known."[10]

Masterson, the gunfighter-journalist, rambled on for a few more paragraphs describing how "drunken bands of young bucks were regularly returning to their villages from the direction of the Short rendezvous, loaded to the muzzle with 'Pine Top'." It didn't take long, in Bat's version, for an alarmed Indian Agent to notify his superiors in Washington as to what was happening. The agent got quick service, for that time and place. Bat reported that the military commander at Omaha soon got an entire company of cavalry after Luke Short. As no one informed the trader that the company was after him, he soon found himself a prisoner in the hands of the government. Masterson described the incident as if he had been there, that his old friend Luke Short "was alone in his little dugout was cooking his dinner, when the soldiers arrived." He was quickly made a prisoner of the government. His crime he was rudely informed was for having unlawfully traded whiskey to the Indians. Soon, everything around the "ranch" resembling whiskey had been destroyed by the commanding officer; Short was tied to a government horse, "his feet fastened with a rope underneath the animal's girth" and was placed in the center of the company, preventing all means of escape. The entire group headed for Sidney arriving there in time to catch the Overland train. Short was "hustled aboard with as little ceremony as possible."

But Luke Short did not submit humbly to this arrest. By his "quiet and diffident manner during the short time he had been prisoner" he had succeeded in having the officer regard him as a "harmless little adventurer, who really did not seem capable . . . of committing a crime or escaping and for this reason did not have him handcuffed or shackled, after placing him aboard the train for Omaha." And what was Luke Short thinking as he rode the rails? "I can beat this for sure," he said to himself, "but supposing the agent should take a notion to call a count of heads. What then? I know there are several young bucks, whom I caught trying to steal my 'Pine Top,' who will not be there to answer roll-call, in case one is ordered. I planted those bucks myself, and, outside of my partner, no one knows the location of the cache." Instead of explaining how Luke Short escaped from the hands of the military, Masterson continued telling his readers that "Luke did not tarry long with the soldiers after the train left Sidney." Somehow he and his unidentified partner managed to obtain "a big span of mules" conveniently hitched to a canvas-covered wagon and were quickly on their way to Colorado. The irony is that if the mule thieves had been captured by the owner a frontier necktie party may have been the result. Good mules were more valuable than horses. This supposedly happened in the fall of 1878.[11]

As it happened, Luke actually was very much involved with the military during the fall of 1878, not as a prisoner but as one who played a much more heroic role. Between October 6 and October 8, 1878, Short was employed as a dispatch courier from Ogallala to Major Thomas Tipton Thornburgh who was in the field. Short was paid $30 for his service. From October 9 to October 20, 1878, Luke served as a civilian scout for Thornburgh. He enlisted at Sidney, Nebraska, at a rate of $100 a month. He only served twelve days and was paid $40 for his service.[12]

The earliest known account of Luke Short's service was given by Luke himself in his March 19, 1886, dictation, in which he inflated his pay rate, but did get the year of 1878 correct. According to his account he was with the expedition under Major Thornburgh. That group started out after the Cheyenne, and only two days before the departure, Short received news that the Sioux had also broken out. Short followed Thornburgh and took the position of scout as he knew the country thoroughly. He was furnished with a fine horse and offered $15.00 per day, which was accepted. Soon after starting out Short met two returning soldiers who with others had been left to guard some ambulances and who had been drawn away by the Indians. The soldiers tried to deter Short from continuing, telling him awful stories of what the hostiles had done, but Luke was not frightened and continued. Two days later he caught up with Thornburgh who "was very much delighted to see him as he was really lost" as his own scouts did not know the territory. A fresh horse was made available for Short and he was ordered to "circle the command" which he refused to do as he had been two days and nights in the saddle without rest. According to Short, Thornburgh said, "You must go[;] you are getting $15 per day." Short replied, "I don't care if I was getting $1500.00 per day. I can't go tonight." Major Thornburgh accepted this, and became "his fast friend from that time to the day of his death."[13]

Short tells a similar story about his service as a dispatch rider in the previously mentioned biography of him printed in the *National Police Gazette* on March 15, 1890. According to Short's recollection, in 1878, the Northern Cheyenne "broke loose from Fort Reno in the Indian Territory, and passing back to Dakota they murdered many people in Kansas on the way."[14] Major Thornburgh led a command of 500 men in pursuit. Then word came from General Crook's headquarters in Omaha, from the Rosebud Agency, that "the Sioux were coming down 7,000 strong from the north on Thornburg [*sic*], and that he would be massacred."[15]

According to Short in the 1890 account, the news was telegraphed to Ogallala and the commander there was instructed to send a courier to Thornburgh "at once" with dispatches notifying him of the danger. No one knew the trail but Luke Short. He was to go to Thornburgh with the news. At 2:00 in the morning Luke started out; at 9:00 the next night, after more than 200 miles, horse and rider arrived nearly dead. Luke Short delivered the valuable messages and Thornburgh, who had no idea of the danger he was in, realized that due to Short's exhaustive work he had "saved the lives of 500 men." Short remained with Thornburgh "until the last Cheyenne had been captured and carried back to the reservation."[16] Whether these two incidents are actually the same one, Short and Thornburgh became friends.

In truth the friendship between the major and the scout wasn't a long one. On September 29, 1879, while leading a command of cavalry to rescue settlers under attack by Ute warriors, Thornburgh and thirteen of his soldiers were ambushed and massacred. This happened at Milk Creek, near present-day Craig, Colorado.[17] At the time of Thornburgh's death, Luke Short was also in Colorado, but by then he was honing his skills as a gambler in Leadville.

Luke Short's obituary in Fort Worth's *Gazette* indicated that his career as a scout began much earlier than the October 6–20, 1878, service under Thornburgh. According to the *Gazette*, "he was one of the bravest and most trusted scouts in the employ of the government, and many a time while acting in this capacity he showed acts of bravery, which then distinguished him as 'The bravest scout in the government employ.'" The paean of praise continued. "He traveled over a wild country on many different occasions where other men had refused to go. He was in the employ of the government for several years and retired from service some time in the 70's."[18]

The *Omaha Daily Bee* also provided an obituary for Luke Short that offered an account of Luke's "most famous feat of arms" as a government scout and Indian fighter, which predated his Thornburgh service by more than two years. According to the *Daily Bee*, Short entered the service as a scout in 1876 "when the trouble between the United States troops and the Sioux Indians was on." After attaching himself to General Crook's command he went into the Black Hills country where "his most famous feat of arms was performed." He was carrying dispatches from headquarters to "a distant outpost one day" when a band of fifteen Indians attacked him. They had hidden themselves among the crags in the foothills, some distance from Short's destination. "The first intimation he had of their presence, as he rode by, was to hear the crack, crack of their rifles and the singing of the bullets around his head. Putting spurs to his horse, he rode straight in the direction of the outpost, turning in the saddle to look for the redskins. Soon they appeared from behind the crags, all riding straight for him. Short returned their fire and dropped the three foremost in quick succession with as many bullets." This was not exciting enough, and the reporter continued: "The survivors urged their ponies and two better mounted and bolder than the others were closing in on him." The brave scout, "deliberately checking his horse's pace," turned in his saddle and "dropped the two Indians, one after the other." The band of fifteen warriors was now but ten and those ten "became cautious and contented themselves with taking long distance shots at the scout, who was soon out of range and safe in camp with his dispatches." Short reportedly remained with General Crook's troops "until Sitting Bull was captured."[19]

Obviously the roles as portrayed by Bat Masterson in his 1907 account of Luke Short peddling "Pine Top" compared to the reports of him and his scouting heroics—including the unerring marksmanship by a man riding a horse against other men riding horses—defies credibility. As with all obituaries, it is not difficult to laud the deceased with actions he never did perform. Who will disagree? Whatever role he really played was over by late 1878 in any case. Luke Short was a man who would constantly reinvent himself. The time had come for Luke to try something new, involving less physical effort and greater financial rewards.

Chapter 3

The Gambler by Choice

> "Today the monotony was broken by the shooting of Chas. Storms by Luke Short on [the] corner of [the] Oriental."
>
> George Whitwell Parsons' *Diary*, February 25, 1881.

Short's 1886 interview with George H. Morrison provides us with the details of his next move after he left scouting for the army. To quote from this six-page document, "In the fall of 1878 he returned to Ogallala, Nebraska and in 1879 went to Leadville" he began, pointing out that Leadville was so crowded at this time that Short paid $25.00 a week just for a place to sleep. "There was more money in circulation at that time than the subject of these remarks ever saw before in all his travels. There was a good deal of betting & shooting [.] [T]here were courts of law in operation yet there were men hung for jumping lots [,] for attempting to rob somebody and for such minor offenses."[1] There were no examples given of what were considered "minor offenses." Morrison's handwritten notes describe the atmosphere in Leadville that would have attracted a risktaker like Luke Short:

> In 1879 there was an election for officers of Leadville and a gambler and candidate for Mayor and Mr. Short saw miners peddling

> tickets and calling out to the voters to come vote the gamblers and miners ticket. This shows the condition of the public mind. During all this time there was no one in distress for money was generally plenty. The New York capitalists were in there with money and the Little Pittsburg[2] and other mines were turning out more carbon than was ever turned out of any one place of like size and under like circumstances.[3]

Short's obituary suggests he may have opened a gambling place on State Street in Leadville, as such a business provided the excitement that Luke thrived on. He traveled from place to place, wherever the fever spread and "his luck was good."[4] This is a fairly accurate description of the man, but it has not been confirmed by other sources that he opened "a gambling place on State Street."

In a third source of information about what Luke might have been doing in Leadville, Bat Masterson provided an account in 1907 that may be more accurate than it first appears. Certainly Bat's earlier story concerning Luke selling "Pine Top" to Indians does not stand up to close scrutiny—but when Masterson wrote about Short in Leadville there was a more authentic feeling, despite Bat's use of invented dialogue. "Luke went to Leadville," Bat wrote, "where everything was then on the boom. Here he began to associate with a class of people far different in manner, taste and dress from those he had been accustomed to." Is the feeling of verisimilitude present in this passage because Bat was writing of his own experience as well as Luke's? He continued, describing how Luke was "thrown into the society of rich mine buyers, as well as mining promoters." It was here that Luke got acquainted with gamblers and the keepers of the mining camp "honkytonks."

> The whole thing was a new life to him, and he took to it like a duck to water. It was the first place where he saw the game of faro dealt, and he was fascinated. He was not long in camp before he was talked about. He ran afoul of a bad man with a gun one day in one of the camp's prominent gambling houses, and the bad man, who had a record of having killed someone somewhere, attempted

> to take some sort of liberty with one of Luke's bets and, when the latter politely requested the bad man to keep his hands off, the bad man became very angry and made some rude remarks.[5]

The dealer, probably anticipating gun fire or at least costly damage to his layout if the matter turned into a brawl, was "frightened half out of his wits."

> He looked to see Short shot full of holes before any one could raise a hand to prevent it. The dealer, of course, didn't have Luke's number. He knew the other fellow, but had yet to become acquainted with the late vendor of "Pine Top" up Nebraska way.

In an effort to smooth matters over, the dealer said, "in his most suave manner, 'I will make the amount of the bet good, rather than have a quarrel.'"

But Luke responded: "You will not make anything good to me. That is my bet, and I will not permit anyone to take it."

In Masterson's lively telling, Luke's antagonist now "growled" out a threat: "You insignificant little shrimp. I will shoot your hand off, if you dare put it on that bet."

> But he didn't. Nor did he get his own pistol out of his hip pocket. For, quicker than a flash, Luke had jammed his own pistol into the bad man's face and pulled the trigger, and the bad man rolled over on the floor. The bullet passed through his cheek but, luckily, did not kill him. There was no arrest or trial. Such things [were] happening all the time in those days in Leadville.[6]

Once again, Masterson elected "to state the story briefly." His account is so purposely vague that it defies challenge. Luke's antagonist is identified only as a "bad man who had a record of killing someone somewhere." Bat notes that incidents like this were "happening all the time in those days in Leadville." Apparently the shooting wasn't considered noteworthy. A search of the Leadville newspapers has failed to produce any mention of the incident. As before, subsequent writers have tried to "improve" upon what Bat wrote. In 1940 Stewart H. Holbrook took Bat Masterson's unnamed "bad man" and christened him "Brown." Holbrook then decided to kill off bad man Brown—rather than have him merely wounded by Luke. According to Holbrook, Brown "became more abusive and finally drew his gun, thinking to frighten the sad little fellow. Luke shot him as quietly as possible, between the eyes, before Brown could pull his own trigger." Holbrook did not explain how Luke shot Brown "quietly" but did state that Luke was heard to say that "he hated the sound of shooting."[7]

William R. Cox, Luke's 1961 biographer, clearly took the ball thrown by Bat Masterson and ran with it. Cox added some wrinkles of his own, such as having Luke draw his Colt from a "leather-lined pocket." Cox also used Holbrook's name "Brown," but essentially it was the same account as Bat's.[8] The story continued to evolve over the years, culminating in this bizarre offering fourteen years later.

> During the Leadville days Luke was provoked into putting a Derringer ball between the eyes of a trouble-maker named Isaac Brown when the latter tried to break up Luke's faro game—a killing that may be termed the "highlight" of Luke's somewhat uneventful Colorado days.[9]

It turns out that Luke Short's "somewhat uneventful Colorado days" may have been more eventful than previously imagined. Nearly a half century after Short was in Leadville, Cyrus Wells "Doc" Shores wrote an account for a Denver newspaper[10] that linked Short to a notorious character named Jim Clark. According to Doc Shores, one time he and Jim Clark went into Leadville and "did quite a bit of business in high grading." At that time the stagecoaches were running into Leadville loaded down with passengers. A "man named Luke Short" came to him and borrowed his double barreled shotgun. Short and another man then went down to the head of California Gulch, south of Leadville, and robbed the passengers.

When Luke Short brought back his double barreled shotgun one night, Clark was out of the cabin, but Short left it with a roll of bills sticking out the muzzle of the shot gun, as well as a note saying, "This will buy some cartridges for your gun." Shores recalled Short as "a small, well built, dark complected nice looking fellow. . . . Any of the old timers will remember Luke Short of Dodge City and different places in the west as a courageous gambler and killer."[11]

There is no known record of Luke Short being charged with holding up a stage and robbing passengers in the Leadville area, or anywhere else, which is not to say that such a crime did not happen. If indeed it did happen the way Shores described it, then Luke got away with the robbery, or possibly such a crime was committed by someone using Luke's name.

On June 1, 1880, United States Census enumerator W. W. Orrick visited household number forty-eight in the community of Buena Vista, Chaffee County, Colorado.[12] Buena Vista was a community some thirty miles from Leadville. Number forty-eight was the residence of someone identified only as M. Murphy, a fifty-year-old liquor dealer. Four others resided there: Rick M. Rumsey and his wife H. P., John D. Rumsey, and Luke Short, twenty-six years of age and born in Texas. This young man, who by now apparently considered himself a Texan, gave his occupation as clerk as had John D. Rumsey. Were Luke and John Rumsey both clerks in the Murphy liquor establishment, or somewhere else, in Buena Vista? Perhaps Luke had a regular job as a clerk but did gambling on an occasional basis. Luke Short did not get into any trouble in Buena Vista so far as known. According to his interview with Morrison, he left Colorado later that month and went to Kansas City.[13]

He was there only a few months when he did get into trouble. According to the *Kansas City Star* a Texan identified as John Jones "was swindled out of $280 on three card monte by one Luke Short, who is now in the calaboose." Two days later the *Star* added further news of the incident, and shared its view of the legal profession at the same time.

> It has been noticed and commented upon that no confidence man has ever suffered in Kansas City the full sentence of anything like the full sentence imposed by law. The last case resembles its predecessors, inasmuch as justice is liable to be thwarted by a keen lawyer. This is the case of Luke Short, who beat the Texan Jones. Desperate efforts have been made to clear him. The last trick turned was by a lawyer, and has proved to be so far successful.

Texan Jones remained in town but was constantly being "coaxed and bulldozed" by friends of the prisoner who were trying to make him leave town. With a touch of humor, the *Star* added that Chief of Police Thomas Speers had provided Jones with "a big horse pistol, with instructions to shoot it off the first opportunity he gets."[14]

On October 11, it was reported that William T. Murphy, described as "a young man who introduced Jones, the Texan, to Luke Short, the confidence man, was arrested by detectives Bryant and Hunt. Short was released this morning."[15] Luke had been held in jail for at least six days. The outcome of the case is unknown, but Luke was soon on the move again. He visited Kansas City for a short time and then went west to locate in Tombstone, Arizona. He was established there by November.[16]

In spite of the attraction of Tombstone, some writers have asserted Luke Short appeared early in that "Queen City of Cowtowns"—Dodge City. Based on his own chronology it now must be accepted that Luke Short never set foot in Dodge City *prior* to his going to Tombstone in late 1880. His 1961 biographer claimed that "springtime 1879 found Luke back at the Long Branch Saloon," indicating that Luke had been there prior to 1879.[17] Cox also claimed that during that period, at Dodge City, Luke first met Wyatt Earp and Bat Masterson. None of this was true, but it would be repeated by other historians, such as Dale T. Schoenberger who wrote "from Leadville Luke drifted down to Dodge City. There he made friends with fellow gamblers Bat Masterson and Wyatt Earp. [They] secured Short employment as a house dealer at Chalk Beeson's and Will Harris's Long Branch Saloon. From 1879 to early 1881, Short seems to have remained in relative obscurity at Dodge City."[18] There would be no obscurity in Tombstone.

The fact was that Luke first met Wyatt Earp, William H. Harris, and Bat Masterson, in that order, in Tombstone. Earp would have been the first that Luke met, since he had been a resident of Tombstone for nearly a year when Short arrived in November of 1880. William H. Harris was next, arriving in the tough silver city about a month after Luke. On January 1, 1881, the *Dodge City Times* reported that "W. H. Harris, one of the Dodge City councilmen, is in Tombstone, Arizona, having left San Francisco. Presume he will wend his way to Dodge."[19] Bat Masterson left Dodge City for Tombstone on February 8, 1881. On February 24 the *Dodge City Times* noted that "C. M. Beeson received a letter from W. H. Harris, which states that W. B. Masterson arrived in Tombstone, Arizona. The old Dodge boys are seeking fortunes in the gold [*sic*] fields of Arizona."[20]

The stampede to Tombstone had, of course, been caused by the discovery of silver and not gold. The attraction that brought Earp, Harris, Masterson, and Short together in Tombstone was the Oriental Saloon, a restaurant and bar located at the corner of Fifth and Allen streets. James Vizina and Benjamin Cook were the actual owners, but the building was leased to Milton E. Joyce and William C. Parker, of San Francisco. Lou Rickabaugh, also of San Francisco, William H. Harris, who had met with Rickabaugh in San Francisco prior to coming to Tombstone, and Richard Clark ran the gambling concession at the Oriental. This establishment, which gained national recognition, opened for business on July 21, 1880. The next day the *Tombstone Epitaph* gave it a rave review, announcing the "spacious corner building" had been transformed into a facility described as "the most elegantly furnished saloon this side of the favored city of the Golden Gate." The *Epitaph* reporter counted the twenty-eight burners, "suspended in neat chandeliers," which afforded "an illumination of ample brilliancy, and the bright rays reflected from the many colored crystals on the bar sprinkled like a December iceling in the sunshine." And that was not all that impressed those in attendance. The saloon comprised two apartments. Entering the main entrance one could admire the bar "beautifully carved, finished in white and gilt and capped with a handsomely polished top." At the rear were a "brace of sideboards which are simply elegant and must be seen to be appreciated." M. E. Joyce had purchased these from the Baldwin Hotel of San Francisco. They were too small for that facility but were suitable for the Oriental. The floor of the back apartment was covered with a Brussels carpet, "suitably furnished after the style of a grand club room, with conveniences for the wily dealers in polished ivory." The furniture and fixtures displayed the "exquisite taste" even to the "handsome stock of stationery." The reporter was obviously very impressed with everything he saw and concluded that Tombstone now "takes the lead" and Joyce and his staff were to be congratulated.[21] One wonders if the many attendees at this wonderful event really did appreciate the fineness of what the *Epitaph* reported.

William H. Harris was well acquainted with Wyatt Earp from Earp's time in Dodge City. Based on their previous friendship, Harris had no problem convincing his partners to engage Earp as a faro dealer at the Oriental. Faro was easily the most popular card game in the Wild West and could be found at nearly every gambling hall. The game itself was often called a "faro bank." Cheating at the game was so common that earlier editions of Edmond Hoyle's book on the rules of games claimed that not a single honest faro bank could be found in the United States.[22] The faro table itself was oval, covered with green cloth, and featured a cutout for the "banker." A deck of fifty-two cards was placed face-up inside a dealing box. The first card was known as "soda," while the last or bottom card was called "hoc." Early card backs featured a drawing of a Bengal tiger, leading to the term "Bucking the Tiger." Luke Short and Bat Masterson both worked for the Oriental, usually in the capacity of a "lookout" hired to protect the game. A "lookout" sat on a high chair to the right of the dealer. His job was comparable to that of a "pit boss" in a modern casino.

Luke Short was serving as the lookout at a faro game in the Oriental when he became involved in his first celebrated gunfight on Friday, February 25, 1881. Within hours of the event, George W. Parsons had recorded his version in his now-famous diary. He wrote of the incident as if he somehow knew that his words would be important someday for history, pointing out that of late there had been "[q]uite peaceable times" but "today the monotony was broken by the shooting of Charles Storms by Luke Short on corner of Oriental [Street]." Hearing shots in Tombstone was apparently so common that Parsons did not make any special note of them as "the first two were so deliberate I didn't think anything much was out of the way" but when he heard the third shot he knew something was different. He grabbed his hat and ran out into the street "just in time to see Storms die—shot through the heart."

Parsons pointed out that both men were gamblers and Short had been "running game" at the Oriental. During the night Storms had become drunk and the trouble brewed, with Storms growing more aggressive. Although drunk and shot through the heart, according to Parsons, Storms "was game to the last" and with "a desperate effort steadying revolver with both hands fired—four shots in all I believe." One cannot help but realize that Parsons had an admiration for the courage of the drunken Charlie Storms, even though he was the aggressor in a matter that resulted in his own death.

Dr. George Goodfellow later took the bullet to show his friend Parsons, who recognized it as a .45 caliber, "slightly flattened." The doctor also showed him a bloody handkerchief, part of which had been driven into the wound. "Short," Parsons noted, "very unconcerned after shooting—probably a case of kill or be killed." As the body of Storms was taken to his room at the San Jose House, the games continued "as though nothing had happened[.]" [23]

Twenty-six years later, Bat Masterson wrote what has become the most famous account of the gunfight between Luke Short and Charlie Storms.[24] This time Masterson was on more certain ground as he was actually present when Short killed Storms. His story varied from Parsons' in some matters. Bat "one morning" had gone into the Oriental where Luke worked "just in time to keep him from killing a gambler named Charlie Storms." In his telling, Masterson pointed out to his readers that there was scarcely any difference between the Short-Storms incident and the "bad man" back in Leadville, only in that situation Short's opponent was only wounded. According to Bat, Storms was one of the best-known gamblers in the west and on numerous occasions had successfully defended himself in pistol fights against "gun-fighters." Bat and Storms were "very close friends," in fact, as much as he and Luke Short were, "and for that reason I did not care to see him get into what I knew would be a serious difficulty." Storms did not know Luke Short. Bat again compared him to the "bad man" of Leadville, and claimed that Storms had considered Short as an "insignificant-looking fellow, whom he would slap in the face without expecting a return."[25] Bat revealed that both men were about to draw their weapons when he jumped between them to prevent gunplay. Like Parsons, Masterson noted that Storms had been up all night and drinking, but in his telling, he convinced him to go to his room and sleep it off. At Storms' request, Bat accompanied him to his room where he remained —at least for a short time.

Bat Masterson returned to the Oriental and began to talk to Luke outside the saloon on the sidewalk about Storms being "a very decent sort of man," when Storms, much to their surprise, stood before them. Bat observed how Storms, without a word, "took hold of Luke's arm and pulled him off the sidewalk, where he had been standing, at the same time pulling his pistol, a Colt's cut-off .45 calibre, single action, but like the Leadvillian, he was too slow, although he succeeded in getting his pistol out." Luke pulled his pistol and placed the muzzle against Storms' heart and pulled the trigger. The bullet "tore his heart asunder" and as Storms fell, Short shot him again. Charlie Storms was dead when he fell. Luke had a preliminary hearing and was exonerated.[26] In Masterson's 1907 version, only two shots were fired, both by Short. In George Parsons' diary entry (written the day the shooting happened) he described hearing at least three shots, ran to the scene, and witnessed Storms surviving long enough to fire at least four shots as he lay dying.

A couple of days later a Tucson newspaper reported the shooting, providing some background information on Storms that was missing from the other accounts. This reporting placed the cause of the quarrel as "a dispute over a faro game." Short worked for Lou Rickabaugh "to protect the game." Storms had been in El Paso and on his way to Tucson stopped in Tombstone. Years earlier he had been a pioneer, having arrived in California as early as 1849. For years he had been a "sporting man," having been in Pioche and Virginia City, Nevada; Deadwood, South Dakota; and Leadville, "in fact all the mining camps." Storms was about sixty years of age, making him more than old enough to have been Luke Short's father, not that the age difference made him any less dangerous. He left a wife in San Francisco.[27]

Leadville, Colorado, was a town that both Luke Short and Charlie Storms knew well. Leadville, for its part, knew Storms far better than it wanted to. Five days after the event, the *Leadville Democrat* provided what remains the most authoritative account of the killing. From the very first line of this obituary the *Democrat* left no doubt as to how the editor felt about the passing of the gambler. "At last," the report began, now foregoing objective reporting, "after courting the grim sentinel of death for years, and not infrequently gloating upon the outrageous Charlie Storms," the "noted sporting man, has found his destiny." Tombstone was described as "a place that is just now being infested by a portion of the rubbish that was once in this city."

According to the *Democrat,* Storms' career was "most eventful" and his "favorite diversion was the handling of a six-shooter with humanity as a target." Storms had arrived in Leadville about two years before and was considered "one of the most successful of the myriads of gamblers that thronged the city." According to this report it was Storms who was enraged over what he believed was the insult from Short, which led to the confrontation. On the morning of the fatal day Storms approached Short and "catching him by the ear" demanded a retraction of the "epithets" Short had used and demanded an apology. We are to accept that Storms actually had Short by the ear; it was done with his left hand as in his right hand he held a revolver. It this situation Luke Short drew his weapon and fired, causing Storms to release his grip on the ear. Storms had enough life in him that as he fell on his shoulder he was still able to fire his weapon. He missed. Short put two more bullets into "the sinking soul of Storms."

The gunfire had attracted others and soon a "multitude had gathered around." Short surrendered to an officer and was escorted to jail and incarcerated. Many were aware of Storms as well as Short, and were sympathetic to the victor; not surprisingly, any "suggestions at lynch law were quickly voted down by all classes." The remains of Storms were taken to the undertaker's establishment where a coroner's jury was empanelled and testimony heard. After hearing all the evidence the jury reached a verdict that Storms came to his death from three pistol wounds at the hands of Luke Short, and that the killing was justifiable.[28]

This account was published on March 2, 1881, five days after the killing. The jury had reached its verdict in a brief preliminary hearing before Justice of the Peace Albert Osborn Wallace. The proceedings most likely took place on either Saturday, February 26, or on Monday February 28. The rival newspaper of the mining camp, the *Tombstone Nugget*, provided a brief summary of the action, but provided no new information, merely reporting Short had an examination before Justice Wallace and "was discharged yesterday, the evidence being conclusive to the court that Short acted in self-defense." From the evidence it was clear that Storms was the aggressor, having stepped out of the saloon, grabbing hold of Short "and stepped out into the street with the intention of killing him."[29]

Luke Short was free to go as there was no further legal action taken. The last mention of the killing, as far as the court was concerned, was contained in a "Disposition of Cause" document which stated that any further action following the preliminary hearing had been "Ignored by Grand Jury."[30] After leaving Tombstone, Luke briefly turned up in

Deming, New Mexico, where an unidentified gentleman writing from Tucson observed him and contributed his thoughts to the newspaper. "California and Nevada may have had some very tough characters in their day," he observed, while visiting, "but it remained for El Paso and Deming to capture the top traffic in that line. While at Deming I saw Luke Short [who] is as mild a mannered person as you would wish to meet, quite good looking, neat in appearance, and a stranger would never take him to be the bad man from Tombstone."[31]

Charlie Storms would be in the news again, over six years after his death, when it was revealed that his real name wasn't Charlie Storms. A gambler named Peter A. Vallet (sometimes spelled Vallat) shot himself in the head with a Colt .45 on June 11, 1887. In reporting the suicide, a Denver newspaper informed its readers that Vallet had resided in Denver for about eight years and had been a faro dealer in "all the gambling establishments in the city." He was a French Creole by birth, having been born in New Orleans, about fifty-two years old, of heavy build, with a very large head and small blue eyes with a black mustache. To add to the physical description, he was "slightly bald, and the head perfectly flat on the top." But perhaps as a surprise to the public Vallet was described as a half-brother to Charles Storms, the gambler who was killed at Tombstone. The two had gone west together.[32]

On June 20 a follow-up item in the Leadville newspaper shed further light on the siblings, in particular Peter A. Vallet. The man was by reputation a "prominent sporting man of New Orleans" whose parents were "highly respectable" in the Crescent City; Charlie Storms was a "full brother" of Vallet. "The two men always passed as half brothers, but those acquainted with their history knew this was not the case. Some irregularities in the life of Charley caused him to change his name."[33] It would be most interesting to learn what the "irregularities" were that caused the brother to change his name.

Luke Short moved to Dodge City during April 1881 and Dodge would be his home base until the final months of 1883, although he made frequent trips to other places to pursue gambling opportunities during those years. One such opportunity presented itself on March 19, 1882, in Salida, Colorado, a community nearly 150 miles southwest of Denver. According to an account published six years later, Luke had gone there to attend a foot race between two sprinters named Ed Campbell, of Leadville, and M. K. "Cyclone Kit" Kittleman, of Pueblo, Colorado. It was a case of a "fixed" race where Short expected his man, Kittleman, to win the race—despite the fact that he had agreed to "sell out to the other side." Luke knew about this and figured he would "double cross" the gamblers betting against Kittleman and make a killing when Cyclone Kit won. Things didn't exactly go the way Luke planned. Short's man "agreed to sell out to the other side to lose the race" but had it understood with Short to win anyway. But—the referee "got a tip, and promised to see the thing through." The track was lined with "the toughest kind of Western sports" and there was upwards of $8,000 riding on the result. But, the surprise was that the "crooked racer" decided to double cross Short himself, and did lose the race by about four feet. Amid the "tremendous excitement," the referee, the stake-holder, and winners intended to divide the spoils at a neighborhood saloon.

But before the money was produced Luke Short strode in, pistol in hand. "Who won that race?" The referee responded with his own question: "Why, don't you see?" Short repeated his simple question. "I guess your man won it by about a foot" replied the referee, "getting out of range." Short, coolly taking the sheaf of bills out of the hand of the stakeholder, commented: "The fact is, gentlemen, you know my man can win, but you did your best to rob me, and I just reversed things on you." Short did get away with the money, perhaps miraculously, as the following day John Cozad, the referee, "was poisoned by unknown parties."[34] John Wesley Cozad was indeed poisoned, but that crime happened more than five weeks after the foot race.

The most extensive report of the race was given by the *Leadville Herald* just two days after the event. It was a lengthy article, which gave a virtual step-by-step account of the race, and its aftermath. The main headline screamed that Cozad "Gave It Away" and further headlined the news that "His Treachery Condemned by the Entire Populace of Salida, and by Everybody Else, Except a Few of the Pueblo Roughs."[35] Although not actually named by the reporter, Luke Short was clearly one of the "Pueblo Roughs" he was describing. The rumors, identified at the end of this lengthy article, were "anything but creditable to Cozad." He had been a sprinter himself, and had run against Kittleman and lost. On that occasion Deveraux, the man who ran the saloon in which Cozad was bartender, lost several hundred dollars. To get back his money this time he bet on Kittleman, "which he would have lost had not the decision of the bartender gone in his favor." A second rumor was that a Pueblo man[36] had approached Cozad in his room and leveling a gun at his head, made him decide in the false manner which he did. Yet another rumor was that for "a miserable five hundred dollars Cozad threw the race." The indignant citizens of Salida "knew no bounds" and the talk was "quite loud" whether to lynch Cozad or simply shoot him.

John Wesley Cozad lived only thirty-eight days after the race. He wasn't shot or lynched, and the persons responsible probably had no connection with the foot race. The *Leadville Daily Herald* published a report the day following Cozad's death. It reminded the readers that Cozad had been the referee in the foot race between Campbell and Kittleman, and he now was tending bar at Deveraux's saloon. Late the previous evening Cozad had been in his "usual health" when he retired to his room. At 2:00 in the morning of April 26 he was found "upon the floor in convulsions and insensible." The physician was unable to revive him. People suspected foul play and three arrests were quickly made. The coroner's report was pending, and a post-mortem examination would be made the following day.[37]

A few days later a wire service report stated that Cozad, "the famous short distance runner," had died at Salida. Authorities believed he had been poisoned as a few hours before his death he had been well. A dance house girl and a man named Streehy, who had Cozad's watch, were arrested.[38]

Chapter 4

Get Out of Dodge

> "Luke Short and L. C. Hartman met upon the street and paid their respective compliments to each other by exchanging shots."
> —*Ford County Globe*, May 1, 1883.

The first time that Luke Short's name appeared in a Dodge City newspaper was during the summer of 1882. It was one of those "humorous" items, which an 1882 audience in Dodge would have found hilarious. Cringe-inducing today, it reflects the racial prejudice then prevalent in Dodge City, as well as the rest of 1882 America. It told of two Chinese gentlemen who had been "added to the population of Dodge City" directly from Trinidad, Colorado, and "brought with them letters of introduction from Bat Masterson to Luke Short. They engage in the washee business. There are four gentlemen from the Celestial Kingdom now residents of Dodge. All were pursuing the wash business. Mr. Fred Wenie provided the new arrivals with quarters. Fred is chief mogul among the Chinese. He speaks their language fluently. But he can't go their diet of rats, mice and rice."[1]

By the time this item appeared Luke Short had been gone from Tombstone for more than sixteen months. During the intervening months he had alternated his time between various Colorado mining camps and, during the cattle drive season, Dodge City. Luke's friend William H. Harris had sold out his interest in Tombstone and provided Luke with employment as a faro dealer at the Long Branch Saloon in Dodge. The Long Branch was owned by Harris and his partner Chalk Beeson. By this time Harris had become a very wealthy man—one of the wealthiest in Kansas. During June 1882 Harris became one of the five incorporators of the Bank of Dodge City and served as vice president of the bank. Harris purchased J. Collar's interest in the C.O.D. brand of cattle, paying about $20,000 during August of 1882. The Beeson & Harris firm then claimed ownership of the C.O.D. brand.[2] Early in 1883 Chalk Beeson decided to sell his share of the Long Branch. The *Ford County Globe*, a Dodge City newspaper, published this notification:

> DISSOLUTION NOTICE
>
> This is to certify that C. M. Beeson, and W. H. Harris doing a saloon business in Dodge City, Kansas, under the firm name of Beeson & Harris, has this day been dissolved by mutual consent. Mr. Beeson [is] selling his interest in the business to Luke Short who will continue the business with Mr. Harris and who assume all the liabilities of the late firm and collect all outstanding accounts due the same.
>
> C. M. BEESON
>
> W. H. HARRIS
>
> February 6th 1883

Alonzo B. Webster was the mayor of Dodge City at the time this notice appeared and he wouldn't be running for reelection.[3] Webster headed a "reform" faction that represented a real threat to the way that Harris and Short preferred to conduct business. The month after Short and Harris formed their partnership, Harris was nominated to run for mayor of Dodge City. Among those who supported him were William F. Petillon,

Clerk of the District Court, and James H. Kelley, the former mayor. Harris also had the backing of the *Ford County Globe*. On March 19, 1883, a "law and order" group nominated Lawrence E. Deger for mayor.[4] Deger had the support of Alonzo B. Webster, the outgoing mayor, and was endorsed by the *Dodge City Times*, the rival newspaper of the *Globe*.

Much of the election was fought out between the two newspapers supporting the opposing candidates. The *Dodge City Times* warned its readers that a Harris victory would provide fertile ground for robbers, drunks, and con men. The *Ford County Globe* devoted most of its coverage condemning editor Nicholas B. Klaine of the *Dodge City Times* for his vitriolic attacks on Harris and his supporters.[5] Deger defeated Harris by a vote of 214 to 143 in the election on April 3. All five of the city council candidates running with Deger were also elected.

On April 23 the Dodge City Council posted two ordinances that were immediately approved by Mayor Deger. Both contained a section stating that the ordinance would take effect on and after its publication once in the *Dodge City Times*, which occurred on April 26. Ordinance No. 70 was defined as "An Ordinance for the Suppression of Vice and Immorality Within the City of Dodge City." Ordinance No. 71 was described as "An Ordinance to Define and Punish Vagrancy." Officers arrested three women employed by Short at the Long Branch on Saturday, April 28, two days after the ordinances became effective. The *Ford County Globe* reported that the arrests were "peaceably accomplished and without any resistance so far as we are enabled to learn." The names of the women were not given and it was justly perceived perhaps that the three were prostitutes, not as Luke later claimed, simply singers in the Long Branch. The report continued: "It was claimed by the proprietors that partiality was shown in arresting [the] women in their house when two were allowed to remain in A. B. Webster's saloon, one at Heinz & Kramer's, two at Nelson Cary's, and a whole herd of them at Bond & Nixon's dance hall." If that was true, "it would be most natural for them to think so and give expression to their feelings." [6] The "expression to their feelings" turned out to be a gunfight between Luke Short and Louis C. Hartman, as will be described below.

The editor of the *Globe*, Daniel M. Frost, always friendly to Luke Short, permitted his style of reporting news to flourish with abandon now, perhaps to reveal to the Dodge City *literati* that he could utilize warlike imagery to great effect.

> The annual revolutionary spirit was again exhibited on our streets yesterday. Wars and rumors of war, was the out-cry all along the line. The smoldering volcano broke forth on this day and wiped out the wicked and ungodly, they having to flee from the wrath that was to come. It was a hot day for the vagrant, the gambler and the inmate of the house of ill fame, but they must yield to the majesty of the law or take the consequences.[7]

Frost continued, toning down his imagery but retaining the style of the mock-heroic, attempting to report the events more prosaically. But he could not resist returning to colorful language in his concluding paragraph.

> Thus the smoldering volcano has burst forth in all its fury, and has stricken terror to the hearts of the inhabitants that so closely surround it and causes one to reflect as to whether or not it will be followed up by a St. John[8] cyclone and sweep away in its train the dispenser of ardent spirits, and thus give us another evidence of the moral and temperance element of our citizens and show that the righteous must and shall prevail in the city of Dodge.[9]

Further details of the arrest, shooting, and subsequent events were provided a couple of days later by Nicholas B. Klaine in the *Dodge City Times*. What has become recognized as the "Dodge City War" was as much a conflict between newspaper editors as between owners of gambling houses. Klaine provided a lengthy report in his story in the rival paper, but to the regret of numerous historians did not provide the names of the three ladies arrested. Klaine did state what perhaps all of Dodge City knew, that the three women arrested were in reality prostitutes, not "singers" as described by Short and Harris. Klaine stated clearly this nomenclature was to evade the ordinance in relation to the vice of prostitution. Once the trio was jailed, further trouble was not anticipated, but later that evening Short and special policeman Louis C. Hartman met. Their exchange of shots was termed by Klaine an assassination attempt. Short fired twice at Hartman; the latter fired once at Short. No one was hit. Editor Klaine, who also ignored objective reporting, stated that with Short arrested and placed under $2000 bond, Mayor Deger learned that "a *conspiracy* had been formed, which had for its object the *armed resistance* to the enforcement of the law and *murder* of some of our best citizens [emphasis added]."

Once Luke Short was jailed, more arrests followed, men who remain obscure in the history of gambling in the Wild West: W. H. Bennett, a "former New Mexico desperado"; Dr. Niel, identified as "a Mobeetie gambler"; Johnson Gallagher, a gambler; and Lon A. Hyatt, also a gambler. Editor Klaine inadvertently overlooked naming the fifth man arrested: he was Thomas Lane. The group was given the choice of leaving Dodge on the eastbound train or else the westbound train, but they had to leave upon orders from Mayor Deger. Short, Lane, and Gallagher went east while the others went west. As if to underscore the seriousness of Deger and his associates, "about one hundred and fifty citizens were on watch Monday night [May 7, 1883], and a large police force is still on duty night and day," according to Klaine. Deger, the police force, and the Dodge City citizens "are determined that the lawless element shall not thrive in this city. No half-way measures will be used in the suppression of either lawlessness or riot." If anyone was concerned about their safety in Dodge, Klaine's assurance should have underscored the idea that all were safe. "Mayor Deger," the editor wrote, "is a resolute, fearless and obstinate officer. All good and law abiding citizens are standing by him in this trying emergency."[10]

Nicholas B. Klaine was as far from an unbiased source as possible to get. He supported the Webster-Deger faction without question. By contrast, the *Kansas City Evening Star* newspaper of Kansas City, Missouri, reported the events in a manner clearly more sympathetic to William H. Harris and Luke L. Short. The *Evening Star* report reminded its readers that Dodge City had long "enjoyed the reputation of being a hard place" and pointed out Dodge was one of the few places in Kansas where "saloons run openly and gambling is legitimized." The previous mayor, "a man named Webster," was described as "the proprietor of a dive, half saloon and the other half a gambling house and variety hall." He was "a representative of the tougher element of the sporting fraternity." The other faction, headed by W. H. Harris, was the representative of "the quieter and more reputable element" and to no one's surprise perhaps "there was bitter feeling between the two." The Kansas City report continued explaining the background of the present "emergency." With Harris losing in the last race for mayor, beaten by "one Deger, Webster's candidate" it was understood by all that it was only a matter of time before all of Harris' supporters would be driven out of town. The report continued relating the Hartman-Short shooting affray, pointing out that "the evidence showed that Short was fired on first. . . . nevertheless [he was] placed under bonds, and next day thrown into jail." The Dodge City marshal, John L. "Jack" Bridges, "a well-known character," had formerly lived in Kansas City, "and traveled principally upon having 'killed his man.'" Curiously the *Evening Star* of Kansas City, Missouri, headlined its contribution with "Ruffians Regime." Jack Bridges was a tough character who had been drawn to Dodge City as one who could handle the rougher element.

According to the Kansas City paper, the quintet of gamblers who were jailed received a visit from the Dodge City "vigilance committee," led by Tom Nixon. Nixon was described as "the proprietor of one of the hardest dance halls that ever existed in the west." This paper agreed with Klaine's story in that here too the five were given the choice of trains: either westbound or eastbound. Then the vigilance committee took possession of the town. As if to intentionally make this a national incident, the correspondents of the *Chicago Times* "and other leading papers" were notified that they would not be permitted to send any telegrams in reference to the situation. To make sure this was carried out, "a body of armed men watched the arrival of each train to see that there was no interference." One of the prisoners had managed to send for legal assistance, but lawyer Nelson Adams was met by a member of the vigilance committee "who leveled a shot-gun at his head and told him not to stop. He passed on."[11] The situation in Dodge was no longer just an attempt by the "moral" clique to run Short out of town, but had become an attempt to stifle the press by preventing outside reporters in to report what was happening in Dodge.

After being run out of town, Luke went directly to Kansas City where he looked up Charles E. Bassett at the Marble Hall Saloon at 522 Main Street. Bassett and Luke had a lot in common, not the least of which was that both had, at different times, owned an interest in the Long Branch Saloon. Bassett was among the earliest settlers in Dodge and knew everyone involved in the incident. He had served as the first sheriff of Ford County, as well as city marshal of Dodge City. Both Wyatt Earp and Bat Masterson had, at various times, served under Bassett as deputies.[12] Luke used Bassett's Marble Hall Saloon as his temporary mailing address, and received a letter from Dodge City. The letter, sent by Otto Muller and dated May 5, 1883, did not contain encouraging news. "Harris feels very downhearted," Muller's letter began, "but is untiringly at work to set matters right. You can form no idea how your enemies watch him at every step and move. No train passes this station without being searched and watched by the Vigilantes for contraband." Positive news was there nevertheless: "Harris and his friends feel confident that Bob Wright on his return to town will take the lead against the suppression of further outrages, and I think also that he is the best man for it. Our best men in town will back him, and I think that before long the '*Reformers*' will be compelled to surrender and lay down their arms." Muller concluded by advising Luke to "not feel discouraged" and to "feel confident that Harris will spare no effort to have everything fixed right and that your friends will assist him all they can."[13]

But feeling confident is not necessarily reality, as Luke learned when his state representative, George M. Hoover, responded to his letter written on May 7. "You know how a Governor acts. With the church element, the Railroad officials and part of the so called immoral element against you he would not interfere in the rulings of a city or mob ruling," Hoover explained. He advised Luke "to either sell your interest in Dodge or else employ some one to look after your interests here and make up your mind to abandon Dodge at least during the present administration." Hoover felt abandoning Dodge was "the only safe plan for both yourself and friends."[14]

Despite Hoover's observation concerning the governor of Kansas, Short and William F. Petillon, the district court clerk, had already been in touch with the chief executive. Petillon had already gone to Topeka in response to a telegram from the governor. "Some affairs of state" commented the report, "need the diplomacy of statesmen." The *Dodge City Times* did "suppose" that the governor's "intercession is desired on behalf of the affairs in Dodge." The paper assured the citizens that the governor "will not interfere with our local laws and the manner of disposing of them. He might execute the State laws which would then render local laws of no use and no consequence."[15]

Luke Short was not sitting idle waiting for others to bring a resolution to his problem. On May 10 he and Petillon left Kansas City to go to Topeka and meet with Governor Glick, with the intention of laying his case before him. His main concern was that the Dodge City authorities had "no right to expel him from town, but if he has violated any laws he should be permitted to remain there and answer the charges."[16]

Short and Petillon had taken with them to the governor a notarized petition they had drawn on May 10, while they were still in Kansas City. The document marks the first of several occasions that Luke spoke for himself—with the assistance of District Clerk Petillon—on the origins of what would later be termed the "Saloon War" or the "Dodge City War." The petition is summarized here as the lengthy original filled five pages.

Short explained to Governor Glick that he had lived in Dodge City for two years, that he was a member of the firm of Harris and Short, and that partner Harris was vice president of the Bank of Dodge City. He also stressed to the governor that during all that time of residence he had not been charged with any crime until April 30, 1883, when he was arrested, charged with assault upon L. C. Hartman. Short claimed he was "entirely innocent of said charge" and that he gave bond in the sum of $2000. He then caused Hartman to be arrested on a charge of assault, and that Hartman's trial was set for hearing on May 2. He explained that on April 30 he was arrested for a second time "but on what charge your petitioner was at the time and is now ignorant." No warrant had been read or shown to him, and he was denied bail.

Further, while in custody in the jail an armed body of men led by Larry Deger, the mayor of Dodge City, came to the jail and ordered him "to leave said city and never to return," threatening him "with great physical danger" upon refusal to do so. He further was told that if he returned "he would do so at his peril." Short named the leading men who accompanied Deger in making the threats: Fred Singer, Thomas Nixon, A. B. Webster, Brick Bond, Bob Vanderburg, Jack Bridges, Clark Chipman, L. C. Hartman, and about twenty-five others, "all heavily armed." Some of these individuals Governor Glick certainly knew, if not personally then by reputation, but just in case, Short explained their positions: Deger was the mayor, Singer was under sheriff, Nixon a proprietor of a dance hall in Dodge, Webster the proprietor of a saloon and gambling house, Bond, proprietor of a dance hall, Vanderburg and Hartman both special policemen, Bridges, a marshal, and Chipman assistant marshal.[17]

Governor Glick was not pleased with what he had read. He telegraphed Sheriff George T. Hinkel, asking for an explanation.[18] Not surprisingly Sheriff Hinkel's telegraph back to Governor Glick was different from the picture Luke Short had presented. According to the sheriff's explanation, Mayor Deger had compelled "several persons to leave the city for refusing to comply with the ordinances." He stressed that "[n]o such mob exists nor is there any reason to fear any violence as I am amply able to preserve the peace." He further explained that he had shown the message to Mayor Deger who pointed out that his act of "compelling the parties to leave the city was simply to avoid difficulty and disorders." He concluded that "[e]verything is quiet here as in the capital of the state" and he assured the governor that if he found he could not preserve the "present quiet" he would "unhesitatingly" ask for assistance from the governor's office.[19]

Governor Glick was still not pleased with the situation in Dodge City and his response was a blistering letter, revealing his anger as well as pointing out to Hinkel that he considered what was happening in Dodge as the revelation of a "monstrous" situation. The "extraordinary state of affairs" was simply "outrageous upon its face." The action of the mayor in compelling citizens to leave town for not obeying the ordinances "simply shows that the mayor is unfit for his place, that he does not do his duty, and instead of occupying the position of peace maker, the man whose duty it is to see that the ordinances are enforced by legal process in the courts, starts out to head a mob to drive people away from their homes and their business." Governor Glick further stated that the idea of meeting the trains to prevent citizens from returning to their homes and businesses was intolerable. If the citizens were "disreputable characters" who disturbed the peace, that would be one thing, but the truth of the matter as the governor understood it revealed it was "simply a difficulty between saloon men and dance houses." He was right. He also condemned the action of the mayor selecting the ordinances against one saloon but not others. If this "state of affairs" were to continue it would bring disgrace upon "your city, upon your county, and upon the state of Kansas." Pressure was being put on the governor to totally change society in Kansas: to close up every saloon and dance hall and gambling place; if the closing up of such places of vice were not done he would station a company of troops in Dodge and "it shall be done."

Governor Glick had essentially heard the two sides of the issue, and had also read of the situation in other Kansas newspapers and realized it was not simply a disagreement between saloon owners now but a matter that could do political damage. Whether Sheriff Hinkel appreciated the gravity of the matter in Dodge is doubtful, but the governor was telling him clearly that he must not permit the mayor or anyone else to trample upon the rights and privileges of others. His concluding statement may have caused Hinkel to wish he had never gotten involved: "The peace of the city is with you, Mr. Sheriff, and I expect it to be safe in your hands."[20]

Short kept the pressure on by now going to the press. On May 11, he and W. F. Petillon gave a joint interview to a reporter of the *Topeka Daily Capital.* Sharing with the reporter the events that had garnered such publicity, Short and Petillon gave "from their point of view, bringing forward a number of facts which have not been presented heretofore." Short was a Texan who had gone to Dodge some two years before with an interest in the cattle business. He had an "extensive acquaintance" with other cattlemen and their employees and in Dodge he engaged in the saloon business with "a man named Harris" and had made their saloon "the most popular and profitable one in the city." Next door to their saloon was another, and while the popularity of Short & Harris' establishment increased, Short "modestly stated" that the popularity of Webster's saloon had declined. Besides the business competition causing friction between the two saloons, the matter of electing a mayor also became controversial. Deger was brought in and began boarding "at the hotel in town, in order to gain a legal residence." This was not all, as the night before the election, the "construction trains of the Santa Fe railroad, manned by men residing at different places scattered along the line, were run into Dodge" and the results of the election were determined by these men who had "obtained control of the election" and voted. Short now was accusing his enemies of election fraud.

The "interview" also provided a word picture of the saloons of Dodge City. They were "all of a similar character," which included bars for drinking, tables for gambling and games of various kinds, arrangements for variety performances—at least singing—and "all employ women who are admittedly of loose character, and are provided with facilities for plying their business." This was now at the heart of the conflict: the ordinances of the new administration prohibited "loose women" from pursuing their solicitations in any public place. If the reporter did not appreciate the intricacies of the questionable electioneering he, and his readers, certainly realized the matter of prohibiting those "loose women" from "plying their business."[21]

The citizens of Dodge were certainly aware of the events happening at the capital. Supporters of Luke Short assembled and prepared a letter that was sent to the governor explaining that they were well acquainted with Luke L. Short who was "driven" from Dodge "by a band of armed men headed by L. E. Deger" and "we hereby give you the facts as they occurred." The letter provided a brief account of the arrest of the three women, the forced exit from Dodge, and the chronology by stating that the events were "a disgrace to the City and are an outrage upon law and good order." Further, during Short's two-year residence in Dodge, "he has conducted himself like a gentleman and law abiding citizen and he has never resisted any arrest or placed [himself] at defiance of the law." In brief: the twelve good citizens of Dodge respectfully requested the governor to take whatever action necessary to allow Luke Short to return to Dodge to "prosecute his rights and defend himself in the court of the County."[22]

On the same date the twelve citizens sent their letter to the governor —May 15—a Kansas City newspaper published a report that must have alarmed the "law and order" faction back in Dodge. The *Kansas City Journal* stated that on the previous day "a new man arrived on the scene who is destined to play a part in a great tragedy." Was this simply media hyperbole, or was the reporter prescient, predicting the tragic results of an inevitable confrontation? The "new man" was Bat Masterson, ex-sheriff of Ford County, described as "one of the most dangerous men the West has ever produced." A few years before, according to the *Journal*, Masterson himself "incurred the enmity of the same men who drove

Short away, and he was exiled upon pain of death if he returned." Further, Masterson was going to visit Dodge City, and within twenty-four hours "a few other pleasant gentlemen [will be] on their way to the tea party at Dodge City." Those named included Wyatt Earp, "the famous marshal of Dodge," Joe Lowe, "otherwise known as 'Rowdy Joe'" and the mysterious "Shotgun" Collins, but "worse than all is another ex-citizen and officer of Dodge, the famous Doc Halliday [*sic*]."[23]

The names of these rather notorious individuals may have caused some citizens of the "law and order" league to begin to doubt the wisdom of their actions, but more respectable citizens were also brought into the matter. On the evening of May 15 an "informal committee of three" arrived in Kansas City to confer with Short and Masterson. The three were G. M. Hoover, banker and representative in the Legislature; Robert M. Wright, a merchant; and C. M. Beeson, "a prominent cattle man." Their business was not conducted lightly, and they remained over night, at which time they would reach "some conclusion." Their intention was to find a solution to the situation in Dodge, a situation which still, according to the sheriff and the mayor, could result in danger to Luke Short if he returned. Nothing certain was reported: Luke Short might be in danger if he returned and stayed any length of time, but if he returned only to settle his business interests—and then leave again—he probably would be safe.[24]

Following this Kansas City conference with Beeson, Wright, and Hoover, Luke Short returned to Topeka, accompanied by Masterson and Petillon. Their return was noted in the *Topeka Daily Capital*, pointing out the trio was staying at the Copeland Hotel. Short was "fully aware" that his return to Dodge would be "strongly objected to and that forcible means will be used to prevent his remaining any time." But, the *Capital* hinted, Short "intends soon" to return. It was as if the reporter was developing the scenes to lead up to the final act of a Shakespearean tragedy.[25]

Webster and Deger certainly kept informed of these events happening in eastern Kansas and chose to go to Topeka and meet with Governor Glick. They reportedly were going to present to the governor "the facts on the situation in Dodge City." Supposedly the governor had been "woefully misinformed." The citizens who left Dodge for Topeka were R. J. Hardesty, G. S. Emerson, Elder Collins, B. E. Rice, S. A. Bullard, P. G. Reynolds, S. Mullendore, T. L. McCarty, Henry Sturm, A. Dienst, F. J. Durand, and L. W. Jones.[26] After hearing this side of the story, Governor Glick ordered his adjutant general, Thomas Moonlight,[27] to Dodge City to assess matters there and report back.

The reporting again suggested a dramatist was at work, describing Tom Moonlight as a "Minister Plenipotentiary to Ford county" for the purpose of negotiating a treaty "by which peace might be restored to that distracted community." Would Short enter into the fray and participate in a bloody battle, the readers may have wondered? Or would Moonlight be able to bring about a peaceful settlement? Further in the report however the matter proved to be more serious than the lightheartedness of the earlier paragraphs. Sheriff Hinkel had given assurance that "ample protection" would be afforded Short if he returned. This was not too comforting to Luke Short, as he explained to the *Capital* reporter: "If the sheriff is sincere in saying so, why has he not got some of my friends on the posse? Instead of doing that he has called to his assistance men known to be my bitterest enemies. I would as soon trust myself in the hands of the mob as to the protections of the sheriff's posse." Short added that he was "convinced" that the plot for his assassination was "perfected" and that he would be killed if he returned to Dodge. The reporter could not resist giving a description of the man who had created such good press. "Mr. Short, who has been observed by many on the streets of Topeka during the last week, would hardly meet, in his personal appearance, the expectations of many who have heard and seen him described as a 'red-handed desperado.'" Short in truth was under medium height, well built and firmly knit, "with nothing in his features or complexion to indicate irregular or dissipated habits." The man was clean shaven except for a "natty little moustasche [*sic*]" who dressed with "great care and good style. He sports a magnificent diamond pin, and yesterday twirled between his fingers an elegant black walking stick with a gold head." The *Capital* knew little of Luke's past history, but in case there was any question "there is no doubt he is able to take care of himself in almost any kind of crowd." The committee of twelve did meet with Governor Glick and after an extended conversation were satisfied that peace would be restored in Dodge, and Mr. Short would be assured that he would be "permitted to return to Dodge and remain there for ten days for the purpose of closing his business." During this ten-day period he would be "perfectly safe against molestation of any kind."[28] Would this be satisfactory to Luke L. Short remained the pressing question.

By this time newspapers across the country started to print wire service reports of what became known as the "Dodge City War." Many of the items profiled Luke who was becoming a favorite among the ladies. One described him as being "a regular dandy, quite handsome, and . . . a perfect ladies man." Luke dressed "fashionably, is particular in his appearances, and always to look as neat as possible." When in Dodge City the man associated with "the very best element, and leads in almost every social event that is gotten up." Luke had created such a positive impression upon the ladies that they were "anxious to get up a petition among themselves to send to the governor" in support of this handsome young man who had been so rudely mistreated by Dodge City.[29] Would the adjutant general and the governor respond to such a petition?

The cast of characters was now well known enough to inspire bad puns, such as this example from an Atchison, Kansas, newspaper, which opined:

> "If Dodge City doesn't Luke Sharp," says the Topeka Journal, "they will be Short a citizen." We hope the Journal will not Harris us with any more puns as the above.[30]

Chapter 5

A Plain Statement and Shots from Short

> "Mr. Short's expulsion from the city is the direct result of his own action and the feeling of the people generally is very strong against him."
>
> —George T. Hinkel, Ford County Sheriff, May 12, 1883.

There were two factions in the "Dodge City War" and to a great extent they waged their battles in the columns of the newspapers, suggesting perhaps that the solid citizens involved realized their differences were not worth killing anyone. Each side presented their beliefs in lengthy newspaper articles. Thirteen citizens of Dodge City "officials" fired the opening salvo in a letter published in the *Topeka Daily Capital* on May 18, 1883 (the same issue in which was printed the interview with Luke mentioned above). The *Capital* editor headlined this missive as "A Plain Statement" that described the troubles as viewed three days before. As one would expect it was quite different from the version of events as reported by Short and his supporters. The lengthy "Plain Statement" began by pointing out that the "commotion" reported in the Kansas City and Topeka newspapers would have their readers believe that Dodge

City was in the hands of a mob, and that the persons and property of peaceable citizens were in constant jeopardy from destruction. In reality the Dodge City citizens continued to pursue "the even tenor of their way" and perhaps the town was more peaceable than it had been for years. The violence being done to persons and property was "all being done in Kansas City and Topeka through the press" while Dodge City itself was "quiet orderly and peaceable."[1]

"A Plain Statement" stressed that what was happening was necessary about every two years, in other words, "a clearing out of an element composed of bold, daring men of illegal profession who, from toleration by the respectable portion of the community, are allowed to gain a prestige found difficult to unseat."[2] But what of the group that was ordered out of town? That element was one which "has to be banished, or else the respectable people have to be bulldozed and browbeat by a class of men without any vested interest or visible means of support, who should be allowed to remain in a decent community by toleration, but who, instead, after gaining prestige, they undertake to dictate the government of the better class."

The facts of the matter had been misunderstood, both to and for the press, as well as the governor. The true state of affairs was quite different, and the Plain Statement reviewed the facts as they knew them: First, at the last election in April Deger and Harris ran for the office of mayor. Harris was described as "a gambler by profession" and was living "in open adultery with a public prostitute"; whatever interest he had in the town was "merely of a local character." Harris supposedly had one item of real estate, a small house on which he paid taxes, and the only reason for him owning that was that it was cheaper to own than to rent. Harris, living in this building with the "public prostitute," resulted in the decent people of Dodge recognizing Harris as a "sympathizer, friend and shielder of the gambler, thus, confidence man and murderer. . . . always found on their bond for recognizance, no matter how glaring the deed or heinous the offense for which they stand charged."[3] It was not clear which sin of Harris was the worst: being a professional gambler, living with a "public prostitute," or owning a small house instead of renting it.

Running against Harris was Deger, described in the "Plain Statement" as "a man of irreproachable character and honesty . . . an old resident of the town [who] was elected by a large majority . . . [and] Harris felt very sore over his defeat." From this defeat it was apparent that he and some of his supporters, essentially the gambling crowd, would be against everything the new administration intended to accomplish. At the first meeting of the new administration it was found necessary to revise ordinances prohibiting "women of lewd character" from loitering around the saloons and on the streets. This ordinance was passed, and a second one proposed concerning gamblers. To a committee of gamblers the council did make concessions, in fact, made all concessions asked, "in order to preserve peace and harmony."[4] The council did not itemize what concessions they made however.

On the second night of the ordinance being in effect, the night of the concessions made, Short, Harris, and one other gambler, "who were loud in their abuse of the ordinance, there being no women down town, went to a house of ill fame, and, according to their spoken words, forced two of the inmates down to their saloon to violate the ordinance, saying they would pay the fines and costs assessed against the women." But did they? The women were tried and fined for the offense but they had to pay their fine and court costs themselves and were then ordered to leave town.[5]

The officers placed the three women in jail. It was after this arrest that Luke Short, the partner of Harris, described as a gambler and hard character in the version of the thirteen officials of the city, "attempted to assassinate L. C. Hartman," a special policeman. He had assisted in the arrest or the women. This assassination attempt occurred at night in front of a general store, which was closed. While Hartman passed by Short and his companion, Short turned and drew his pistol and said, "There is one of the son's of ---, lets throw it to him" and immediately fired two shots at Hartman. Somehow Hartman fell down but was not hit, although Short and his companion believed Luke had hit him, or perhaps even killed him. Short and his companion started to the nearby saloon of Tom Land. Hartman had now recovered himself and fired a shot at Short, which also missed.[6] Strangely, according to the officials, although the women were locked up one night, Short and Harris were not, having intimidated the officials to not incarcerate them. Luke Short was considered the "leader and spokesman" for the group. In case Short's name was not recalled, the letter stated that only a few weeks earlier Short had "pulled out his pistol and beat one of our most respectful citizens over the head until he was carried home on a stretcher, and his life was despaired of for several days."[7] Continuing, Luke Short was described as a ruffian, a "man that killed his man, an old gray headed man 57 years old, in Tombstone, Arizona, and has been run out of that and other places by the respectable people."[8] Short was also an "intimate friend" of Jack McCarty, as "notorious and well-known three card monte and confidence man . . . who recently died near this place after being convicted of highway robbery and about to receive his sentence of ten years."[9]

According to these thirteen citizens, the saloon of Harris and Short was "a refuge and resort for all confidence men, thieves and gamblers that visit the town." Any statements about Webster's saloon, on the other hand, were false. It was apparent to the mayor and councilmen that this element led by Harris and Short was going "to violate, encourage, shield and protect" all violators of the city's ordinances. Short, in addition to surrounding himself with this low class of people, had attempted to assassinate an officer of the law in the discharge of his duty, had bulldozed the city officers, and had violated, aided, and abetted in the violation of the laws. Supposedly after all this the mayor and "a large number of citizens" determined to arrest Short and six other associates, locked them in the calaboose for one night, and then allowed them to leave town the next day.[10] It was clearly a matter of St. George, on a white stallion, fighting the dragon, which was covered in evil blackness.

To the claim that a mob was in control of the town, the thirteen responded that there was no mob, that the group was "*bona fide* citizens armed to aid the officers if necessary in the enforcement of the laws." Much of the confusion and misunderstanding in Dodge City was due to intentionally misrepresenting the facts and that was done by none other than the district clerk William F. Petillon, a Ford County citizen who lived about six miles north of Dodge on a claim of 160 acres.[11] He was recognized as "a Harris man." To further complicate matters, Jack McCarty had been arrested on a charge of highway robbery and had given bond for $2000. Harris was one of the bondsmen, and Short, having no real property, convinced a citizen who had real property to sign the bond. Short deposited the amount to secure the party's appearance. During McCarty's trial it became evident he would be convicted, but after conviction and before sentencing, McCarty escaped. Upon his escape clerk Petillon was applied to for the bond, but he could not give it, "as he did not know where it was. He had it the last day of court and was the one seen to have it last." The bond was never found, and it was "impossible to obliterate from the minds of a great many respectable people here that Petillon knew why and where that bond disappeared."[12] The inference was clear. And Petillon was a clear supporter of Harris and Short.

In sum, since the condition of Dodge City then was deemed an orderly and law-abiding community, it was believed it would stay that way if Luke Short and his associates disappeared. But if they were allowed to remain it would be "against the will and without the consent of a majority of the law-abiding citizens . . . and if the Governor, through his interference and encouragement, forces these men back on us he does so at his peril, and if there is bloodshed as a result the responsibility will not rest entirely with the Governor,[13] who, had he not given the matter encouragement, it would have passed unnoticed, as an occurrence frequent in all cities desirous of being law-abiding, and of good government." The document was dated at Dodge City on May 15, 1883. It was signed by Mayor L. E. Deger, Councilmen H. B. Bell, H. T. Drake, Henry Sturm, George S. Emerson, and H. M. Beverley. The seven others were Police Judge R. E.

Burns, City Treasurer N. B. Klaine, City Clerk L. C. Hartman, Assistant Marshal C. E. Chipman, City Attorney Fred T. M. Wenie, City Marshal J. L. Bridges, and City Physician T. L. McCarty.[14]

The letter was notable not just for who signed it, but who did not sign it as well. The thirteen signatories were among the hardest of the hard-liners opposed to Short and Harris, so the appearance of their names was no surprise. It was also no surprise that "moderates" in Dodge City, such as Robert M. Wright and George M. Hoover, elected not to sign the document. What was surprising was the absence of a signature from Alonzo B. Webster, who some believed to be the person actually pulling the strings in the administration of Mayor Deger. The other missing signature belonged to the man that Luke Short regarded as the actual author of the letter: Mike Sutton, a highly successful attorney at law.[15]

Luke Short could not ignore this published statement, and by May 21 had composed his "Shots from Short" as it was headlined, and it appeared in print in the *Daily Kansas State Journal* of Topeka, datelined May 23, 1883. Needless to say, Luke's version was radically different from the "plain statement." First of all that "plain statement" was a "malicious statement" and needed to be refuted. For those who had any direct knowledge of the circumstances that brought about the "recent state of affairs at Dodge" it was apparent that the purpose of its being written was to justify those who participated in "running me away from the town; as not one word of truth appeared in the statement, which was unquestionably written by an advisor and principal director of the mob, and who is too cowardly to openly identify himself with them." Short was not cowardly and he identified the author of the document as Mike Sutton, one who had been "playing the part of 'Judas' in this matter all through." Luke claimed that Sutton had the "carefully prepared statement" written to show that it was "a fight between the city authorities on one side and the gamblers, thugs, thieves and prostitutes on the other," which he denounced as "a base malicious falsehood, at least so far as my side of the question is concerned." Short denied that he or Harris ever had "championed the cause of thieves, thugs and prostitutes" since they had a business in Dodge City, "which is more than can be said of those who opposed us."[16]

The matter of Harris not having any interest in the city, that he owned only one little house worth $400, could not be ignored. According to Luke, Harris bought the little house and paid for it honestly, which could not be said about how Mike Sutton obtained his, "by jobbing and swearing a poor unfortunate creature into the penitentiary . . . in order to get possession of his little household."

Also the matter of Harris living in an open state of adultery with a prostitute was raised. Luke called it an "infamous lie." As for living with a prostitute, "I consider that a rather broad assertion to make and consider such things his own private affairs and no body's business." What if it was true, that Harris was living with a prostitute? If the accusation was true Luke considered it nothing more than what Sutton, Webster, Deger, Chipman, Hartman, "and others of that outfit have done in the past, and are doing at present." According to Luke, Alonzo Webster had abandoned his family for a prostitute; Tom Nixon had done the same, and "there are only those who cannot get a prostitute to live with, who have not got them . . . all the thieves, thugs and prostitutes who have been in town in the past two years have been directly or indirectly connected with the city government. These assertions," Luke stormed on, "I am prepared to prove in any court of justice in the world."[17] It was a safe statement to make, as who would want to testify in court to such accusations?

Short was also peeved that his killing of Charlie Storms was brought up, and that he had allegedly "been run out of every country I have lived in." This was an "infamous" statement to make. He assured his readers that there was not a "civilized country under the face of the sun" that he could not go to with "perfect safety" except Dodge City. There was no law preventing Luke from living in Dodge, but there was "a band of cut throats and midnight assassins" who had "banded together" solely for the purpose of keeping all those out of the place who would oppose them at the polls, or be competitive to them in their business. And the Storms matter was not overlooked: he reminded the readers that he stood trial in an Arizona court and was "honorably acquitted."[18]

Nor was the question of ownership of land overlooked: remember the remarks made about Petillon and his 160 acres. To Luke, who may have been on shaky ground at this point, the delegation who went to see the governor and who claimed to represent the moral element of Dodge, was

> principally composed of tramps, who do not own a single foot of ground in the country, and never have, and I want to specially refer to the two leading spirits and spokesmen of said delegation, the Rev. Mr. Collins and Capt. Dinst [*sic*], —one an itinerant preacher, who by his peregrinations, through charitably disposed committees manages to eke out a miserable existence, and who, on the eve of the last municipal election at Dodge, sold the influence of his congregation and his own, for fifteen dollars; the other, Capt. Dinst, it is positively asserted by the most reputable citizens of Dodge City, was engaged in robbing a safe at the flouring mills owned and operated by one H. F. May.[19] He is a man wholly without character, and cannot get employment of any description with any responsible parties.

Then Luke remembered the accusation against his friend W. F. Petillon that he had stolen a bond. Luke averred that Petillon could not have done that as he never had the bond in question. Petillon was prepared to prove he did not do what he was accused of doing. "It is a fine accusation for such a man as Mike Sutton," continued Luke, apparently fearing nothing, "to make against such a man as Pettilon [*sic*]. There is not a responsible man in Ford County that believes Pettilon stole the bond, but there is not an honest man in the county but believes Sutton would steal a bond or anything else that he could get his hands on." Luke bravely continued: "and they base their opinions on his past record as an official of the county."[20]

And what of the past record of Sutton? "Every inhabitant of the county knows that not over eight months ago he resigned his position as county attorney in order to accept a two thousand dollar fee to defend one of the most cold blooded murderers that ever appeared in any court of justice. He knew that by resigning, he could defeat the ends of justice." How, questioned Luke, and then provided the answer: the man whom he had appointed in his stead was wholly incompetent to conduct a successful prosecution and the result was an acquittal and "a red-handed murderer turned loose upon the world to repeat his crime."[21]

Another matter could not be ignored—the shooting at L. C. Hartman. Certainly the accusation that Luke tried to assassinate this law officer was "a lie on its face." If it were true then why didn't they try and convict Luke of the attempted murder? They did not try to do so as they had no evidence, Luke answered his own question. They knew that "their policeman attempted to assassinate me and I had him arrested for it and had plenty of evidence to have convicted him, but before it came to trial they had organized a vigilance committee and made me leave, so that I could not appear against him." Short was still fuming now, "And this is what they call justice and the law abiding element clearing out the lawless characters. If it be true, it is a sad commentary on Kansas justice and those who are supposed to execute the law."[22]

Would not Luke return to Dodge on their pledge that he could remain for ten days and "that during that time I will not be in imminent danger of being murdered?" And if he overstayed the ten days they "would not be responsible for any personal safety." Luke slyly stated this was a "very liberal concession on their part" but he had no desire to accept. Short feared he would meet the same fate as the late General Canby "when he accepted the invitation extended to him by the Modocs."[23]

Luke finished his missive stating that he would rather trust himself in the hands of wild Apaches than trust to the protection of such men as Webster, Nixon, and Deger, "with Mike Sutton, in the background to perfect the plans of my assassination." When he would return, Luke assured the readers, it would be when his enemies least expected him, and it would not be "in answer to any invitation which they may extend to me."

Luke concluded with his own threat. "In conclusion I will say that they may be able to keep me out of Dodge City by brute force without the sanction of law, but there are many towns in America that I will keep them, out of, or make them show a valid cause for remaining."[24] Perhaps Luke Short did give the thirteen citizens who had signed the "plain statement" something concrete to think about. They certainly realized that the little gambler was no pushover.

Chapter 6

The Dodge City Peace Commission

> "There seems to be a general opinion, now very frequently expressed here, that a few of the ring leaders ought to be allowed to fight and kill each other off if they want to."
>
> —*Daily Kansas State Journal,* June 7, 1883.

Luke Short and Bat Masterson were both on the move on Monday, May 21, 1883. Luke went to Caldwell, Kansas, where his arrival was considered important news. Caldwell was a cattle town nearly two hundred miles southeast of Dodge City. The *Caldwell Journal* provided a brief reminder in case the readers had not been following other Kansas news, introducing him as Luke Short, "about whom the fuss at Dodge City was kicked up," as sufficient notice as to who the man was. He was described as "a quiet unassuming man, with nothing about him to lead one to believe him the desperado the Dodge mob picture him to be. He says the whole trouble arose from business jealousy on the part of Webster, Nixon and others. As to his plans he has nothing to say, but he is determined to take all legal measures to secure his rights."[1]

On the same date that Luke arrived in Caldwell, a train carrying Bat Masterson stopped at Dodge, before going on to Colorado. Nicholas B. Klaine of the *Dodge City Times* noted his presence at the stopover, merely saying that Masterson passed through on "the cannon ball train." Some citizens of Dodge went to the train but they could not gain access to the sleeping car, which contained "the redoubtable Bat." The unexpected statement was that "No one in Dodge wants to offer Bat any harm as long as Bat offers no harm himself." Why would there be a concern? Bat was a good friend of Luke Short, and, according to Klaine, the country "has been anticipating some fearful things judging from the promulgation of the proposed movement of a notorious gang." The people of Dodge had anticipated such a denouement; few people, Klaine noted, "believed the statements in the Kansas City papers about the proposed action of the gang."[2]

Things remained quiet until May 31, when Wyatt Earp returned to Dodge. The former city marshal arrived in the city from the west, "looking well and glad to get back to his old haunts, where he is well and favorably known."[3] Earp was too well known as far as Sheriff George T. Hinkel was concerned, however. Within hours of Earp's arrival Hinkel sent a telegram to Governor Glick, asking if he could send Colonel Moonlight to Dodge "tomorrow" with the power to organize a company of militia. Hinkel had "ample reason" for asking this which, he assured the chief officer, he would give to Colonel Moonlight so that he could communicate it directly to the governor.[4] What Sheriff Hinkel chose not to reveal to the governor was that he was fearful of what might happen if these noted men assembled to do harm to any Dodge City citizen; Hinkel knew he would be helpless in such a situation.

On Sunday, June 3, Luke Short and some supporters boarded a train in Kinsley, Kansas, and headed straight for Dodge City, less than forty miles away. Short and Earp (who had joined Luke in Kinsley) were accompanied by W. F. Petillon as they rode the rails to Dodge. They expected to be joined in Dodge by "Shotgun" Collins and Bat Masterson.

Unless the city authorities backed down, there would be some "lively news" from Dodge.[5] The press may have hoped for such lively news, knowing the circulation of their newspapers would increase, but Sheriff Hinkel and others became nervous.

The *Ford County Globe* avoided lengthy descriptions of Luke's coming home and reported the news in a manner to suggest that it was time to settle scores, alerting its readers that "Luke Short . . . has come to stay." [6]

The day after his return—Monday, June 4—Luke was in the Long Branch Saloon, well protected by several gun-toting supporters, many of whom had been awaiting Luke's arrival in Dodge for days. Backed into a corner Mayor Deger could only issue another proclamation. The mayor ordered the closing of all the gambling places. Deger's action, supposedly, was brought about because Short and friends had failed to fulfill the compromise agreed upon, that he and several other "hard characters" should leave town. As soon as this proclamation was issued, every gambling house did close its doors. "Whether the trouble will end there," the *Leavenworth Times* wondered, "it is hard to determine."[7]

Never considered as the most diplomatic of men, Bat Masterson appeared now to extend an olive branch, but with a sprinkling of sarcasm, in a letter to friends in Topeka. Bat wrote that upon his arrival at Dodge a "delegation of friends" met him to escort him "without molestation" to the Harris & Short establishment. He considered all the "inflammatory reports" that had been common in the press about Dodge City and its citizens had been "greatly exaggerated"; whatever "war paint" had been applied to the warriors' faces had been washed off by the time he had arrived. Certainly with tongue in cheek he continued: "I never met a more gracious lot of people in my life. They all seemed favorably disposed, and hailed the return of Short and his friends with exultant joy." From his sarcastic tone Bat segued into declarative fact: "I have been unable as yet to find a single individual who participated with the crowd that forced him to leave here at first." Bat added that he had conversed with many citizens and "they are unanimous in their expression of love for

Short. . . . [H]e is gentlemanly, courteous and unostentatious—'in fact a perfect ladies man.'" Bat's mastery with a six-gun was well-known; his talent with the Queen's English was no less so; he proved to be a master at articulating his thoughts without resorting to the Colt revolver.

Mutual friends of Luke and Bat were already in Dodge, among them Wyatt Earp, Charles Bassett, and Frank McLean, and were making the Long Branch their headquarters. Short contributed to Masterson's letter, pointing out that all the gambling houses were closed by the mayor's proclamation, but hinted that they would open soon. Luke was well aware of the economic impact on the town. "The closing of the 'legitimate' calling has caused a general depression in business of every description, and I am under the impression that the more liberal and thinking class will prevail upon the mayor to rescind the proclamation in a day or two."[8] Was Luke Short subtly describing the mayor and his supporters as part of a non-thinking class of citizens? Certainly businessmen would resent any action of the mayor that would have a negative effect on their business.

Masterson was not exaggerating when he mentioned there could be a "general depression in business" in Dodge City. Among the many readers of Bat's letter was Adjutant General Moonlight, who wrote Sheriff Hinkel that "the cattle trade will soon begin to throng your streets, and all your citizens are interested in the coming. It is your harvest of business and affects every citizen, and I fear unless the spirit of fair play prevails it will work to your business injury."[9]

By this time the events in Dodge City, whether accurately reported or not, were newsworthy beyond the borders of Kansas. A New Orleans newspaper reported that all gambling had been stopped, and Luke Short, at his place of business, was "defiant." Reportedly Short had returned to Dodge with "no flag of truce" but was willing to obey the law. He was defying "the mob" and had "caused a change in his favor." With no gambling allowed, there were no games and "dozens of gamblers were idle."[10]

Important figures other than idle gamblers also became concerned. Who would have believed that Luke's actions would cause the governor of Kansas and the president of the Santa Fe Railroad to make it clear to the Dodge City officials to find a peaceful solution to the matter? The pressure of the citizens on Deger was one thing, but the governor and the Santa Fe as well? The *Evening Star* of Kansas City, Missouri, now reported that there was a "band of noted killers" at Dodge. Besides Earp, Masterson, and Bassett, Doc Holliday was now there and with his presence trouble could occur at any moment. Charlie Bassett was there in Kansas City for "quite a time" with Colonel Rickets of the Marble Hall; if anyone was unfamiliar with Bassett he was described as "a man of undoubted nerve and has been tried and not found wanting when it comes to a personal encounter." The names of Masterson and Holliday were too well known "to need comment or biography." Notices had been posted up ordering these men classed as killers out of town, and "as they are fully armed and determined to stay, there may be hot work there to-night."[11]

There was no "hot work" in Dodge that night, but the conflict known as the "Dodge City War" concluded the evening of June 7. Although there were a few minor points yet to be worked out, Adj. Gen. Thomas Moonlight brought about a peaceful settlement between the two "warring factions." The Short faction were "in the ascendancy" but were "peaceably disposed. There is no danger of trouble."[12] So reported a Topeka newspaper.

The gunfighters who came to Dodge to support Luke Short had represented a very real threat, but it wasn't their formidable presence that finally brought the opposing factions together: it was simple economics. Some people could even interject some humor into the situation. An Atchison, Kansas, newspaper pointed out that the troubles between the two factions finally settled satisfactorily and "everything is as pleasant there now as a basket of chips." Adjutant General Moonlight could very well feel satisfied with the results: no fatalities, not even a wounded warrior on either side. In fact, the Dodge City folks felt better than they had for the previous four or five years. The officers realized and "willingly admit, that in running Short out they made a horrible mistake, which has cost the town thousands of dollars."[13] If there had been a question before, no one now could claim ignorance that in reality it was a question of following the money. The question of living in open adultery with a "public prostitute" or the degree of vice was not now so important as it had been not too long before.

On Saturday, June 9, 1883, the two factions had a final meeting. At that time all those who had been run out of town were back, with no fear of assassination or further trouble. In fact, the gambling houses were ready to open but there was to be a "door shield" or screen door, shielding the activity in one room from another. At a new dance house just opened that Saturday night, the former enemies met and settled their differences. Everything was now "lovely and serene." All opposing factions, both saloon men and gamblers, agreed to stand by each other for the good of their trade. They all realized the result was for their common good, but Mayor Deger, all three-hundred-plus pounds of his honor, was still standing firm on his proclamation. He would have no support as most of his "most ardent supporters" had gone over to his "enemies." If Mayor Deger had followed his own best judgment and not the advice of others who had only their selfish interests at stake he would have had much better success in his actions as the city's leading citizen. "No one knows this now any better than himself."[14]

On Sunday, June 10, 1883, Wyatt Earp and Bat Masterson were preparing to return to Colorado on a westbound train. Before leaving they got together with Luke and five others to pose for a group photograph. The historic photo was taken inside of what amounted to a large tent, which was serving as the temporary studio of Dodge City photographer Charles A. Conkling.[15] It has become one of the most reproduced photographs of Wild West gamblers and gunfighters. From the very beginning the group portrait was known as "The Dodge City Peace Commission." Forty-four days after it was taken, the photo was reproduced, as an engraving, in the July 21, 1883, issue of the *National Police Gazette* which noted,

> the "peace commissioners," as they have been termed, accomplished the object of their mission, and quiet once more reigns where war for several weeks and rumors of war were the all absorbing topic. All the members of the commission, whose portraits we publish in a group, are frontiersmen of tried capacity.

Standing in the photo, from left to right, were William H. Harris, Luke Short, Bat Masterson, and William F. Petillon. Seated, left to right were Charles E. Bassett, Wyatt Earp, Michael Francis "Frank" McLean, and Cornelius "Neil" Brown. Prints were made of the photo and given to each of the eight "Peace Commissioners," as well as others who had supported Luke. One of those prints was found in Fort Worth in 1918 and may have been Luke Short's personal copy.[16]

Editor Nicholas B. Klaine of the *Dodge City Times* noted that "the photographs of the eight visiting 'statesmen' were taken in a group by Mr. Conkling, photographer. The distinguished bond extractor and champion pie eater, W. F. Petillon, appears in the Group."[17] Klaine never missed an opportunity to take a swipe at Petillon. The reference to his being a "champion pie eater" does not refer to Petillon having won a contest at a country fair. The fact was that Petillon was notorious for scooping up slices of pie at the various Dodge City saloons that had a "free lunch" counter. There were several newspaper references, over the years, commenting on Petillon's fondness for pie.

So now the Dodge City War was over, but Governor Glick kept his promise to commission the militia for Dodge City, just in case. They were appropriately named the "Glick Guards" and supporters of both groups during the saloon war composed the company. Pat Sughrue was selected captain; James H. Kelley his lieutenant; others were Dr. Samuel Galland, a former Deger man; Neil Brown, William H. Harris, W. F. Petillon, Luke Short, solid pro-Harris men; Clark E. Chipman was pro-Deger of course. Two others whose names failed to appear in the vast literature concerning the "troubles" were Isom Prentice "Print" Olive and William M. Tilghman.[18]

A couple of months after things calmed down in Dodge City, Luke Short was interviewed while in Kansas City. Nicholas B. Klaine reprinted a portion of the interview in the *Dodge City Times.* The reporter asked Luke if he was running his business as he had been before the "agitation occurred."

"Yes, sir; I am going ahead as usual. I returned to stay. Those men made a bad play and could not carry it out." As to whether or not the trouble might break out again, Luke responded: "It may be at the election this fall, but I do not think it will be like it was formerly. If it breaks out this time it will mean a fight. The next election [will] take place in November. The sheriff will then be elected." And who will be the candidate for the other side? "The present under sheriff, Fred Singer, while ours is Pat Shugrue [*sic,* Sughrue]."[19]

But not all was serene and peaceful in Dodge City, at least for some of those involved in the recent difficulties. On August 22, 1883, Luke swore out a complaint and had Police Judge Robert E. "Bobby" Burns arrested. Editor Nicholas B. Klaine reported it in the columns of the *Dodge City Times.* He was not pleased. Burns was brought before Justice Rufus G. Cook and was "charged with misconduct in office and the collection of illegal fees." Judge Burns had "incurred the enmity" of many who had come before him officially. In Klaine's reporting Burns had "inflicted heavy fines" on those appearing before his bench. Klaine, without specifying in detail what Burns had allegedly done, commented that there was "a certain clique in this city that feel the legal halter drawing tighter and tighter, with an ultimate tightening of the grasp never to be loosened." The law was coming down upon "indecent and illegitimate traffic" and the handwriting was on the wall.[20]

The case against Burns was finally dismissed. Luke Short was rapidly losing interest in Dodge City, and was often out of town. The results of one excursion, to Kansas City, on September 10, 1883, were reported in a Medicine Lodge, Kansas, newspaper. The incident was "a scene of revelry" in the barroom of a well-known hotel in Kansas City. The scene reportedly had a "decidedly western flavor" and if there was a "tenderfoot" present then his mind was "filled with terror." What brought about this scene was that a large group of western cattle men had gathered during the afternoon and by nightfall had become "uproariously drunk." Luke Short was among the group but apparently he was not one of those who had imbibed so heavily. All might have gone unnoticed except some of the group drew their revolvers and "began to rake up old grudges against each other." Someone threatened Luke Short who of course returned the threat. Some onlookers decided they were too close to what might happen and blended into the background. Two policemen were stationed on the outside of the door where the gathering was held. Since nothing more than words resulted from the drunken threats the "more drunken of the party were put to bed and the others gradually cooled down and dispersed."[21]

After leaving Kansas City, Luke went to Texas to explore opportunities in Dallas, San Antonio and Fort Worth. He returned to Dodge to settle up his affairs there. Both he and William H. Harris had decided to sell the Long Branch. Once they found buyers, they published a "card" in the November 20, 1883, issue of the *Ford County Globe*:

> We take this opportunity of informing our numerous patrons and friends that we have sold out our interest in the Long Branch saloon and billiard hall to Mr. [Roy] Drake and [Frank] Warren, who will continue the business and are authorized to collect and receipt for all accounts due us. Any accounts against the late firm will be settled by us. Thanking past patrons for their many favors shown us, and trust the new firm may receive a like generous treatment at their hands.
>
> W. H. Harris
>
> Luke Short

November 19, 1883.

The *Ford County Globe* also noted Short's departure: "Luke Short came up from Texas during the past week, spending several days here, during which time he sold his interest in the Long Branch and returns to Fort Worth, Texas, accompanied by W. B. Masterson."[22] Nicholas B. Klaine also reported the departure of Bat and Luke in his signature style:

> Gen. Bat Masterson and Col. Luke Short . . . left on Friday evening [November 16, 1883] for Ft. Worth, Texas. The authorities in Dallas and Ft. Worth are stirring up the gambling fraternity, and probably the "peace makers" have gone there to "harmonize" and adjust affairs. The gambling business is getting considerable "shaking up" all over the country. The business of gambling is "shaking" in Dodge. It is nearly "shook out" entirely.[23]

During December Luke Short left Fort Worth and went to Kansas City where he looked up Charles E. Bassett. On December 28 Short and Bassett showed up in Dodge City, both looking well, showing they had been kindly treated by their friends in the east. They intended to remain in Dodge until after the holidays.[24] This would not be Luke's final visit to Dodge City, as there were still old scores that he wanted to settle in Dodge—but that fight would be waged mainly from his new base of operations in Fort Worth.

CHAPTER 7

THE WHITE ELEPHANT IN PANTHER CITY

> Gamblers Luke Short and Wm. Attenbury "were acquitted by a first class-intelligent jury."
>
> —*Galveston Daily News*, August 27, 1884.

The February 2, 1875, *Dallas Daily Herald* published an article stating that Fort Worth was such a boring city that a panther was found sleeping in the streets. Intended as an insult, the story was enthusiastically adopted by Fort Worth residents who began calling their town "Panther City."[1] In 1876 the arrival of the Texas & Pacific Railway created a boom and transformed Fort Worth, and its stockyards, into a major player in the wholesale cattle industry. The city would be Luke Short's home base from 1884 until his death in 1893. Although Short spent long stretches away from the town during those years, Panther City would—for better or worse—be the place that he considered "home."[2]

Luke Short returned to Dodge City during May 1884, and his friend William F. Petillon, then editor of the *Dodge City Democrat*, had a little fun at his expense by writing that "Luke Short is here from Fort Worth.

He will remain until after the arrival of St. John and Campbell, as he is anxious to meet these learned gentlemen."[3] John P. St. John, an ex-governor of Kansas, and A. B. Campbell were ardent prohibitionists, and the last kind of people that Luke would be "anxious to meet." That summer both Luke and his attorney, Nelson "Net" Adams, sued the city of Dodge in the District Court at Larned, Kansas. Nicholas B. Klaine, ever ready to be critical of Short, reported that Luke had sued Dodge City having determined the damages were in the amount of $15,000. Mayor Hoover was served with notice of the suit while in Larned but there was no immediate response. Klaine then reminded his readers who Short was, the "conspicuous figure" in the spring of 1883 "Dodge City trouble," although certainly no one really needed to be reminded. Attorney Adams had sued the city some weeks previously for $5,000 damage, Klaine pointed out, reminding his readers that Adams "was also in that ugly little matter" as a lawyer. Just how Short was damaged $15,000 worth was also undetermined, but how Adams could have lost $5,000 was apparently easily seen. Perhaps this was simply an additional slam against the attorney. [4]

Dodge had elected George M. Hoover as mayor on April 7, 1884, replacing Lawrence E. Deger. It was the new Hoover administration, with newly elected city council members, who had to deal with the suits from Adams and Short. Nelson Adams finally agreed to settle for $1,750, a fraction of the $5,000 he was asking. Short and Adams both settled for far less than what they sued for. They probably knew what they had asked for was far more than what they had actually "lost."[5]

Back in Fort Worth, on August 26, Luke made a courtroom appearance where he was the defendant. He and William Atterbury were both charged with being vagrants, although they were professional gamblers. City Attorney J. W. Swayne prosecuted with F. W. Ball while William Capps appeared for the defense. After a "hard fight" by the counsel the jury returned a verdict of not guilty in each case.[6] A Dallas newspaper commented: "This makes seven different cases with seven different juries and not one verdict of guilty. Public sentiment, so called, is not against gambling, or the law and the evidence fall far short of what they should be."[7] As in Kansas, there were active reformers in Texas who were out campaigning for the closing of saloons and gambling houses. As the Dallas newspaper indicated, "public sentiment" did not yet reflect the reformers' zeal, however. The *Daily News* of Galveston certainly agreed, saying that Short and Atterbury "were acquitted by a first class-intelligent jury."[8]

Occasionally the reformers managed to get the saloons and gambling halls shut down, but whenever an opportunity presented itself they soon opened. These places had been shut down while the grand jury was in session, exactly why not stated, but when the grand jury adjourned they opened again. The night of September 27, 1884, saw "a number of gambling saloons" opened and they "did a rushing business." Games were in full progress above the White Elephant, in Dickson's Hall over the Horse Head Saloon and in the hall above the Occidental. Although there were large crowds of men going into these establishments, "everything was conducted with order" and the scene on Main Street was "animated up to a late hour."[9]

Luke Short's name will always be associated with three of the most celebrated saloons in Wild West history: the Oriental in Tombstone, the Long Branch in Dodge City, and the White Elephant in Fort Worth. Jake Johnson, Luke Short, and James A. "Alex" Reddick became the new owners of the White Elephant in December 1884, along with several other investors who owned similar shares in the business.[10] The announcement of the new partnership was publicized: "The White Elephant saloon has changed hands. Messrs. G. Burgower and Nath Bernstein selling out their interest to Messrs. Jake Johnson and Luke Short. Mr. Sam Berliner still retains an interest in the place. If the new management keeps an orderly a house as the old it will deserve the patronage of the public."[11]

The White Elephant was hardly a corner bar, or one of those swinging-door saloons so frequently featured in movie and television westerns—anything but. Some considered the bar and billiard parlor the "Pride of the City." The White Elephant arguably was "the largest and most magnificent establishment in the state." With a change of proprietors one might fear there would be a drastic change, but with the new proprietors "it loses none of its life, popularity or vitality by the change, but, to the contrary [Johnson, Short and Reddick] who now have the control and management is a guarantee within itself of its continued success and prosperity." Senior partner Jake Johnson had resided in Fort Worth "for many years, making a good and liberal citizen, and a gentleman who is liked by all classes of our people, and we can say as much for the other gentlemen." Short and Reddick were equals and no doubt the success of the White Elephant would "continue to be as brilliant and attractive as of your [*sic*, yore]." Reading the description one might wonder if there was anything equal in the entire country, not to mention Europe. The furniture was "the most elegant and costly"; the walls were "handsomely decorated with mammoth plate mirrors while glittering chandeliers hang suspended from the ceiling, illuminating the entire building." And to quench the thirst of the gambler, cowboy, businessman, gunfighter, lawman, or deputy marshal? There were "the very finest wines and liquors, ripe and aged, consisting of Scotch and Irish whiskies, French brandy and Holland gin, fine old rye and Bourbon, Scotch Ale, London and Dublin Porter." The bartenders, Ed B. Brown and Johnny Mallory, were "princes of good fellows" and were always "courteous and obliging." Of course.

If one wanted to be a little more active there were some ten or a dozen or more billiard and pool tables which were of "the latest improved and also beautiful design, and kept in excellent order." For the weary traveler or anyone who had "an hour or so hanging heavily over them" the White Elephant was the best place to be, where "those in attendance are always polite and active in their efforts to please their numerous patrons."[12]

Jake Johnson, Luke's partner, was one of the wealthiest citizens of Fort Worth. Using today's dollar values, he would have been a millionaire several times over. Johnson always had some investment going on that would provide entertainment for the citizens of Fort Worth while adding to his already impressive wealth. In January of 1885 Jake Johnson had, besides his interest in the White Elephant, a driving park, along with J. D. Reed, N. Harrold and A. J. Rose. The amount paid was reported at $9,000. It would be known as the Fort Worth Driving Park.[13]

Former "Peace Commissioner" Michael Francis "Frank" McLean also owned a share of the White Elephant. He had spent only a short time in Fort Worth, but it was enough for him to decide to settle there. Once McLean made his decision he prepared to return to Lawrence, Kansas, to get his wife and child.[14] Before he left, the gang at the White Elephant threw him a going away party. Although he wasn't tubercular, McLean was as thin as the consumptive Doc Holliday, and the *Fort Worth Daily Gazette* decided to have some fun at the underweight gambler's expense. McLean,

> one of the proprietors of the White Elephant, departed for the land of [Kansas Governor John P.] St. John Thursday [February 19, 1885] evening. His many friends and admirers in the city, knowing of the velocity of the winds in that state and knowing Mc's thinness (he having served in a museum as a skeleton for three years), combined together and purchased an elegant cane for him to cling to, which was presented at 8 p.m. on the evening of his departure, with a neat and appropriate speech by the business manager, Chas. Cunningham. Among the donors were E. B. Brown, John L. Ward, Sam Berlini [Berliner?] of trumpet fame, and many others. Toasts were responded to by several guests, and the programme was varied by McLean swallowing his cane.[15]

The thin man was back in Fort Worth, with his family, two months later. With no house for his wife and child McLean settled his family in the Hotel Lindell.[16] Frank McLean had not picked that hotel at random. The 1885 Fort Worth City Directory listed Luke Short as also boarding at thc Lindell Hotel. During May 1885 at least three of the "proprietors" of the White Elephant had to pay the routine fines that were assessed against gamblers at the price of doing business. In May Jake Johnson,

Dixie Lyons, Frank McLean, Sam McConnell, Luke Short, Louis Maas, and others paid a $25 fine.[17]

On June 28, 1885, Luke Short found himself cast in the unlikely role as the referee of a boxing match. Only a couple of years earlier Short had been indifferent to the sport, but constant prodding from Bat Masterson had finally turned him into a boxing enthusiast. As far as known, this marked Luke's only appearance as the "third man in the ring." It had not been Short's intent to become a referee, but the "hard-glove fight" took place between the "St. Joe Kid" of Fort Worth and "Kid" Bridges of Gordon, Texas. The contest, for $200 a side and gate receipts, took place at the first siding west of Weatherford on the Texas & Pacific railroad. A special train left Fort Worth at two o'clock with about seventy passengers. At Weatherford Kid Bridges, known as "the Gordon coal miner" and his backers, with a number of Weatherford people, boarded the train and the entire party proceeded to the place agreed on for the fight, which was reached a little after four in the afternoon. The spot for the ring was immediately selected in a close field on the side of the track and the ring was enclosed. But then there was a hitch: neither P. H. McDonald, the second for Kid Bridges, nor John Clow, the second for the St. Joe Kid, could find a man they both knew and were willing to agree upon for the important position of referee. After a great deal of discussion and some squabbling, they both finally agreed upon a man who had never before refereed a fight: Luke Short. According to one witness, when both fighters left their corners they presented a "fine appearance, but it was plainly evident that the St. Joe Kid was greatly overmatched in size and weight." Overmatched indeed, as Kid Bridges was six feet two inches tall, and weighed, when stripped for fighting, 175 pounds. The St. Joe Kid was only five feet eight inches in height and weighed but 152 pounds.

Both men left their corners "looking confident" and at the end of that round "both men went to their corners very little worried." The next four rounds "did not amount to much" and on the sixth round the St. Joe Kid "put in several good body blows, but was never able to reach

Kid Bridges' face." About the middle of round seven Kid Bridges "led out with his left on the St. Joe Kid's side and followed with his right, taking the St. Joe boy right under the chin and knocking him silly." The St. Joe Kid "fell like a beef" and lay several seconds without moving. Then P. H. McDonald jumped into the ring to attend to his fighter, at which point John Clow claimed a foul and took his man out, ending the fight.

"Great excitement followed" as the Gordon men, who favored Kid Bridges, claimed their man had won the fight fairly, and the St. Joe Kid's followers claimed a foul. Luke Short made a wise choice in not making a final decision amidst the "great excitement," putting off announcing his decision until he was in a safer place. "Under the rules," the *Gazette* reporter wrote, "a foul was unquestionably made by the second of Kid Bridges who had no right to get in the ring until time was called, and Mr. Short, the referee, so decided, giving the fight to the St. Joe Kid."[18]

As with so many western personalities, there are exciting incidents for which there is no contemporary record. For Luke Short there are many stories that are of questionable provenance. One, in particular, seems to have no provenance at all. The story appears to have originated in a 1958 magazine article by Tom Bailey. The publication that Bailey's article appeared in was in no danger of being confused with a respectable historical journal.[19] Bailey claimed that his article was based upon a 1903 book by a gambler named Charles "Rusty" Coe, who wrote his book with the aid of a co-author. The problem is that no one has ever seen a copy of this 1903 book—except for Tom Bailey.[20] The story that Bailey related had Charles Coe sitting in on a poker game at the White Elephant Saloon during August 1885. His fellow players were supposed to have been a nearly all-star cast of sporting men that included Luke Short, Wyatt Earp, Bat Masterson, and Jim Courtright. When the showdown came, Short is supposed to have produced a hand that Coe beat with two kings. Could it have happened?

The many things wrong with this story were best summed up by Jim Courtright's best biographer, who wrote: "First of all, the game was said to have taken place in August 1885; Courtright was on the run at the time and far away from Fort Worth. Secondly, such a monumental clash of prominent western sporting men, witnessed by dozens, would not have escaped the notice of city journalists, but no mention of this great game appeared in the papers. And lastly, Courtright was simply not in the same gambling league with the other players named."[21] The noted quartet gambling together remains one of those incidents a historian might wish to have happened, but as there is no provenance at all we must accept it is a figment of Bailey's active imagination. Short and Courtright would meet in the near future, however, near the White Elephant, with five shots from a Colt's .45 as the victor, not a pair of kings.

During August 1885, one of the partners in the White Elephant had to deal with a family health crisis. Elsie Belle McLean, Frank's wife, was seriously ill and was taken by her husband back to their home in Lawrence, Kansas. They arrived in Lawrence on August 11 after being in Texas four months. The local newspaper reported that Mrs. McLean had been ill with typhoid fever and had been brought back "as soon as she could be removed."[22]

Frank McLean was back in Fort Worth on October 1, 1885, when it was reported that "deeds of trust and chattel mortgages were filed with the county clerk yesterday as follows: Luke Short and M. F. McLean to F. W. Ball, and undivided one third interest in the White Elephant saloon to secure W. H. Ward in payment of a note of $1,000."[23]

Chapter 8

Sporting Men of Fort Worth

> Budd Fagg and Luke Short had "skipped, vamoosed the ranch, or in other words forfeited their bonds."
>
> —*Dallas Daily Herald*, November 18, 1886.

Luke Short was just one of many sporting men of Fort Worth in 1885 and 1886. He is the one best remembered today, but there were many, many others. Some of these men were his close friends, while others proved to be dangerous enemies. Luke's name often appeared alongside the others in newspaper reports of their frequent court appearances. Some of these sporting men had monikers that could have been created by Damon Runyon: Cheese Hensley, Saloon Galloway, and Hotel Hurd to name just a few. Others with more conventional names such as Charles B. Dixon, Nat Kramer, Sam McConnell, and Charles Wright would all play their part in Luke's career as a sporting man of Fort Worth.

J. H. "Cheese" Hensley was a wealthy cattle man and gambler who became very combative when drunk—which was often. On one occasion in Fort Worth this "good-hearted fellow" and "everybody's friend when sober" consumed too much of "the beverage of Gambrinus [beer]" and imagined himself "a second edition" of John L. Sullivan and sought a fight. Sam McConnell was the "first available timber" and the pair went at it in front of the Horsehead Saloon. Both had received bruises before friends separated them. Later that evening Hensley "ran up against" Tom Stephens at the corner of Second and Main. Another fight ensued but this time the police interfered and arrested both parties.[1]

Luke Short of course would rarely be accused of fighting with his fists, but he did appear in court alongside several who did. On the fifteenth of September in Tarrant County Court, Charles Dixon, Dixie Lyons, Sam McConnell, G.H. Day, and Short were together, charged with the offense of exhibiting a faro bank. All pled guilty and paid a fine of $25.00 for what amounted to a license fee to gamble.[2]

Luke made another appearance at the Tarrant County District Court on November 3 and entered a guilty plea for assault. Others on the court docket, including Cheese Hensley, elected for a trial by jury. The Dallas newspaper, which seemingly took great interest in the happenings in the neighboring Tarrant County courts, reported that the jury found Hensley guilty of the charge of betting at a faro bank and he was fined $10. Other matters of interest included Bill Cooper being fined $50 for permitting a game of "stud-horse poker" in his saloon; A. L. Brown pled guilty to an assault charge and was fined $10. Jeff Davis was charged with carrying a pistol; he pled guilty and was fined $25. Bill Petty was charged with betting at faro but the jury acquitted him. Not so with Luke Short who was charged with aggravated assault and was fined $25.[3]

But at times Luke Short appeared not as a defendant but one on the other side of the court room with the prosecution. This time Luke was in Bowie County, the farthest most county in northeast Texas, bordering the states of Arkansas and Oklahoma, in the final days of 1885. Luke Short had caused J. A. Odenheimer to be arrested on a charge of swindling "to the tune of $700." He appeared in circuit court in Texarkana and was honorably discharged, "the testimony failing, in the mind of the court, to make out a case against him." Later that same day Odenheimer, "fell like a brick house upon his chief prosecutor," Luke Short. He was arrested and charged with "malicious prosecution." Further, Luke was charged with a damage and defamation of character suit for the sum of $20,000. Short was in custody of the sheriff, and reportedly he immediately telegraphed home to make his bail while Odenheimer "promenades the streets in as nonchalant manner as the proudest of his race."[4] James A. Odenheimer and Luke Short finally arrived at a settlement: Luke withdrew the complaint against Odenheimer and the latter gave Short a check in the amount of $500.[5] Apparently that resolved the matter to the satisfaction of both parties.

Luke Short and Jake Johnson were among the sporting men of Fort Worth who made an almost routine appearance in the Tarrant County District Court. On March 29, 1886, both appeared and entered their plea of gambling and then paid the $25 fine. Charles Sexon and Jose Wilson also appeared and made the same plea and paid the same fine.[6]

Trying to keep track of Luke Short's partnership in the White Elephant Saloon has proven to be a challenge to historians. Most of them have the identity of Luke's partners, on a given date, wrong. In all fairness to them, the ownership of the White Elephant changed hands several times during Luke's association with the business. Adding to the confusion were small share holders, such as Frank McLean, who were listed in the newspapers as being among the "proprietors." The chronology, as far as Short is concerned, began during December 1884 when Jake Johnson, Luke Short, and James A. "Alex" Reddick became the principal owners. Late in 1885, or very early in 1886, Jake Johnson sold his share of the White Elephant to John L. Ward. Then during May of 1886 Alex Reddick sold his portion to William H. Ward, the brother of John L. Ward. That latest change in ownership was announced in a special "Dissolution Notice" appearing in Fort Worth's *Daily Gazette* on May 15, 1886: "The partnership existing between Ward, Short & Reddick has this day been dissolved by the sale of J. A. Reddick's interest in the business to W. H. Ward. The new firm name will be Ward Bros. & Short."

Luke and Frank McLean were back in the Tarrant County District Court on June 8, 1886, both fined $10 for "betting at faro." [7] That fall Cheese Hensley was in trouble again, only this time the results were far different. It was a deadly affray much more serious than a gambling disagreement. Cattleman Hensley was shot three times by Ben Kaufman, a bar keeper, around midnight. It was initially reported the shots proved fatal. Hensley was often drinking and this time in his cups threatened the life of Kaufman, who defended himself. Kaufman was exonerated. Hensley was a "well known" member of the Hensley Brothers ranch and cattle firm, who had "large transactions in Chicago, Kansas City and St. Louis."[8]

The report of Cheese Hensley's death, like that of Mark Twain, had been "greatly exaggerated." Against all odds, he did survive. Once he was able to have visitors, Luke Short went to Dallas, checked in at the Windsor Hotel, and went to the hospital to see his friend.[9] Nine days after Luke's visit, it was reported that Hensley, "the Fort Worth cattle man who was shot by Ben Kaufman, and whose life had been despaired of, has so far improved as to be able to be removed from the city hospital to a private boarding house."[10]

Just as Bat Masterson had transformed Luke into a boxing enthusiast, Jake Johnson was responsible for making horse racing a major part of Luke's sporting agenda. Johnson and two partners had opened the Fort Worth Driving Park in January 1885. Luke had bought his own race horse and planned to drive the two-wheeled sulky himself in a race scheduled for November 1886. Luke had gained weight in his easy lifestyle, shunning any type of physical labor, but now he attempted to lose those extra pounds in order to have a good showing driving his horse "Tobe."[11] Luke ought to have lost more weight, as he came in dead last in a field of five. The others who paced past Short were Tom Witten, E. H. Keller, F. L. Twombley, and J. H. Martindale. Keller and horse "Cisco" crossed the finish line first with a time of 2:12-1/2.[12] Whatever Luke's embarrassing time was did not receive attention.

Luke Short's frequent arrests and fines for gambling were an annoyance, but were considered by him to be a necessary expense—just a part of the cost of doing business for a sporting man. On November 15, shortly after his embarrassment at the horsetrack, he and three other noted sporting men were arrested. Besides Luke, those arrested were Sam McConnell, Donney Hunt, and Bud Fagg. The warrants from Dallas charged them with running gambling games during the fair. All gave bonds to appear in court in Dallas.[13]

Gambler Budd Fagg's surname often appeared in court documents misspelled as "Faag," "Fogg," and sometimes "Fog." His first name was occasionally recorded as "Bud," but he usually signed his name as "Budd." Neither Luke Short nor Budd Fagg had any intention of keeping their court date. As the *Daily Herald* of Dallas reported, almost as a comic relief item, the "festive gentlemen" allegedly had left for Arkansas, had "skipped, vamoosed the ranch, or in other words forfeited their bonds."[14] But Short and Fagg were hardly the only sporting men of Fort Worth who had "vamoosed the ranch." In county court on November 18 there were over 400 gambling cases called, among them twenty-five Fort Worth gamblers, "who moved to Dallas for temporary enterprise in faro during the fair" but none of the defendants responded. The court learned later that there had been "an excursion to Arkansas." The bonds in the cases for Fagg and Short were declared forfeited, and alias warrants issued for their arrests. The others whose names now joined Fagg and Short were Donny Hunt, Jim Illie, Jim Ellis, Sam McConnell, Saloon Galloway, Little Frank, Hotel Hurd, Charlie Atkins, Charles Dixon, John Norton, Jim Reed, Tom Roberts, Charlie Reagan, M.F. McLean, Jim Thurman, Nat Kramer, H. Owens, and six others. If all had given bond the forfeiture would have amounted to $100,000, and if the accused had "stood their ground and been found guilty" the fines and costs would probably have amounted to $20,000. But with the new law then in effect, imprisonment would have been obligatory, and "the poor farm would have acquired a large contingent for use in preparing the soil for next year's cotton crop." When Sheriff Henry Lewis called the names of Luke Short and the others, no one replied, and "almost thirty miles over yonder, there was no need for a defense." It was no secret that the new county attorney would bring "unmerciful disaster" to those indicted gamblers who had fled. It was not believed any of them would return soon.[15]

The *Herald* clarified its reporting, stating that besides Fagg and Short forfeiting their bonds, other Fort Worth gamblers charged with gambling on the Dallas State Fair Grounds had forfeited their bond as well. They included Jim Illie, Donny Hunt, Jim Ellis, Sam McConnell, Saloon Galloway, Little Frank, Hotel Hurd, Charles Atkins, Charles Dixon, John Martin, Jim Reed, Tom Roberts, Charles Reagan, M.F. McLean, Jim Thurmond, Nat Kramer and H. Owens.[16] Once this gaggle of gamblers had had their fill of Arkansas they returned to Fort Worth. The indictments in Dallas were still left hanging for the moment, but members of the group, including Luke and Jake Johnson, decided to settle some old charges against them in Fort Worth. What was news was that the Court of Appeals had "wiped out the imprisonment clause in the gambling law" and the "sporting fraternity" concluded it was probably a good time to settle old cases against them in Tarrant County court—in other words, pay the fines. Fifty of the cases were taken up and disposed of in short order. Jake Johnson, who had six indictments pending against him, pled guilty to two cases, was fined $25 in each and the other four were dismissed. Luke Short had six indictments against him and he was able to settle on the same basis. F. M. McLean had two against him; he pled guilty in one, was fined $25, and the other was dismissed. Charles Hodley had two indictments against him and he settled on the same basis as Luke: pled guilty on one and the other dismissed. Out of the fifty cases there were pleas of guilty in seventeen, with the fines amounting to $425. There were additional court costs as well of course.[17]

Dallas took notice of the settlement that the sporting men of Fort Worth made with the Tarrant County Court in Fort Worth. The city then sent out this feeler to the gamblers of Fort Worth, advising them to come to Dallas and settle up there. Those gamblers who were indicted in Dallas

County but who resided in Fort Worth "have had the thumb screws of the law put to them over in that burg, and Luke Short and others settled." Since they had not yet settled in Dallas, it was advisable for them all to come in and settle their bill. The gamblers were assured that the court would "settle on a fair basis, as much the law will allow."[18]

During the new year of 1887 Luke would settle with the court in Dallas, but before that could happen there was the more serious matter of two killings, one by Luke and the other by his brother Henry. The two killings happened only sixteen days apart.

Chapter 9

Dead Man in a Shooting Gallery

"When I saw him do that, I pulled my pistol and began shooting, for I knew that his action meant death."

—Luke Short, to a *Fort Worth Daily Gazette* reporter, February 9, 1887.

Eighteen eighty-seven would be Luke Short's crowded year. It would be the year that included the gunfight he is best remembered for, as well as the year he married the love of his life. It was also a year when Luke Short finally attained the celebrity status as a sporting man that Bat Masterson had achieved. The event-filled year began with Luke's younger brother, Henry Jenkins Short, killing a man in the town where Luke's parents and other family members lived—San Angelo, Tom Green County, Texas—a thriving community over 200 miles southwest of Fort Worth.

The man killed was Charley Schuyler, the proprietor of Schuyler's meat market. Henry Short and two other brothers—John Pleasant and Josiah—ran a meat market as well. The tragedy took place at 6 p.m. on the evening of January 23, 1887. Initial reports indicated that Schuyler was shot twice, the bullets entering the back and coming out the front, either one of which would have been fatal. After he was shot he ran approximately fifty yards before he collapsed and died.

The press was eager to report the sensational news, so eager that initial reports were printed even before the coroner's jury had concluded its findings. It appeared that Schuyler was passing by Henry Short's shop, when a "few words were exchanged, and then the shooting commenced." Most witnesses claimed there were three shots fired, a few claimed four. No one claimed the victim had a pistol, and evidently Schuyler was running when hit. Early the following morning a deputy sheriff found a .38 caliber Smith & Wesson pistol on the ground in the direction in which Schuyler was running. One cartridge had been fired and one cartridge had snapped, or misfired. The friends of Schuyler claimed it was not his pistol and no pistol was found on the body. Then John and Josiah Short were arrested and, and, according to a newspaper report, Henry Short disappeared. Schuyler as well as the Shorts all had many friends in San Angelo, and the killing by a brother of Luke Short created much excitement in the town. Schuyler had been married in Fredericksburg only three months before the shooting, which caused many to sympathize with his bereaved widow. He was to be buried at 4 o'clock the afternoon of January 24.[1]

The Short family did not have a reputation as being brawlers or desperate people, but rather stood well in the San Angelo community; the men were thought of as quiet and industrious. The press could not resist pointing out that Henry Short was the brother of Luke Short, thus giving the latter additional notoriety.[2] Rather than disappearing as the paper reported, Henry had gone to Fort Worth to enlist the aid (and funds) that his brother Luke could provide for his defense. Luke and Henry returned to San Angelo on January 29 and Henry voluntarily surrendered to Sheriff J. Willis Johnson and gave bond for his appearance in the district court. Luke Short intended to stay for a few days; he expressed the belief that his brother would come clear on a trial.[3]

The money that would be needed to defend Henry Short would have to be provided by Luke, who had already put up the money for Henry's bond. The amount for his defense was more than Luke had on hand and in order to raise it he approached Jake Johnson. Johnson agreed to purchase Luke's one-third interest in the White Elephant on February 7. The press informed the public that with this "little business deal" Luke did not contemplate any change of base, "but will continue to call Fort Worth home."[4]

One historian has suggested that this transaction was prompted by problems that Luke was having with Timothy Isaiah "Jim" Courtright. It was further suggested that Luke needed the money to start fresh in another town, where he wouldn't have to worry about Courtright. It was finally suggested that there may have been a presentiment, on Luke's part, that he was about to be killed in a gunfight between himself and Courtright. None of these latter-day musings have any basis in fact.[5] At this point if there were indeed any real problems between Luke Short and Jim Courtright, the fact that he had to provide finances for his brother, who was charged with murder, now became Luke Short's top priority. Besides the money he needed for his brother's defense, Luke would be needing cash for his own looming legal problems with the Dallas court. Jake Johnson was an assured source for the kind of cash he needed.[6] Jake Johnson had no real interest in again being a partner in the White Elephant but Luke needed help and he agreed to buy Luke's share. Within nine days, Jake sold that one-third interest to William H. Ward.

The names of Jake Johnson, Luke Short, and occasional lawman Jim Courtright will probably always be linked together in the lore of Wild West gunfights and gunfighters. Ironically it was not that long since Johnson provided Courtright a special gift and now Johnson was providing Short assistance. Courtright had been the recipient of a "very handsome gold watch," which was nothing more than a gift from Johnson.[7] Obviously Johnson and Courtright both had developed a friendship in the Panther City, as well as Johnson and Short.

The last person Luke Short was thinking about as he signed over his interest in the White Elephant on February 7, 1887, was Jim Courtright. Courtright was the president and general manager of the Commercial Detective Agency, a business that was also known as the T. I. C. Agency, after the initials of his full name Timothy Isaiah Courtright. Its letterhead used an open human eye in place of the middle initial, suggesting his agents were always vigilant. The early years of Jim Courtright remain obscure, in spite of the efforts of highly respected historians. Courtright was born in the northern state of Illinois about 1847. Later some historians have claimed he served in the Union army, first as a drummer boy and then as a soldier when he picked up the rifle of a fallen comrade. Further claiming he fought valiantly against the enemy he supposedly was wounded several times during the course of the war. In spite of these alleged heroics later historians have found no record of any service by Courtright, or any name of a similar spelling, as having served in any capacity during the war.[8] No marriage record of Courtright's has been found, although it is claimed he eloped with Sarah Elizabeth Weeks, a girl all of fourteen years of age, shortly after the war's end.

Although so much of Courtright's early life is the creation of later writers, by the early 1870s he and possibly his wife and family were in Fort Worth where he began his service as a lawman. As a lawman Courtright became highly regarded as efficient and respected by his peers —in the beginning. Fort Worth voters elected him city marshal in 1876, again in 1877, and to a third term in 1878. In spite of his previous success at the polls, Courtright lost to Sam Farmer in the election of 1879. This unexpected loss may have been the reason that Courtright began the downward descent from being a respected lawman to one who became more of a rogue officer. With Fort Worth having rejected him, and several difficulties which did not brighten his reputation as a fearless lawman, he located in Lake Valley, New Mexico, where he was chosen city marshal in the fall of 1882. [9] He even was commissioned a deputy U.S. marshal, but his actions as a regulator there resulted in a charge of murder, a charge that forced him to return to Fort Worth and which would not be resolved for several years, though he was eventually cleared of the charge.

Certainly these actions of Jim Courtright were not at all of Luke Short's concern, as he had his own to deal with. What may have been true or may have simply been rumor was that the so-called "detective agency" was also a front for Courtright's protection racket. With his reputation as a deadly man with a gun Courtright had convinced many of the saloon owners to pay him a certain percentage of the house winnings on a monthly basis. Luke Short refused, even offering to pay Courtright to stay out of his place of business.[10]

Short's outward display of civility in regard to Courtright ended with an event that received newspaper coverage all across the country, forever linking the names of Short and Courtright. "Jim Courtright Dies" screamed one headline, with a sub-headline: "A Bullet from Luke Short's Pistol Pierces His Heart and He Expires Without a Word." The shooting was called "one of the most startling tragedies" that had occurred in Fort Worth "for many days." The killing took place a few feet north of the entrance to the White Elephant, just in front of the little shooting gallery operated by Ella Blackwell. The affair created intense excitement and within seconds the street was blocked with a mob of excited men eager to see the result of the shooting, eager to learn all the details of the homicide.

It was about 7:30 in the evening when policeman W. B. "Bony" Tucker, District Clerk Taylor, and Bony's brother Rowan, calmly discussing what they might do that evening, heard the crack of a pistol. Within moments they heard another, then two more followed by another—in all five shots. The men ran to where the shots had occurred, only a few blocks away. Arriving on the scene they observed Luke Short standing only twelve or fifteen steps north of the shooting gallery. Short, with a pistol in his hand, was the only one standing, and detective Tucker bravely approached and grasped the pistol, a Colt's .45. Brother Rowan grabbed the shootist to subdue him, although Short had given no sign of any resistance to the officers. By then another officer, J. W. Pemberton, had approached and the scene of the shooting was controlled. Luke Short, well known to all present, was standing, but remaining calm. A few feet away was the body of T. I. "Jim" Courtright, partially inside the shooting-gallery, his feet stretched out onto the sidewalk.

Tucker, who had no doubt experienced this type of situation before, bent over Courtright but he could not speak. In his hand was a pistol, a Colt .45, the same kind of weapon as the one that had killed him. Examining it Tucker determined the chambers were full of cartridges, indicating he had not fired a shot. Three of the five shots had taken effect: one had broken his right thumb, one went through the heart, and one had struck him in the right shoulder. The heart shot proved to be fatal and within five minutes Jim Courtright was dead. Sheriff B. H. Shipp, Marshal W. M. Rea, and the Tucker brothers then took Short to the county jail.[11]

That evening one of the most widely known sporting men of the west was secured inside the doors of the Tarrant County jail. Courtright could not give his version of events, but Luke Short explained what had happened:

> Early in the evening I was getting my shoes blackened at the White Elephant, when a friend of mine asked me if there was any trouble between Courtright and myself, and I told him there was nothing. A few minutes later I was at the bar with a couple of friends when some one called me. I went out into the vestibule and saw Jim Courtright and Jake Johnson. Jake and I had talked for a little while that evening on a subject in which Jim's name was mentioned, but no idea of a difficulty was entertained. I walked out with them upon the sidewalk, and we had some quiet talk on private affairs. I reminded him of some past transactions, not in an abusive or reproachful manner, to which he assented, but not in a very cordial way.[12]

Assuming the sporting man was quoted correctly, this exchange between the reporter and the gambler proves Luke Short was quite capable of articulating his thoughts in a clear and concise manner. He continued, now getting to the heart of the matter that resulted in the gunfight.

> I was standing with my thumbs in the armholes of my vest and had dropped them in front of me to adjust my clothing, when he remarked "Well, you needn't reach for your gun," and immediately put his hand to his hip-pocket and pulled his. When I saw him do that, I pulled my pistol and began shooting, for I knew that his action meant death. He must have misconstrued my intention in dropping my hands before me. I was merely adjusting my clothing, and never carry a pistol in that part of my dress.[13]

The remains of Jim Courtright were taken to his home on East Second Street where his wife and three children, the eldest a girl of about fourteen years, were "almost distracted with grief." According to the *Gazette* reporter, who apparently accompanied the remains, the "heart-rending sobs over the body of the lifeless husband and father were pitiable to hear. It was a sad, sad ending for them."[14]

In thinking over the tragedy the reporter also provided a summary of Courtright's life, which was essentially accurate. He also could not help but ponder the results. He recognized the fact that Jim Courtright "was a splendid shot. His dexterity with the six-shooter was known far and wide. He could manipulate a weapon as well with one hand as another, and in a desperate emergency his coolness and self-possession never left him. He was quick, too, as lightning." If Courtright was such an expert with a revolver why did the shooting gallery incident result as it did? The answer to that question was simple: Courtright's pistol failed to operate smoothly; if it had, perhaps the two men would have shot each other, resulting in a double tragedy. Officers who examined Courtright's weapon found that the revolver's cylinder had failed to turn, making it useless when it was needed most.

The funeral of Timothy Isaiah "Jim" Courtright took place from his residence at 3 o'clock the afternoon of February 9. Friends and brother Odd Fellows stayed with the remains during the night. He was interred with the ceremonies of that order. "Peace to his ashes, and in the land whither his spirit has fled may it find the rest and peace his troubled life knew not here."[15]

There may have been more to the difficulty than was first reported. City Attorney William Capps, who witnessed the shooting, believed there had been a conspiracy to murder Short. When the smoke had cleared Capps immediately called on officers to arrest Charley Bull, Courtright's partner, claiming "it was a job put up to murder Short." It supposedly went back to the time when Courtright had been a fugitive from New Mexico justice and "certain parties" wanted him to return to Fort Worth "for the alleged purpose of putting Luke Short out of the way." Courtright did come back but the scheme "miscarried and was dropped." When gambling opened up in Fort Worth, Courtright, "so it is said," extracted a certain sum each month as an inducement for him and his detective aide to keep their mouths shut. This protection money was paid him on a regular basis, and Courtright wanted Short to pay his "share" on the basis of his keno operation. "Short refused to put up, and it is claimed that Courtright made threats to make Short bite the dust."[16] If indeed Short refused to pay up in this protection racket, then Courtright felt justified in enforcing what he believed was his right to do.

The inquest was held on February 9. That morning an excited crowd appeared at Justice Smith's office to hear the testimony presented before the jury of inquest. The jury returned a verdict that briefly stated that Courtright came to his death from pistol shots fired by Luke Short. That afternoon, the examining trial was set for two o'clock before the same justice. The courtroom was now filled with the crowd anxious to hear every word. County Attorney Robert McCart represented the state while Alexander Steadman and William Capps represented Short.

The first witness, Ike Cantrell, testified that at 8 o'clock he was standing on the corner of Main and Second and had seen Jake Johnson, Luke Short, and Jim Courtright "in close conversation." After the shooting, which he did not witness, he took a pistol from Courtright's holster on his left side. He had "heard Courtright say the night before that dirt had been done to him in the White Elephant." On cross-examination Cantrell stated that Courtright had two "scabbards" but the one on his right side was empty.

B. F. Herring followed Cantrell. He was standing in the shooting gallery and heard the report of "a large pistol." Courtright fell "into the door close to me. The man doing the shooting stepped up to the door and fired four times after Courtright fell." He stated that he had not seen the beginning of the row nor had heard any words. He did know Courtright.

Ella Blackwell was the operator of the shooting gallery, but she was quickly released as she had only heard the shots.

William Allison was behind the counter of the shooting gallery when the "trouble came up." As Courtright fell, he testified, he saw him pull a pistol out of his pocket. "He was pulling it from the right hip pocket. By the time he fell to the floor he had the pistol clear out. He made no effort to shoot after he fell; he was not able. The man that shot him fired one shot while Courtright was falling and three after he fell."

W. A. James had seen Courtright the night of the shooting and the night before that saw him in John Stewart's saloon and heard him say to one "old gentleman"—McCarty—that "God had made one man superior to another in muscular power, but when Colt made his pistol, that made all men equal." Courtright inadvertently said Short's name, but they both then decided not to call any names. James testified that Courtright said to him that "he [Short] had lived over his time. No man on earth, he said, had any percentage over him. He said that this would be settled within a week; that he hadn't been treated with respect up stairs over the White Elephant. When he heard the shooting he was satisfied that Courtright was into it." Cross-examined, James stated that when Courtright made these remarks he was "considerably under the influence of whisky at the time" and when drinking he was "usually inclined to braggadocio."

Jake Johnson was the only man who saw the start of the shooting as he had been conversing first with Courtright and then Short. He was close enough to the two men to hear what was said. Short had his thumbs in the armholes of his vest when Courtright said, "You needn't be pulling your gun" to which Short answered: "I haven't got any gun here, Jim." Then Courtright drew his Colt .45 and then Short drew his and fired. Courtright fell at the first shot fired. Jake Johnson was as good a friend of Courtright as he was of Short.

Policeman John J. Fulford did not see any part of the difficulty but got to the scene "about the time the last shot was fired." He saw Courtright on his back, "a little inclined to the left." In his right hand he had a pistol, which Fulford took. In the scabbard on the left side he had a pistol as well. Officer J. W. Pemberton took Short's pistol from him and it was in his possession at the time of the inquest. According to Fulford, Courtright did speak as he was dying. "Ful, they've got me," were the only words he uttered. These words were no doubt very softly said as in a whisper. It is not surprising that other witnesses did not hear them.

That concluded the testimony. The question of bail was then raised, and Justice Smith and Attorney Steadman agreed on the sum of $2,000. Within minutes, the sum was arranged with Jake Johnson, W. T. Maddox, Robert McCart, and Alex Steadman becoming Luke Short's bondsmen.

Luke was never brought to trial for the killing of Courtright. Likewise his brother, Henry Jenkins Short, seems to have avoided prosecution in the January 23, 1887, killing of Charles Schuyler, although the details remain unclear.[17] Just nine days after buying Luke's one-third interest in the White Elephant, Jake Johnson sold it to William H. Ward. Johnson and Ward simply "made a trade" with Ward buying out Johnson's interest in the White Elephant.[18] Eight days later the *Gazette* announced the dissolution of the firm the proprietors of which were Johnson and Short and Ward. It now became the property of the Ward Brothers. To a drinking man or a gambler—or any kind of sporting man—who actually owned the establishment was not a necessary aspect of the trade to know. Luke Short's name would continue to be associated with the name of the White Elephant, regardless of who the actual owner was.

Luke Short, Budd Fagg, and other sporting men of Fort Worth finally settled with the court in Dallas after forfeiting their bonds for missing the November 1886 court appearance. Fagg, C. M. Wright, and Nat Kramer were each fined $10 and costs for gambling. All the cases against Short were dismissed, with no explanation.[19]

By this time Luke Short and Bat Masterson, both notorious sporting men of the west, had achieved enough celebrity status to inspire satirical press notices such as this:

> Orth Stein, the reprobate journalist now in jail in El Paso, is whiling the time away writing sketches of noted western men for the *St. Louis Post-Dispatch* in his own graphic and breezy way. In a late issue he gives a pen and ink portrait of Luke Short and Bat Masterson, in which the former figures as a great Biblical student, and the other as quite a dandy, if not a dude with a strong penchant for the stage.[20]

Illustration Gallery

Illustration 1. Luke Short

Courtesy the Jack DeMattos Collection.

Illustration 2. Michael Wayne Short and Judy Ohmer.

Courtesy Dr. Judy Ohmer.

Illustration 3. Where Luke Short Gained Fame.

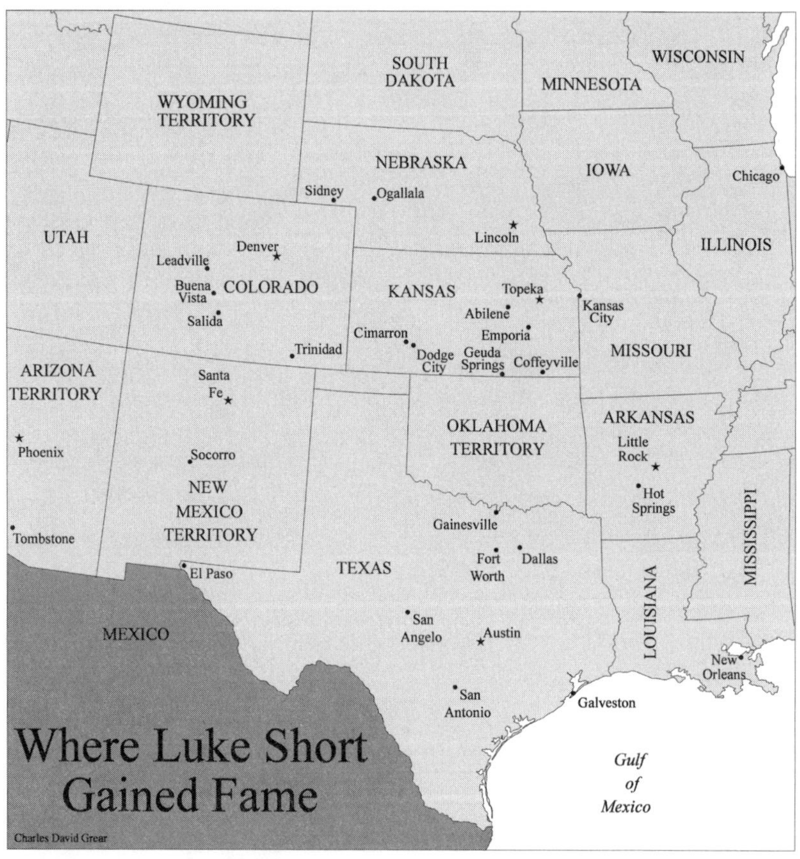

Courtesy Charles David Grear.

Illustration 4. Charles William Berger (1909–1987), the man who called himself "Luke Short II." Photo by Jack DeMattos in Tombstone, Arizona, on June 15, 1980.

Courtesy the Jack DeMattos Collection.

Illustration 5. Hetty Brumley Short.

Courtesy Dr. Judy Ohmer.

Illustration 6. John Pleasant Short (1848-1919), the oldest of the seven Short brothers. He married 16-year-old Louisiana "Lou" Brown (1854-1940) in 1870.

Courtesy Dr. Judy Ohmer.

Illustration 7. Luke Short at age twenty-three in 1877. The original tintype measures a mere 1-7/8 x 3-1/8 inches and remains the earliest likeness of Luke Short.

Courtesy Dr. Judy Ohmer.

Illustration 8. Wyatt Earp (1848-1929). Short and Earp first met in Tombstone at the Oriental Saloon where Earp was a faro dealer and Short was the "lookout" who protected the game.

Courtesy the Jack DeMattos Collection.

Illustration 9. W.B. "Bat" Masterson (1853-1921). Short and Masterson first met in Tombstone early in 1881. It was the start of an enduring friendship between the two men cut from the same green cloth.

Courtesy the Jack DeMattos Collection.

Illustration 10. William H. Harris (1845-1895).

Courtesy the Kansas State Historical Society, Topeka.

Illustration 11. This plaque outside of the building that housed Tombstone's Oriental Saloon marks the location of two of the town's celebrated gunfights.

Courtesy Dr. Judy Ohmer.

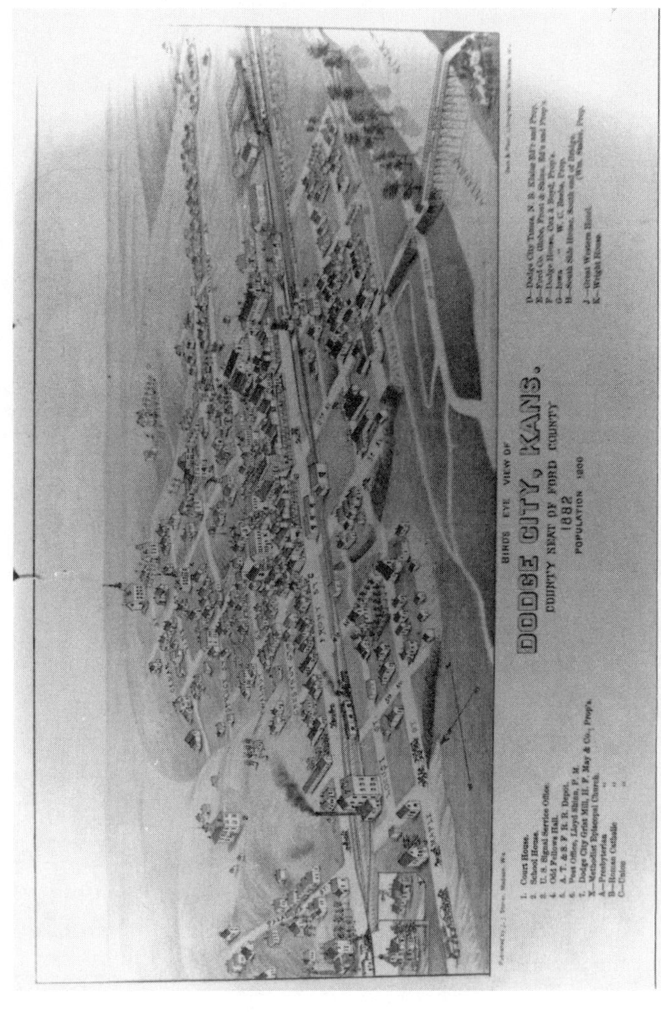

Illustration 12. This is how a lithographer viewed the town of Dodge City in 1882, the year before the "Dodge City War" broke out.

Courtesy the Boot Hill Museum, Dodge City, Kansas.

Illustration 13. Luke Short as he appeared around 1883.

Courtesy the Robert G. McCubbin Collection.

Illustration 14. Dodge City as Luke Short knew it. A view of Front Street looking west from Railroad Avenue.

Courtesy the Boot Hill Museum, Dodge City, Kansas.

Illustration 15. Chalkley McArtor Beeson (1848-1912).

Courtesy the Boot Hill Museum, Dodge City, Kansas.

Illustration 16. Alonzo B. Webster (1844-1887).

Courtesy the Kansas State Historical Society, Topeka.

Illustration 17. Lawrence E. "Larry" Deger (1845-1924).

Courtesy the Boot Hill Museum, Dodge City, Kansas.

Illustration 18. Nicholas B. Klaine, editor and publisher of the *Dodge City Times*.

Courtesy the Robert K. DeArment Collection.

Illustration 19. Luke Short at age twenty-nine from an image made in May 1883. After being told to "get out of Dodge" Short went to Kansas City's Marble Hall Saloon at 522 Main Street to plot his return. During his brief stay in Kansas City Luke walked a few blocks from the Marble Hall to the studio of photographer David P. Thomson at 612 Main Street and sat for this photograph.

Courtesy Dr. Judy Ohmer.

Illustration 20. George Merritt Hoover (1847-1914).

Courtesy the Kansas State Historical Society, Topeka.

Illustration 21. Governor George W. Glick (1827-1911).

Courtesy the Kansas State Historical Society, Topeka.

Illustration 22. Robert M. Wright (1840-1915).

Courtesy the Kansas State Historical Society, Topeka.

Illustration 23. Dr. Samuel Galland. Despite being an ardent prohibitionist, Dr. Galland was one of Luke's staunchest supporters during the "Dodge City War."

Courtesy the Kansas State Historical Society, Topeka.

Illustration 24. Dr. Samuel Galland's Great Western Hotel. Dr. Galland would not permit the serving of alcoholic beverages at his Great Western Hotel, which was where Luke Short rented rooms. As co-owner of the Long Branch Saloon, Luke was hardly inconvenienced when he felt the need for a drink.

Courtesy the Boot Hill Museum, Dodge City, Kansas.

Illustration 25. Sheriff George T. Hinkel (1846-1922).

Courtesy the Kansas State Historical Society, Topeka.

Illustration 26. Michael Westernhouse Sutton (1848-1918).

Courtesy the Kansas State Historical Society, Topeka.

Illustration 27. Thomas Clayton Nixon (1837-1884).

Courtesy the late Bob Fleming, Nixon's great-grandson.

Illustration 28. "The Dodge City Peace Commission." Photographed by Charles A. Conkling, June 10, 1883. This print, taken from an original copy, has not been cropped or retouched. Standing left to right: William H. Harris; Luke L. Short; Bat Masterson; William F. Petillon. Seated left to right: Charles E. Bassett; Wyatt Earp; Michael Francis "Frank" McLean and Cornelius "Neil" Brown.

Courtesy the Robert G. McCubbin Collection.

Illustration 29. Another view of the Dodge City Peace Commission mounted with identification on the card.

Courtesy the Robert G. McCubbin Collection.

Illustration 30. On Saturday July 21, 1883, *The National Police Gazette* published this engraving based upon the iconic group photograph taken by Charles A. Conkling just forty-one days earlier. It was the first occasion that a version of this group portrait was reproduced for a wide audience—and the first time it was provided with the caption it remains best known by, "The Dodge City Peace Commission."

Courtesy the Chuck Parsons Collection.

Illustration 31. Frederick Singer (1852–1890).

Courtesy the Kansas State Historical Society, Topeka.

Illustration 32. Patrick F. Sughrue (1844-1906).

Courtesy the Kansas State Historical Society, Topeka.

Illustration 33. Henry Jenkins Short (1859-1917) Luke's younger brother and the great-grandfather of Michael Wayne Short (1957-2010).

Courtesy Dr. Judy Ohmer.

Illustration 34. Henry Jenkins Short and Della Bouldin (1877-1964) in a photograph made on their December 20, 1898, wedding day.

Courtesy Dr. Judy Ohmer.

Illustration 35. Luke Short, at the height of his fame as a professional gambler, Luke Short brought a whole new meaning to the term "dressed to kill."

Courtesy the Kansas State Historical Society, Topeka.

Illustration 36. Timothy Isaiah "Jim" Courtright. This photograph was made sometime between April 6, 1876, and April 1, 1879, when Courtright was serving as city marshal of Fort Worth.

Courtesy the Robert G. McCubbin Collection.

Illustration 37. The "beautiful and accomplished" Hattie Buck.

Courtesy Dr. Judy Ohmer.

Illustration 38. On the left, Hattie Buck Short, from an image made about 1887. There is no known photograph of Mr. and Mrs. Luke Short together. On the right, Luke Short as he may have appeared about the time he was married to Hattie Buck. The boutonnière suggests it may be a wedding photograph.

Courtesy Dr. Judy Ohmer.

Illustration 39. Exterior view of the Cimarron Hotel in Cimarron, Kansas, as it appears today. Luke Short and his wife spent at least one night in this hotel when it was new. It was established in 1886 by Nicholas B. Klaine, a one-time enemy of Luke Short. Kathleen Holt, the current owner, has preserved the original integrity of the hotel as well as the registration book signed by Luke Short.

Photo Courtesy Pat Parsons.

Illustration 40. An interior view of the beautiful Cimarron Hotel, less than twenty miles west of Dodge City, Kansas.

Photo Courtesy Pat Parsons.

Illustration 41. Bat Masterson (seated) and Charlie Mitchell at Minnehaha Falls, Minnesota. This photograph was made in 1886. Three years later Masterson, Mitchell, and Luke Short would all be in Jake Kilrain's corner at the Heavyweight Championship fight between Kilrain and John L. Sullivan.

Courtesy the Robert K. DeArment Collection.

Illustration 42. Charles E. "Parson" Davies (1851-1920) Image taken from *The Biographical Review of Prominent Men and Women of the Day* by Thomas W. Herringshaw.

Courtesy the Jack DeMattos Collection.

Illustration 43. Jake Kilrain (1859-1937).

Courtesy the Robert K. DeArment Collection.

Illustration 44. John L. Sullivan (1858–1918).

Courtesy the Robert K. DeArment Collection.

Illustration 45. The Sullivan-Kilrain Fight of July 8, 1889. This is how the fight was depicted in *The National Police Gazette*. It was the last world title bout fought under London Prize Ring Rules, meaning the last *bare-knuckle* Heavyweight bout. Both Sullivan and Kilrain shaved off their mustaches for the fight.

Courtesy the Robert K. DeArment Collection.

Illustration 46. Richard K. Fox (1846-1922), editor and publisher of *The National Police Gazette*.

Courtesy the Jack DeMattos Collection.

Illustration 47. William B. "Will" Short (1867-1890), the youngest of the ten Short children.

Courtesy Dr. Judy Ohmer.

Illustration 48. The Leland Hotel in Chicago as Luke Short knew it. Image taken from *The New Chicago Album*.

Courtesy the Jack DeMattos Collection.

Illustration 49. William F. "Old Hoss" Hoey (1854-1897). Luke Short nearly shot the comedian by mistake.

Courtesy the Jack DeMattos Collection.

Illustration 50. Ticket for the Sullivan-Corbett Fight. Luke Short attended the Heavyweight title fight with Bat Masterson and Charles E. Bassett.

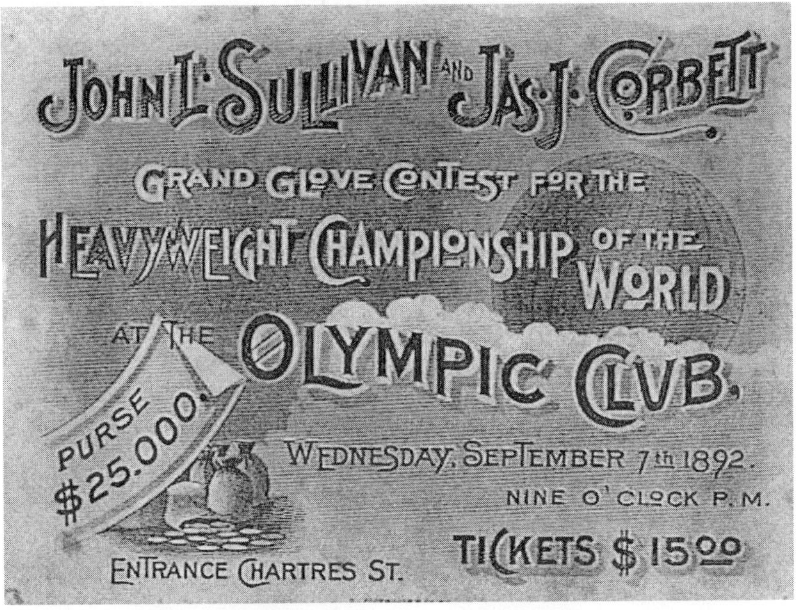

Courtesy the Jack DeMattos Collection.

Illustration 51. This is a retouched version of a photograph of Luke believed to have been made at the time of his 1887 wedding to Hattie Buck (appearing elsewhere in this gallery). It remains the last known likeness of Luke Short.

Courtesy the Robert G. McCubbin Collection.

Illustration 52. George Washington Short (1860-1935). George and Hattie accompanied Luke's body on the long train ride from Geuda Springs to Fort Worth.

Courtesy Dr. Judy Ohmer.

Illustration 53. Luke Short's grave at Oakwood Cemetery, Fort Worth.

Courtesy Tom Todd.

Chapter 10

Mrs. Luke Short

> "Luke Short came there, to the hotel where I was staying, with his wife, the beautiful and accomplished daughter of an Emporia banker, whom he married under romantic circumstances."
>
> —A.G. Arkwright in the *New York Sun*, July 25, 1897.

She was indeed a beautiful woman. It was also true that her family resided in Emporia, Kansas, although her father was not a banker. From March 15, 1887, until his death on September 8, 1893, she was Luke Short's wife. Her full name was Harriet Beatrice Buck but she was always called "Hattie." Her father was Oscar Buck, who was born in Illinois on January 16, 1836. Her mother, Cynthia Allen, was born in Texas on March 26, 1839. They married in Coles County, Illinois, on July 23, 1857.[1] Cynthia and Oscar had eight children, the first five of whom were born in Coles County: Mary Alice on July 7, 1858; Harvey Joseph on March 27, 1860; Eva K. on September 20, 1862; Harriet Beatrice on October 5, 1863; and Nora E. on September 29, 1866.

By 1870 the Buck family had relocated to Ottumwa, Coffey County, Kansas. The seven family members who existed at that time were listed on the United States Federal Census as Oscar, age 34; Lyntha [*sic*], age

31; Mary, age 12; James [*sic*], age 10; Eva, age 7; Hattie, age 6 and Nora, age 4.[2] The family gained a couple of new members in Coffey County, Kansas: William A., born on November 8, 1871, and Grace on April 18, 1874. The nine family members were still living in Coffey County when the Kansas State Census was enumerated on March 1, 1875. Once again the enumerator seemed to have a problem when it came to Cynthia and Harvey Joseph Buck. The nine Buck family members were listed as Oscar, age 38; Cyntha [*sic*], age 34; Mary A., age 16; Harry [*sic*], age 15; Eva, age 12; Hattie, age 10 [*sic*]; Nora, age 8; William A., age 3 and Gracy, age one year.[3]

The family briefly had ten members when Josephine E. Buck was born on January 16, 1878. Two months later, on March 21, 1878, however, the oldest child, Mary Alice Buck, died at the age of nineteen. This was the first death in the family whose members were not destined to live long lives. By the time the 1880 U.S. Census was enumerated the Buck family had moved to Emporia, Lyon County, Kansas, and consisted of nine members. Oscar Buck was employed as a carpenter in Emporia. Once again, the enumerator employed creative spelling when it came to listing some family members, who were identified as Oscer [*sic*], age 44; Centha [*sic*], age 40; Harvey, age 20; Eva, age 17; Hattie, age 16; Nora, age 13; William, age 8, Grace, age 6; and Josephine, age three.

Early death remained a reality for the Buck family. On September 13, 1883, Eva K. Buck passed. She was just one week shy of what would have been her twenty-first birthday. The head of the family, Oscar Buck, died around the same time. The exact date of his death remains unknown, other than it happened sometime between 1880 and 1883. The 1883 Emporia City Directory listed Mrs. C. A. Buck; women were listed in city directories only if they were single and living on their own, or widowed.[4]

When the 1885 Kansas State Census was enumerated on March 1, 1885, Cynthia Allen Buck was described as "widowed" and living in Ivy, Lyon County, Kansas, with her three youngest children. The Buck family was recorded with C. A. Buck as head of household, age 44; children

William, age 14; Gracie, age 11, and Jossie [*sic*] Buck, age seven.[5] The three oldest surviving children are missing from this census. At the time it was enumerated, Harvey would have been 24, Hattie would have been 21 and Nora would have been 18. Where these three were living in 1885 still has not been determined.

It also hasn't been determined exactly where or when Hattie Buck and Luke Short first met, but it can now be stated with certainty that they were married in Oswego, Labette County, Kansas, on March 15, 1887.[6] The bride and groom went to Fort Worth shortly after the wedding but didn't remain there long. Luke and Hattie boarded a train in Fort Worth "for a brief stay at Hot Springs."[7] The arrival of Luke and Hattie at Hot Springs was recalled, years later, by one A. G. Arkwright who wrote that "by a singular train of events" he became "intimately acquainted with him [Short] ten or twelve years ago." The occasion was during a vacation Arkwright was taking at Hot Springs, and Luke Short came in the hotel where he was staying "with his wife, a beautiful and accomplished daughter of an Emporia banker, whom he married under romantic circumstances." Arkwright recalled him as "a short, well-built young man with a round, smooth face, very black eyes, and muscles like steel springs and catgut." Short dressed well and plainly, "habitually wearing a suit of dark blue clothes and a black sombrero. His manner towards those persons he liked was pleasing."[8]

Luke and Hattie remained in Hot Springs for nearly two months; their lengthy stay there was perhaps due to health problems Luke was experiencing. By May the couple was back in Fort Worth, Luke appearing "much improved in health."[9] Luke and Hattie were only in Fort Worth eleven days before leaving town again, now heading for quite a different setting: Minnesota. A local paper noted Luke Short and his wife had left "for a summer's sojourn among the Minnesota Lakes."[10] Did the notorious Luke Short and his bride actually arrive in Minnesota and spend the summer there, or did their plans change? No contemporary record places him there. It is known he was in Kansas City on June 8. His stopover in Kansas City was noted, the reporter unable to merely report his presence, but also stressing his ability with the six-guns: "Luke Short whose dexterity in getting the 'drop' on his opponents in barroom and gambling affrays has caused him to be feared and respected for several years past by his sporting associates throughout the Southwest, made his appearance in this city this morning."[11]

A week later, on June 15, William H. Harris married a much younger woman in New York State. Luke's former business partner had, by this time, become a noted "turfman." Harris and Short enjoyed a friendship that endured to Luke's death, and involved several business partnerships. Given this, it seems likely that Luke and Hattie attended William H. Harris's wedding. Hattie, who was twenty-three, was about the same age as the bride. Based upon later reports, it also seems very likely that the two couples then went to take in the races at Monmouth Park, located in the fashionable seaside resort of Long Branch, New Jersey.

From New Jersey, Luke and Hattie followed the racing circuit to the enormously popular resort of Saratoga Springs, New York. A reporter from the *Albany Evening Journal* caught up with Luke on July 25. The unidentified correspondent not only had a sharp eye for detail, but also a flair for words. "If the prismatic hues of the rainbow be figuratively induced to represent every known shade of humanity," he began, "one can easily find at Saratoga, during a 15-minute walk up Broadway last evening in the under-tow I fell in with a quiet little man with a sharp nose and a bright greenish-blue eye." The "quiet little man" was Luke L. Short. He was wearing a "high Greely hat" or top hat such as the well-dressed gentleman of 1887 would naturally wear, and a "close fitting diagonal blue suit with a jaunty sack coat." His shirt was of the latest style, of course, with a "silk embroidered front." According to this observer, Luke's left ear was small and the "auricular anatomy on the right side of his bullet-shaped head was still smaller." Luke Short also "tolerated an erratic appearing mustache and walked with the easy grace of a fatigued Albany policeman."

The reporter mentioned that he had "met the same individual at the Monmouth race track" at Long Branch, New Jersey, a few days before. At that track the "spruce little man of 35 [*sic*, 33] with a round face was pointed out as Luke Short" who in case the readers did not know, was the "proprietor of the White Elephant in Fort Worth, Texas." Then the correspondent warmed to the violent aspect of his narrative, bringing out some details of the Luke Short-Jim Courtright gunfight. The significance of this contribution by the unknown observer of humanity is in the final paragraph: "Short is a quiet unostentatious fellow and denounces the talk prevalent in the east about the bloody Wild West as overdrawn. Unless an unfortunate is struck by a stray ball, he is just as safe on the frontier if he minds his business as he would be at Saratoga. Short is accompanied by his wife and is doing the racing circuit."[12]

Luke and Hattie's departure from Fort Worth was as noteworthy as was their return. The Shorts arrived back on the nineteenth of August; among the well wishers was a reporter who wrote for the next day's edition:

> Luke Short was welcomed home by many friends last night. He has been enjoying the glorious atmosphere of the Catskills and the Adirondacks, and the leading seaside resorts. He says the interest manifested in the east concerning Texas by all sorts and conditions of people is astonishing, and that a boom of magnitude is surely heading this way.[13]

Luke and Hattie were on the move again the following month, when they arrived in Cimarron, Kansas. On September 26, 1887, they checked into the New West Hotel where Luke signed the register "Luke Short & Wife." What Luke was doing in Cimarron, located less than twenty miles west of Dodge City, remains a mystery. The New West Hotel had been built a year earlier, at a cost of $15,000, by none other than Nicholas B. Klaine—who had been on the side opposed to Luke during the "Dodge City War." Initially called the Klaine Hotel, the owner soon changed the name to the New West Hotel.[14] We are left to wonder if Luke would have stopped at this particular hostelry had it still been called the Klaine Hotel.

Perhaps Luke knew and didn't care. The "Dodge City War" was more than four years in his past, and Dodge City itself was no longer a cattle town. Someone decided to be funny when Luke and Hattie registered at the New West Hotel. Whether it was a bored hotel clerk, or Luke himself, the handwritten notations, for Monday, September 26, 1887, read as follows:

Luke Short & Wife..........Longwood

J. P. Pretty.....................Prettyville

Chas. H. Wood............ Jonesville

Short Luke....................Shortwood

Luke Shortwood............Short[15]

Most likely Luke and Hattie only stayed at the New West Hotel for one night. By September 30, 1887, they were back in Fort Worth, where things were anything but funny.

Chapter 11

The War on the Gambling Fraternity

> "He is the most popular man of his class and, when not professionally engaged is really disposed to be quiet and pleasant in his manners. Oddly enough he is a well posted Biblical student, and fond of arguing on religion topics."
>
> — *Omaha Daily Bee*, March 13, 1887.

When Luke returned to Fort Worth he found himself caught between two opposing factions that had one thing in common: they both wanted him gone. On one side was the "reform" element that embraced prohibition and wanted all vices, including gambling, curtailed. On the other side were certain Fort Worth sporting men who wanted Luke out of the way for reasons that had nothing to do with reform. If Luke Short served as a flash point for these disparate groups, his friend Jake Johnson was someone whom neither side seemed inclined to challenge.

Being a sporting man was an avocation for Jake Johnson. He was a millionaire who could afford to gamble as a hobby. He was a highly successful businessman who always made sure that he gave back something to "Panther City," and Fort Worth loved him for it. Luke Short was a sporting man only, never giving back to the city. He may have thought of Fort Worth as his home, but he would never become an accepted member of the community in the way that Jake Johnson was. Luke and Hattie rented an expensive suite in the Mansion Hotel, while Jake Johnson was busy building a house that was an actual mansion.

In early June the citizens of Panther City could watch Jake Johnson's handsome residence on the south side, costing $15,000, take recognizable shape. There were other dwellings equally fine on the drawing boards, but none would equal the mansion that was Jake Johnson's.[1] What may have been a little-known fact was that Jake owned the land that those other dwellings would be constructed on. He was also powerful enough to publicly ridicule a state-wide prohibition vote that was coming up. The betting on the results of the prohibition election in August was quite heavy. Jake Johnson, being a sporting man of considerable wealth, staked about $10,000 on the state giving a majority of 50,000 against the prohibition amendment.[2]

In Fort Worth, Mayor H. S. Broiles, who was pledged to reform, was having no luck enforcing the "Sunday laws" already in place that were aimed at saloons. Reportedly the "saloon men" were paying no attention to the law, which required them to remove all screens and other devices that obstructed the view through the open door or place of entrance into their saloon. That they intended to test the constitutionality of the law was apparent. An unidentified attorney had advised them that "the law will not stand a test in the Court of Appeals." As yet there were no arrests of anyone violating the law, but "it is probable that some will be made upon information filed with the county attorney."[3]

Jake Johnson continued to take bets on the Texas prohibition bill being defeated. An item in the *Gazette* pointed out how the press interpreted Johnson's antics. The "anti-prohibitionists" were feeling in good spirits, what with Johnson walking "with head erect and smiling face, elated over the fact that he has got up several thousand dollars bet on the result of the 4th of August, in which he backs the antis to win by a majority of 50,000 votes." If any prohibitionists thought otherwise, then there was now a "golden chance to win a good deal of tin" as Johnson was so confident he was willing "to take all other bets of the same sort and allow the same odds."[4]

Jake Johnson won his bet. The statewide prohibition amendment failed to pass on August 4, 1887. Fort Worth and Tarrant County did vote for prohibition, but they were in the minority. In response, an irate Mayor Broiles promised to put new teeth into the Sunday Law that had been in place before the vote, which had long been considered a joke by the saloon owners who ignored it. On August 6 the mayor gave the city marshal "strict orders" to enforce the Sunday law, especially against the saloon men. He claimed that he intended to put a stop to saloons running with open doors on the Sabbath, even if he had to resort to extreme measures. Mayor Broiles "contends that now, more than ever before, it is his duty to close the saloons on Sunday, because of the majority given for Prohibition in this city and county." Previously policemen had been instructed to arrest saloon men only once a month for violating the Sunday law, but Broiles' new policy now was "to make arrests for every drink they sell on Sunday."[5]

Luke's friend Cheese Hensley had miraculously recovered from the wounds that he received in Dallas on October 26, 1886. Apparently the experience did little to curtail his combative nature, however. He was fined $25 in the Recorder's Court for having assaulted M. Schwartz following his recovery[6] He was not the only combative sporting man in the city, as in late September Luke Short and Charles B. Dixon experienced an "altercation," as the *Dallas Morning News* reported in its "Fort Worth Frolics" column for October 1, 1887. According to the report there was a "feeling of uneasiness in gambling circles here caused by an affair . . . in the Cabinet Saloon." The affair was between Charles Dixon, "alleged proprietor of a faro room" and Luke Short, the "reputed head of the keno layout." The keno game had been running "only a few nights" but that was enough "to create a ripple." That morning Dixon and Short met in the

Cabinet Saloon and were taking a drink together, but then Short verbally assaulted Dixon and then emphasized the point—not by drawing his six-shooter, but by striking Dixon over the head with an umbrella. What remarks had been made were not recorded, but Short later explained that he had been receiving "a number of anonymous letters" of late, and that he had traced them "to where they came from." He "intimated" that if keno could not exist then everything in Fort Worth should be closed.

The law responded quickly: two warrants were issued for Short that evening, one charging him with assault and one for carrying a pistol. Trouble was anticipated, and perhaps hoped for by the Dallas and Fort Worth press. Short accused Dixon of "jabbering" but Dixon denied it. It was the intention of the sheriff to raid the place the night of the altercation, but for some unknown reason the raid was not made. Meanwhile, people all over Panther City were talking about this latest incident; some certainly would have preferred Short using his pistol instead of the umbrella.[7]

Then on October 1 Luke's keno operation was closed. It was "closed up" before any game even started. No certain cause was known, but "the supposition is that the sheriff's office had something to do with it."[8]

Charles Dixon, who had been assaulted with Luke's umbrella, now decided to respond to Luke's charge that he was the author of the "anonymous letters" with a "card" of his own, which he placed in the *Fort Worth Daily Gazette.* Dixon expressed himself very well in this notice, stating that it had been said on the streets that he was "charged" to have "written or caused to be written, a number of anonymous letters to parties in this city, and as such charges are calculated to injure me in the estimation of those who have known me ever since I have lived in Fort Worth, I take this method of denying any knowledge of any letter or letters of this character with which I am charged with writing or having written." Dixon continued his denial of ever having said anything against the White Elephant Saloon, or against any business or person connected therewith. "I have never gone to any private citizen, officer, city or county," he insisted, "and made any statement, request, or representation to them, with malicious intent, that would have tendency in any way whatever to affect them or their business." He further accused whoever did write the letters of being "some person too cowardly to father them" as being a "low, despicable character" and in order to protect his good name he had turned the matter over to "an attorney who will use every effort to unearth the author of them in order that the blame may rest where it properly belongs." Dixon provided the card for publication in the *Evening Mail*, the *Fort Worth Gazette*, and the *Dallas Morning News*, as in Dallas he had "a number of friends who I do not wish to censure me for jobs with which I have no connection and of which I know nothing."[9]

As one might expect, Luke Short defied the order to close down the keno games he ran in the club rooms of the White Elephant.[10] The Dallas newspaper reported the games were still running, with a most eye-catching headline: "The Keno Numbers Still Cried Out." In spite of the sheriff "some time ago" ordering the proprietors of the keno rooms to stop running the game, "it is still in full blast every night and is pretty well patronized." Again the subject of the anonymous letters was raised. Now there were anonymous letters written to the owners of the building threatening to have them prosecuted for renting their building. Also anonymous letters were written to insurance agents "for the purpose of influencing them to withdraw their risks" and anonymous letters were also written to various officials "in the effort to induce them to enforce the law." Because these anonymous letters were failing "to produce the desired effect," another scheme was now in place. Broadsides were circulated throughout the city and sent through the mails and otherwise, from an anonymous source "calling the attention of officials to the fact that keno is being run in open defiance of law, and setting forth in graphic language the blighting effect this kind of gambling has upon those who 'buck' against it." The intent was clear, emphasized by the fact that the source of these circulars also called on Judge R. E. Beckham to call a special session of the grand jury in order that not only those who run the game, but also those who play against it, would be indicted and prosecuted. An abundance of testimony was guaranteed to be furnished by parties "who have been spotting keno players." And if one wondered why the broadsides were anonymous, the answer was that the parties against whom it was directed were "dangerous men, handy with the six-shooter, and that it would be worth a man's life to let it be known that he was moving against the game." No other kind of gambling was mentioned in the anonymous circulars.[11]

Charles B. Dixon apparently hadn't forgiven Luke for striking him with an umbrella on the last day of September. On October 15 Dixon decided to sue. The suit attempted to recover the sum of $5,000 from Luke Short "by reason of an assault made by the latter on the plaintiff coupled with the use of opprobrious epithets."[12]

The grand jury met and returned bills of indictment against Luke Short and several other members of the Fort Worth gambling fraternity on November 1, 1887. The grand jury's report to Judge Beckham returned 111 bills, most of which were against parties charged with violations of the laws against gambling. Reportedly they were not through with their work; this fact resulted in a "decided feeling of uneasiness" among the sporting men of Fort Worth.[13]

Cheese Hensley had met with the grand jury and named names, causing that "feeling of uneasiness" among some of those named. The result was not good for Hensley, as some decided to take out their frustrations on him personally. On the night of November 3 Hensley "was rounded up by a lot of gamblers . . . who had it in for him, but he got the best of the crowd by knocking one down, and then leaving when a base ball club was brought to bear against him."[14] Hardly the image of the Wild West combatants: using a baseball bat against a crowd instead of pulling a Colt's or a Smith & Wesson.

This late turn of events may have caused Luke to take a little vacation from Fort Worth. On November 11 he left the Panther City for San Angelo where his brothers lived. He may have intended to stay for a week or longer.[15] Luke went alone, or at least Hattie did not go with him. She was entertaining a guest from another state, Mrs. G. W. Randall of Columbus, Ohio.[16] This is the earliest known Fort Worth newspaper item that mentions "Mrs. Luke Short." Unlike "Mrs. Jake Johnson," who was frequently noted in the Fort Worth newspapers, Hattie received only an occasional mention.

A couple of weeks after this item on Hattie appeared, Tarrant County Attorney R. L. Carlock struck a deal with the three most notorious sporting men in Fort Worth. It may have been a surprise to some, but others may have seen the proverbial writing on the wall. The deal was an understanding with Luke Short and Charles Wright, "proprietors of the gambling house over the White Elephant," and Charles Dixon, "proprietor of the house over the Cabinet" to close their houses. The agreement insisted that they would not be held responsible for the acts of any one to whom the rooms might be leased, "their connection with the games to cease entirely." In consideration of this, some of the cases against men in the house would be "pigeonholed, and pleas of guilty to be entered in a number of cases under the old law." The agreement was to take effect that night, as the night before "gambling went on as usual." Attorney Carlock had been elected over a year before, and his present term would not expire until November 1888.[17]

The news perhaps made some people feel that righteousness was finally taking hold and the Sunday Law would be respected. The *Gazette* announced in its December 2 issue that Luke Short and Charles Wright "have positively severed all their connection with gambling, directly or indirectly, and they will live up to the adjustment." Charles Dixon had visited the County Attorney and told him he had paid all his fines, his house was closed, and he was out of the Fort Worth gambling scene. [18]

Luke and Hattie left Fort Worth and headed for Dallas where they checked into the Grand Windsor. The 126-room hotel was not only brand-new, but parts of it were still under construction when they checked in.[19] It would probably have been better for Luke if he had remained at the Grand Windsor Hotel a while longer.

Instead, on December 12, 1887, he was back in Fort Worth at the White Elephant, acting "crazy drunk," shooting off a pistol, and being placed under arrest.

Chapter 12

The State of Texas v. Luke Short

"You are just as certain to be killed as you live."
—Anonymous to Luke Short, September 1887.

There were periods when Luke Short seemed to be spending about as much time in courtrooms as he did in gambling halls. During the final years of his life, this accelerated. Most of his court appearances were for gambling infractions. While other sporting men paid their fines and went home, Luke usually filed an appeal. After being arrested at the White Elephant on December 12, 1887, for carrying a pistol, he was found guilty on January 6, 1888, by County Judge Sam Furman in the Tarrant County Court. When he was fined $25 and sentenced to twenty days in the county jail, his attorneys filed an appeal. His conviction was reversed and remanded by the Texas Court of Appeals at Austin on May 2, 1888. Ordinarily, a "bare bones" description such as this would suffice to describe the case against Luke, but this was no ordinary case.

The transcript of Luke's appearance before the Texas Court of Appeals provides, among other things, the text of some of those anonymous letters that had been making the rounds in Fort Worth since September 1887.[1] Two main points were considered in Luke's appeal. First, an individual at this time and place could legally carry a pistol if that individual "was at his usual place of business." Second, that individual could legally carry a pistol if the individual had reasonable grounds for fearing an unlawful attack upon his person, and that danger was imminent.

According to state witness S. P. Maddox, one of the arresting policemen, on the night of December 12, 1887, he had arrested Short in the White Elephant for carrying a pistol. He testified he had observed Short withdraw a pistol from his hip pocket and discharge it into the floor of the saloon. Maddox claimed he "had to overpower" Short in making the arrest. At the time Short claimed he had a commission and had the authority to carry the pistol. At the time there was a large crowd in the saloon and Short was "crazy drunk." The state closed.

John D. Thompson testified that he owned a half interest in the building in which the White Elephant Saloon was kept. During the fall of 1887 he had received an anonymous letter, which he had lost, but its substance was that if keno was continued in the building it would be destroyed by "dynamite, giant powder or some other powerful explosive."[2] In this lost communication Short was termed a "desperado and murderer." Thompson attached no importance to this threatening communication.

Jake Johnson, for the defense, also testified regarding letters he knew the defendant had received through the U.S. mail. Witness W. H. Nanny and Short had employed a detective identified only as Thomas to "discover the authors of said anonymous letters" but Thomas reported his inability to do so.[3] J. B. Littlejohn also testified for the defense that during the fall of 1887 he had received an anonymous letter through the mails—since lost or destroyed—in which the patrons of the White Elephant were referred to as "desperadoes and murderers." The letter also threatened that if keno continued to be played, the saloon would be blown up by dynamite or giant powder. Further, the letter warned Littlejohn to cancel the insurance policies his company was carrying on the building and contents. Littlejohn paid no attention to the letter other than to read it.[4]

The next witness for the defense was W. H. Ward, who testified that he was one of the owners of the White Elephant. He had his headquarters there with a desk in the office at which he conducted his correspondence. He also had a drawer in the saloon safe in which he kept his important papers and other valuables. Ward testified to certain letters that were exhibited as having been received in his presence, letters delivered by the mail carriers of Fort Worth.

Cross-examined, Ward stated that in December 1887 Luke Short owned an interest in the White Elephant, "for which he paid witness the sum of one thousand dollars." Witness Ward paid United States and state and city and county taxes, and several licenses were taken out by the witness in his name. The firm of Ward Bros. & Short had been dissolved about November 1886. After that Ward was the sole proprietor of the saloon, until "perhaps, two months before the arrest of the defendant in this case, when he sold defendant one thousand dollar interest mentioned. No papers passed in that transaction, and nobody but witness and defendant knew anything about defendant having this interest until prosecution was instituted."[5]

The first of the threatening letters mentioned by the witness was placed in evidence and was dated at Fort Worth, September 12, 1887. It was directed to Luke Short, advising him that "We have just written a letter of advice to Jake Johnson, and now very cordially invite you, without delay, to leave the city, and without further notice; and if you do not you may expect to abide by the consequences, which, when administered, will be of a rough nature, be assured." This was the opening statement. It continued to explain that "We"—with no indication as to the identity of the "we"—were "approximating too nearly to the completion of disciplined civilization" to have men such as Short in their midst. The letter writer was quite familiar with Short's history, and did not wish his presence in Fort Worth any longer. Such men as "Texas bullies, murderers and black-leg gamblers" must "hunt a clime more congenial to their nature and raising." The "we" now became a "respectable community" and he—Luke Short—was "recognized" as a "high-handed murderer and associate of robbers and murderers" and if he did not leave he would "be served in such a manner as will prove hostile to your better feelings."

Curiously the letter writer did reveal he was no ignorant ruffian, but used terminology that reflected he was an educated man.

> We think you have a great deal of audacity to try to arrogate to yourself the privilege of remaining in a respectable community. Now without further notice, in causing us to give publicity to the fact that you must go at once, for I tell you we do not intend you to remain in our midst. You know you are not a worthy subject for the association of gentlemen of culture, and men who have been raised by respectable parents, and your impotence is only surpassed by your deeds and your ignorance. Now we intend to get rid of you, and it doesn't matter how, but will devise such means if you attempt to remain that we will rid the community of your presence FOR GOOD. The time has arrived when the country has no need of such men, and they must and shall go.

The envelope was addressed to Luke Short, Fort Worth, Texas, and postmarked at Fort Worth on September 13, 8:30 p.m., 1887, with a cancelled two-cent stamp and was introduced as evidence along with the letter.

The second letter and envelope were introduced, but proved to be more threatening and direct, even mentioning Luke's wife. The letter again advised Short to leave; his presence would not be tolerated. Even more direct, it stated, "You are just as certain to be killed as you live." The time of his death did not matter, maybe some time later or maybe in a few days, yet Luke had "got to go, if we have to poison you." More name-calling followed. Luke was a "black hearted murderer, instead of going around hunting men in quiet with their hands in their pockets, as you did with Courtright, you can find plenty in this city who are ready and waiting as you know, but you cowardly cur, you dare not insult them." Strangely, the letter writer, now referring to Luke as "a low down dog" advised him to "fill yourself with whisky and go down to the whoar [*sic*] house and beat a poor, degraded, fallen woman over the head with your pistol."[6] A further insult—clearly garbled—followed: "Outside of a few gamblers and whoars [*sic*] can associate with your so called wife with respectable people."[7] The final threat was that besides Short being forced to leave, "We intend to make it hot for all your kind, and don't you forget it. Keno will close up."[8]

The third letter in the transcript was directed to W. H. Nanny, warning him that the game of keno had to end in Fort Worth. There was no need to explain what negative results followed the game, no need to enter into the details "as to what it has done in our city, such as disturbing mothers, wives and suffering children, because we know you are thoroughly acquainted with these facts." Again there was the threat of danger to the property where keno was played. The letter writer now wanted from Nanny "suberdition," which was probably meant to be "subordination." The owners of property, such as Nanny, could no longer "evade the law, ignore the wants of the poor and suffering, by acting in concert with noted murderers, desperadoes and the scum of creation, who have no ability to follow a respectable business, to longer pile [*sic*, ply] their avocation here without paying a heavy penality [*sic*]." The letter writer reminded Nanny that he was only one of many, a "united body" and if keno was opened than "we will burn the infernal building before it shall run. . . . So now you have one notice, and you had better heed it and abide by it accordingly."

The next letter, dated at Fort Worth on September 12, was included in the transcript. This was directed at Jake Johnson and again the question of economics entered into the subject, suggesting that was perhaps as important an issue as the moral question of keno and its detrimental effect upon people. The letter writer stated that since he—Johnson—associated with "certain noted characters" he had to be warned that there were certain individuals "in our midst that civilization does not need and will not tolerate longer." Fort Worth was "now a city of enlightened people; stand as peers with other cities, and must protect our interest, that we may reflect good credit abroad and compete with growing interests of others more advanced."

Following this introductory paragraph, the letter writer got to the true purpose of his communication. Luke Short was "one of the worst noted characters in our country" and he was guilty of "high handed murder"; now the subject of Courtright's death was raised. According to the letter writer Courtright was "willfully and wantingly [*sic*] murdered, without a shadow of show for his life" and that Short had made it clear that he would do that to anyone "who does not coincide or concur in his views . . . without a moment's notice."

The correspondent was familiar with Short's history, and pointed out that during his absence, while at Hot Springs, there was "comparative piece [*sic*]" and the city "enjoyed the quietude of an enlightened age."[9] "The day has passed" the letter writer continued, "when a community will sit quietly and submit to outlaws, desperadoes, murderers and low down roughs, and such as he will be warned, and it will be well for him if he takes the advice, for we are determined he and like characters shall go." Luke Short, according to the letter writer, had "some of the worst characters brought here, and were here at his call, and were in full companionship with him and like characters" and instead of making the White Elephant a "resort for gentlemen" it had become a "resort for desperadoes and murderers, and a refuge for outlaws and roughs from every quarter." In brief, Short and his associates had made the White Elephant a house "to compare favorably in crime to its ponderous name." The men who came to the White Elephant were men who came to "sap the life-blood, vampire like, never once reflecting a credit or aiding in any way to its advancement." Short was a man "void of honor" and it was the duty of Jake Johnson to assist them "in getting rid of such low down characters" as Luke Short.

The court provided a clear and concise opinion in the case of *Texas v Luke Short.* It reviewed the matter concerning Short being a silent partner in the operation of the White Elephant, and declared that it had been proven "abundantly" that he had received prior to the date of the arrest "several anonymous letters threatening his life" and that Short "had endeavored to procure . . . the aid of a detective and a deputy sheriff to assist him in ferreting out the authors of the letters, and without avail." The opinion of the court was that "the verdict and judgment" pronounced against the evidence and therefore "the judgment is reversed and the cause remanded."[10] Luke Short had proved to have made a wise decision in having the case appealed.

Chapter 13

The Sport of Kings and a Palace Royal

"The wonder to me is I have not killed you before."
—Luke Short to Fred May, in *Dallas Morning News*, September 9, 1888.

With his appeal won, Luke Short left Fort Worth, having decided to expand his gambling interests to include thoroughbred horseracing. His friend William H. Harris was a noted "turfman," as was Jake Johnson. Both had been trying to interest Luke in the sport for some time. Luke and Jake, along with their wives, attended the inaugural running of the Futurity Stakes on Labor Day 1888. That event was held in New York at the Sheepshead Bay racetrack, on Coney Island. One-quarter of those in attendance were women. Two of those women were Mrs. Jake Johnson and Mrs. Luke Short.[1]

A thoroughbred racehorse gelding named Proctor Knott won the inaugural running of the Futurity Stakes, which was then the richest race run in the United States. The owners of Proctor Knott collected $41,675 in prize money from that 1888 win.[2] Jake Johnson won big also that day, and had further bragging rights when it was reported that he owned three brothers of Proctor Knott. At the time they were training in Tennessee.[3]

There is a story, possibly apocryphal, of a Manhattan encounter Luke Short had with a noted trouble maker named Fred May. It circulated while Short was still alive and also appeared in many of his obituaries. May was allegedly "a jewel of a man" when he met up with Luke Short, before his "dissipation had wrecked his constitution as well as his fortune." May had "nerves of steel and knew naught of fear." The incident in question happened in one of the up-town restaurants and the conversation was "rather free." Short made some remark about an actress who was then "the idol of New York." May took exception and stated that the man who would say that was a coward and no gentleman. Short "calmly looked May over from head to foot and then let his eyes travel back from foot to head." This obviously unnerved May and he demanded of Short what was the matter with him. "I was merely thinking where I would hit you" responded Short, and without moving a muscle, Short continued: "The wonder to me is I have not killed you long before." May started to advance then but Luke drew his pistol, and said "Don't you take another step." May, unarmed, looked steadily at Short and then remarked: "Well, as you seem to have the best of it, I guess I'll leave," and with a shrug of his shoulders walked out.[4]

Fred May was a self-styled clubman, sportsman, and yachtsman who hailed from Baltimore.[5] During a dispute there, he had for sheer spite ridden a horse up the steps of the Barnum Hotel. No longer welcome in Baltimore, May and his sister Caroline moved to New York City. When publisher James Gordon Bennett (who was then engaged to Caroline May), urinated in May's fireplace, May challenged him to a duel. On the day selected, Fred May fired his pistol in the air, which ended the duel. During the 1880s May became one of a long line of lovers who attended the world-famous actress Lillie Langtry.[6] The actress who was then the idol of New York, who Short made a remark about which offended May, was certainly Langtry.

The question remains: did such an encounter between Luke Short and Fred May really happen? The *Kansas City Times* published a suspiciously similar story, which predated Short's Labor Day 1888 visit to New York by nearly a year. According to the *Kansas City Times* article, the incident took place on September 28, 1887, a date when Short can be located at Fort Worth.[7] More importantly, the version appearing in the *Times* described a Fred May adversary who was not named Luke Short. In this episode, Fred May was described as the "imperturbable and blasé man about town" who had a "close call" in Valkenburg's Saloon under the Albermarle Hotel. His antagonist this time was Mike Duffy, "regarded as the most dangerous man in New Orleans." Duffy was cool, calm, resolute, and dangerous, in many respects the typical gambler of the time. He was in Valkenburg's Saloon visiting with several friends when May walked in. He joined the group and was introduced to Duffy, whom he apparently did not know, or perhaps misunderstood the name. Someone mentioned the name of Lillie Langtry and her latest production, "As in a Looking Glass."

After some few minutes May stood up, dropped his hat upon the table and said "I don't care to have that lady discussed here," staring at Duffy who happened to be speaking at the time. Duffy looked across at May a few moments and then said: "Mrs. Langtry is a public character. She advertises herself as such, forces herself down the public throat, and as such any man in the world has a right to discuss her in public whenever and wherever he pleases."

May savagely responded: "No man can do it here."

Duffy responded with a southern drawl, "Oh, yes he can. I can and I will. I have a good mind to send around to her house now and see if she won't go out to supper with me."

May was now angry and shouted to Duffy "You are a liar." Both men jumped to their feet and Sergeant Hickey threw himself on May who jumped toward Duffy. May was hustled out of the room by friends just in time to miss a ball from Duffy's revolver.[8]

By October 1888 Luke Short and Jake Johnson were back in Fort Worth. Luke was no longer connected with the White Elephant Saloon in any way. For his part, Johnson was about to open a "resort" called the Palais Royal designed to rival the White Elephant. Johnson's partner was Victor Foster. Luke undoubtedly owned a piece of the action, but remained the most silent of silent partners.[9] In October a reporter visited the Palais Royal and gave it the most glowing review imaginable, headlining it as a "Super Resort." His review appeared two days prior to the official opening date, which was October 23. It was described as "one of the finest and most costly sample rooms in the entire country." The proprietors, Jake Johnson and Victor Foster, had completed all the arrangements and intended their reception to be "one of the most brilliant and pleasant affairs ever witnessed in Fort Worth." The gushing report continued to say the establishment "will be arrayed in all its splendor, choice plants and beautiful pictures will adorn the place, while a profusion of cut flowers will fill the air with perfume rare." Sound had not been forgotten, as "the leading orchestra" would enliven the occasion with "inspiring music."[10] The unforgettable experience would delight those gentlemen and ladies from 7:00 to 10:00 o'clock that evening.

The *Gazette* report assured its readers that "the public generally" would find that the Palais Royal was the finest sample room not only in the south and west, but also of the entire country. Was this mere hyperbole from a Fort Worth newspaper? Of course not, as prominent "connoisseurs" from New York, Washington, Chicago, Cincinnati, "and other large cities" had declared that "there is nothing in the way of fixtures, decorations, arrangements, etc., that excel those of the Palais Royal." The bar fixtures were especially noteworthy, "entirely different from anything in this country." They were of "antique oak, richly carved and polished with French plate and stained glass trimmings." The front window design was "beyond all question, the most unique piece of work ever produced." The praise for the carvings and arrangements and fixtures and the tile on the floor went on and on. All was "in elegant taste" of course. To many patrons, the stock of imported wines, liquors, and cigars was perhaps more important than the etchings on the glass doors. "They are of the best," as we would expect, "and with their fine old Kentucky and Tennessee whisky (some less than eight years old) ought certainly to bring to the Palais Royal the trade which they so richly deserve."[11]

Luke Short was now in charge of the club rooms in the opulent setting of the Palais Royal. But he never was in a position where he could leave his pistol at home, whether it was in a leather holster hanging from a gun belt or hidden in a leather-lined pocket. For those who may have forgotten the constant danger of the sporting man's world, in the decidedly less opulent club rooms above the Cabinet Saloon, Charles B. Dixon, Luke's sworn enemy, made a gun play on October 28, 1888.

About 8 o'clock on the morning of October 28, five pistol shots rang out at the corner of Main and Third Streets, attracting a large crowd within minutes. The shootist was a saloon owner named W. F. Whitlow; the target proved to be Charles B. Dixon. In spite of the five shots fired, apparently only one hit Dixon, striking him in the left thigh, a wound not believed to be dangerous. Some misunderstanding had precipitated the matter, the disagreement beginning over a faro game in Dixon's house. Whitlow had retired to the saloon on the ground floor. After Dixon had closed up he went below and he and Whitlow "engaged in conversation." It was thought to be all over by some, but Whitlow had obtained a pistol, and "when the two men were standing in a narrow passageway, at the foot of the stairs, Whitlow drew his pistol." Dixon reached forward, perhaps defensively to protect himself, but Whitlow fired twice, hitting Dixon once. Bartender Buck Smith jumped to the scene and tried to disarm Whitlow. Before he could, Whitlow had fired three more shots. Two of the shots passed through the front door and entered a street car passing on Main Street. Fortunately no one was hit in the street car. Smith by now had managed to disarm Whitlow, but his pistol was perhaps empty. Whitlow ran out the back way across the street into the saloon that he owned. Dixon stood on the street holding onto a post, bleeding "quite badly." Friends called for help; Dr. J. P.

Burts[12] arrived quickly and dressed Dixon's wound. He was taken to his residence. Whitlow had by now locked himself in his saloon but friends finally convinced him to surrender.[13]

Whitlow was placed under bond of $500 and taken home. He had been drinking during the night, and this was the "excuse" for the difficulty. Dixon had not been armed as he had anticipated no trouble. Buck Smith's prompt action prevented Whitlow from killing Dixon. Within a few days a report informed the public that Dixon was "improving steadily" and the injury was only temporary.[14]

The presidential election between incumbent President Grover Cleveland, who was a Democrat, and Benjamin Harrison, a Republican, was held on November 6, 1888. The only thing Luke Short had in common with Harrison was that they each stood five-foot-six inches tall, in shoes. A humorous item in the *Gazette* left no doubt about whom Luke Short was backing. Budd Fagg was quoted as saying that he was for the Democratic ticket "straight" and he would work for it. Luke Short was quoted as saying, "I am a Democrat in principle and I shall work to-day for the straight Democratic ticket."[15]

Cleveland lost. Eleven days after the election Luke was in Dallas with one of Fort Worth's most combative sporting men. Nathan Brooks, Luke Short, and Cheese Hensley "were involved in a row last night, and Hensley got his hand cut badly."[16]

As far as Luke was concerned he was ready for new adventures in new locales. Most of these adventures would happen far from Texas. His odyssey began in what would, during the years that followed, become his home away from home—Chicago.

Chapter 14

The Main Event

> Luke Short, "the noted sporting man of Fort Worth . . . will go anywhere in the world for Bat."
>
> —*Chicago Daily Tribune*, July 3, 1889.

Luke Short would spend part of each year, from 1889 until 1893 in Chicago. He usually went there during the summer months to get relief from the Texas heat as well as to attend thoroughbred horse races. Hattie always went with him on these extended visits that often lasted weeks and sometimes months. Hattie and Luke stayed at the Leland Hotel on Michigan Avenue. She undoubtedly loved everything about Chicago, from fine restaurants to theaters, and of course, the shopping. Most of all she would have appreciated not being judged negatively, as she was in Fort Worth, because of whom she was married to. In Chicago, if Hattie was judged at all it would have been for her beauty. She had the ability to turn heads in a metropolis with no shortage of beautiful women. By 1889, Luke had attained celebrity status and was well known even in the "Second City."[1]

By this time Luke was occasionally in the headlines, and not for participating in a gunfight. In July 1889 he was among the party going with Charles E. "Parson" Davies to New Orleans to attend a prize fight. Luke was described as "the noted sporting man of Fort Worth, Tex." He was then in Chicago attending the races and said he was "not interested in the fight and does not expect to take any side in the affair, but will go because his friend 'Bat' Masterson insists on his doing so." Luke explained that he would "go anywhere in the world for Bat."[2]

Charles E. "Parson" Davies was of course the leading athletic promoter in the United States from the late 1870s until 1897. It was Davies who had arranged for John L. Sullivan's championship fight with Paddy Ryan. On this particular occasion he was promoting what would be the last bare-knuckle heavyweight championship match fought between Sullivan and Jake Kilrain.[3]

The festive party traveled in a Pullman sleeper, with Davies in charge. With Davies in charge it was no question of being well provided for, as that was one of his many trademarks. They expected to arrive in New Orleans Sunday, July 7. Among those identified as being with the party were Sheriff David Foley of Gogebic County, Michigan, and "Luke Short of Fort Worth," suggesting he was among the notables of Chicago.[4]

The Sullivan-Kilrain fight was the last world title bout fought under London Prize Ring Rules, meaning it was the last bare-knuckle championship fight. The gathering spot for the 3,000 fight fans was New Orleans, where they boarded special trains that would take them to the "secret location" of the fight. That secret location was in Richburg, Mississippi, where the two fighting giants faced each other. The two men "faced each other in the 24-foot ring and there did battle for the largest stakes ever fought for, $20,000, the *Police Gazette* champion belt and the championship of the world."[5]

The *Gazette* backed the "gladiator" Kilrain who "was far from being a well man when he entered the ring." Nevertheless he insisted that the fight go on, refusing to disappoint "those who had placed confidence in him, or place his patrons in a compromising position." The two men were of the same height, age, and physical capabilities and "professional prowess," both equal in "everything that goes to make a first-class pugilist of the heavy-weight class." Kilrain faced Sullivan under a "broiling Southern midday sun" and fought for seventy-five rounds, lasting two hours and sixteen minutes. Enduring that, the *Gazette* waxed poetic in describing the defeat: "This certainly was not the action of a coward, this decidedly was not the action of a craven. Jake Kilrain . . . has proven to the satisfaction of his friends, and even to those who favored his opponent, that he is neither." Apparently there were rumors that the referee was not "altogether impartial" in his decision and that he was "not wholly and fully informed as to the technicalities of the London Prize Ring Rules" but nevertheless the *Gazette* had to accept that the championship belt and the $20,000 stakes went to Sullivan. The *Gazette* concluded it had desired only to "see a fair, square fight, with no favor, and that the battle should be won or lost on its merits." That had been done and thus the *Gazette* greeted the victor.[6]

There were many notables at ringside but the presence of Luke Short and Bat Masterson caught the eye of a Pittsburgh, Pennsylvania, reporter who headlined his article "A Bad Couple Side by Side" which may have amused the pair, if they happened to notice it. "Bat Masterson, of Denver, with a record of 22 men in his book of lives" was how this reporter began his item, apparently with no cause to honor integrity in reporting as Masterson had no such number of kills in his "book of lives." But Masterson was "far from being the typical desperado in manners and dress, being polished and well-spoken in the extreme" and "chatted with Luke Short, of the same place." This was another error in reporting, providing two in the opening sentence. Luke Short's book of lives was "almost as good as that of Masterson" and "the pressure [presence?] of this pair at the ringside made more than one man hope that everything would go off smoothly, as both were primed and loaded."[7]

Bat Masterson was not there at ringside merely to observe the action. He was the designated timekeeper for Kilrain, and came under fire from some sources for how he handled his role. Reportedly Luke Short, Johnny

Murphy, and "twelve other good men were scattered around the ring side where they would do the most good in case of an emergency."[8]

"Jake won't get the worst of it" said Masterson when he came to New Orleans, and he didn't. Masterson gave Sullivan the worst of it, "all the way from ten to twenty seconds in every round. Sullivan's timekeeper was Tom Costello of Cleveland, "but he seemed to let Masterson run it to suit himself." From the reporting of the *Cincinnati Enquirer* one might get the impression that the crowd was filled with gunmen ready to fire. "It is said," reported the *Plain Dealer* of Cleveland, "Masterson's men each had one of Sullivan's crowd picked out in case there was trouble. In this they had no percentage over the Sullivan party. To offset the Masterson gang the Sullivan party engaged some good people. All the western crowd were marked."[9]

Not every newspaper agreed with the *Cincinnati Enquirer*, whose report was picked up by Cleveland's *Plain Dealer* and no doubt others. Most newspapers came to Bat's defense including a newspaper from Little Rock, Arkansas. "One of the most important yet most unassuming men at the fight between John L. Sullivan and Jake Kilrain was Bat Masterson, of Denver, a man with a wonderful record" was how this report began, noting only that his record was "wonderful" and with no mention of how many men he may have killed. Masterson "is known and appreciated all over the West" and was considered almost a Colorado attraction as Pike's Peak or the Garden of the Gods. For those newspapers who declared that he headed a gang of killers who were determined to have Kilrain win the fight no matter what, they were "partly right and partly wrong."[10]

The gang of "killers" were all there but their instructions were clearly to "cover all over blood" anyone who attempted to mob the fight in favor of "the big man from Boston," Sullivan. This report explained that two months before the fight arrangements had been made to send Masterson and "a few of his friends" to New Orleans. From the minute Kilrain arrived in the Crescent City until he left it "a badly defeated man, the quiet, gentlemanly Masterson was always at his side, and attracted almost as much attention as did Kilrain."

Luke Short did not receive near the press' attention as did Masterson in this instance, but his name was included among the party with Masterson. Luke Short, Bud Fagg, Jack Murphy, Joe Copeland, and Mike Ryan were men "with a personal history that would shine red on the bloodiest of theater stories, and with nerve enough to do battle with the supporters of Sullivan who were gathered at Richburg on that great day." Following the fight's end, the supporters of Kilrain returned to their special Pullman car, "loaded down with delicacies, both edible and palatable, and quietly stole back to their respective homes."[11]

Luke Short's return to Chicago on July 12, 1889, was noted by several newspapers in the "Second City." He had returned from the fight at Richburg with a new enthusiasm for boxing and a new ambition for himself. He now wanted to be a boxing promoter; he wanted to live the life style that Parson Davies enjoyed as Chicago's leading sportsman. Luke Short knew it would be useless to try and compete with Davies in Chicago, and he never really considered it. Instead, Luke Short wanted to pursue his new dream in a place where many did not want him—the place called Fort Worth.

Chapter 15

Luke Short—Prize Fight Promoter

> Luke Short has gone to San Angelo "to attend the funeral of his brother Will, who was killed by a herd of stampeding cattle on the Tankersly ranch."
>
> —*Dallas Morning News*, April 4, 1890.

By October 1889 Luke Short was back in Texas attending the annual fair at Dallas. The fair drew huge crowds, including gamblers and confidence men. Luke would have been drawn there by the horse races, which were a major part of the fair. On October 21 the leading Dallas newspaper reported that "Luke Short of the panther city is in this city."[1] Luke was also seeking investors in Dallas to help bankroll his scheme of bringing a heavyweight championship fight to Fort Worth, or a nearby location. One possibility was a proposed fight between the champion, John L. Sullivan, and Peter Jackson, who was managed by Parson Davies of Chicago. A location for the match (which neither fighter had agreed to) prompted bidding from several sporting men, including Short. By now Chicago was well aware of who Luke Short was. The *Daily Inter Ocean* reported that Short, "who is numbered as one of the prominent figures of the Richburg battle" had cabled Charles E. "Parson" Davies offering $20,000 to have a fight in Fort Worth. He stated that state laws "legalize prize-fighting."[2]

Luke's offer was taken very seriously in sporting circles. Chicago's leading newspaper, the *Daily Tribune*, recognized Short as one who could arrange such a contest. If the match between Sullivan and Jackson did occur, however, it would probably be at the California Athletic Club. "After all the offers of big money for a match between them were examined," reported the *Tribune*, "it was clear that only two were reliable. Those were made by Luke Short of Fort Worth, Texas, and the California Athletic Club." However, even though Short "could pay all that he offered and guarantee men protection and fair play . . . he could not successfully bid against the rich California organization."[3]

Never one to be discouraged by such as the statement in the *Tribune*, Luke decided to up the ante by writing to Richard K. Fox, the editor and publisher of the *National Police Gazette*, at that time the sporting man's "Bible." On January 11 Luke informed Fox that he had written Parson Davies to inform him that the National Bank of Fort Worth had agreed to subscribe a purse of $20,000 to $30,000 for a "fistic encounter" between the *Police Gazette* champion, John L. Sullivan, and "the colored champion of Australia." Luke continued pointing out that the "battle" could be fought in the area of Fort Worth or Dallas, and "neither of the pugilists or their backers, or anyone interested, will be interfered with before or after the fight." The amount of money should have been attractive enough, but Luke proposed to erect a "large amphitheater which will hold 5,000 spectators," which should have been a decisive factor.

Luke had already written John L. Sullivan but as yet no reply had reached him. Luke had heard from Davies who assured Luke that Peter Jackson was willing, "and if Sullivan is as eager as Jackson the match can be ratified at once." Luke Short, once he had decided to become a boxing promoter, did not intend to delay. He assured Fox in the letter that he sent on January 11 that the Texas laws allowed prize fighting, and all that would be necessary for each fighter would be to purchase a license of $500. Luke also stated in this letter, which was quoted in a newspaper, that he was ready to give both fighters $20,000, but added: "I am still ready to give them $20,000. If you [Fox] think $25,000 or $30,000 is a sufficient inducement, the bank will authorize me to give it."[4] Luke Short, now enthralled by becoming a promoter, was ready to have the builders start erecting the amphitheater.

Luke had not received a reply from Sullivan, but in early February he received a reply from Richard K. Fox of the *National Police Gazette*, which was not encouraging. Luke must have shared the contents with a Dallas reporter as we know of them from the *Morning News.* It was not a matter of the amount of money involved, but according to the published report, John L. Sullivan objected "to fighting with the negro." Even though this statement underscored Sullivan's prejudicial attitude toward a non-white athlete, he did express his willingness "to meet Jackson in a championship contest if there is money enough put up." A further explanation followed: "A championship fight is a bare-knuckle affair. Jackson won't fight with anything but 4-ounce gloves, and besides he hasn't challenged Sullivan to a fight, and he has declared his intention of not doing so." Even though the prospect of contracting the two pugilists was bleak, in case anything changed, the offer of $30,000 from Fort Worth would be "a strong bid for the fight." Short assured the reporter that the offer would remain open, and that the money was in the bank.[5]

In spite of Luke's eagerness for his success in the promotion endeavor, events beyond his control continued to occur in his life. On February 8, 1890, Luke's father, Josiah Washington Short, died in San Angelo, Texas, of an unknown cause. Luke was in Dallas but for some reason he did not learn of his father's passing until three days later, on February 11. According to the dispatch received on that day he learned of "the sudden death of his father at the ripe age of 78 years." [6] He could not attend the funeral of course as the burial probably occurred the day after his death.

On February 11 a troupe headed by Jake Kilrain, William Muldoon, and Mike Cleary came to Dallas from Fort Worth to put on a boxing and wrestling exhibition at the Dallas Opera House. As part of the entertainment, challenges were made to anyone who might want to take on any of the athletes. Lightweight champion Louis Baznia, nineteen years old, offered $25 to any local 250-pounder who could go four rounds with him. The challenge was met by a twenty-two-year-old local bricklayer named Tom James. For three rounds he made a major effort to avoid getting hit. But in the fourth round Baznia hit James on the right side of his neck and he fell to the canvas. He could not be revived. After all efforts to bring him around failed, James was declared dead. Kilrain, and no doubt many others, wept while efforts were made to revive him. Under orders of the Dallas County Attorney, Police Chief Jim Arnold ordered the entire troupe held until the investigation was completed.[7] In order to come up with the bail for all the members of the troupe a wire was sent to Luke Short.

Luke received the telegram in Fort Worth on the fourteenth, asking him to go to Dallas and "assist the Kilrain-Muldoon combination in getting bail. He left on the 3:30 train for that purpose."[8] The coroner's inquest was held on February 21 and the following morning Justice John Henry Brown rendered his verdict, that there was "no just or reasonable ground for holding Louis Baznia to answer for a violation of the laws of Texas." Following the issuance of the verdict, the entire party then repaired to the Windsor for supper. Even with the tragedy still fresh in everyone's mind, not surprisingly a large number of admirers called on Muldoon and Kilrain to congratulate them on the outcome of the inquest. At 7:30 the group "jumped into hacks in waiting" and left for the depot with the crowd cheering. At the depot the crowd, estimated at 2,000 fans, "stared the wrestlers and pugilists out of countenance until the train pulled in and took them aboard."[9]

On the same day that the verdict was rendered Luke spoke to a reporter for the *Dallas Morning News* concerning the status of a championship fight in Texas. There had been a rumor that Kilrain would retire from the ring. "There is nothing more in the report more than Mr. Kilrain will temporarily retire in order to regain perfect health," Luke explained. "He told me while here that he would shortly go to Hot Springs and spend several weeks [there.]" In case the readers were wondering what was the matter with Kilrain, Luke continued: "He has touches of rheumatism in the shoulders and hands, and he will have to get rid of this before he can keep his place in the ring."

The reporter continued with a question concerning the proposed fight in Fort Worth. "I have received a letter from [William] Muldoon stating that he would see Sullivan as soon as possible after the Mississippi matter is settled," Luke explained. "Muldoon told me when here that he wouldn't back anybody but Kilrain against Sullivan. He has a high opinion of Jackson, but didn't think he would last long against Sullivan in a bare knuckle fight. He considers Kilrain the most dangerous opponent Sullivan could have." The reporter was aware of Luke's intentions to have a major fight in Texas and inquired if the Irishman would fight in Texas. Luke of course had the answer: "Sullivan told Muldoon that he would rather fight here than in California. He knows that I would give him a fair show, which he doesn't think he can get out there." Luke, knowing what he said would get to Sullivan and Muldoon and perhaps Jackson as well, continued: "I won't have anything to do with anything but a first-class fight, and if it takes place here it will likely be a contest to settle the championship of the world, and I believe it will be between Sullivan and Kilrain."[10]

On March 2, 1890, a Rochester, New York, paper reported that Charles Mitchell, a British fighter, was considering coming to the Fort Worth area. Mitchell had announced that he would be coming to America in April, and on his arrival he would "throw down the gauntlet to any man in the world, challenging them to battle according to London rules." This was to be done for $2,500 and within 150 miles of Fort Worth. The report indicated Luke Short and Bat Masterson would be Mitchell's backers.[11]

Knowing that Luke had $30,000 in the bank to stage a championship fight caught the attention of fight managers who wanted to interest Luke in their own fighters. Sometimes they caught Luke by surprise. A Dallas newspaper item reported that a dispatch from Bloomington, Indiana, announced the "probable meeting" between Billy Myers and Jack Hopper for a "finish fight with two-ounce gloves," Queensbury rules with $1,000 a side on April 10, in Fort Worth. It was a genuine surprise to sporting men, including Luke Short who "knew nothing of it." Short assured the press that he was after one particular fight, and that would be between Sullivan and one other heavyweight, and he preferred him to be Kilrain. Whenever the two men were ready for the fight Luke stated that there was $30,000 in the bank for it. And what of the case in Mississippi against Kilrain, who had been convicted of participating in an illegal prizefight? Luke opined: "Jake told me that he expected as much, and in such an event he would go at once and serve the sentence, which is only two months in jail and a fine of $100." Would serving this sentence be injurious to Kilrain? Luke had the answer: "He won't suffer from confinement. Mr. C. W. Rich, on whose farm the fight took place, has a contract with the county to work convicts, and Jake will practically have his freedom. When Jake gets through with Mississippi I expect to have some news."[12]

Both Sullivan and Kilrain had been arrested for participating in what Missisippi said was an illegal prizefight on July 8, 1889. Sullivan was arrested in Nashville while Kilrain was nabbed in Baltimore. At his trial Sullivan was found guilty, paid a $500 fine and left the state. Kilrain wasn't as lucky: he was found guilty, paid a $500 fine, and was *sentenced to six months in jail.* Colonel Charles W. Rich, who owned the land the fight was held on (and who the town of Richburg, Mississippi, was named after) was allowed to "buy" Kilrain's sentence. The Mississippi Supreme Court reduced Kilrain's sentence from six months to just two. Jake Kilrain spent those two months as a guest, under "house arrest," in the mint julep atmosphere of Col. Rich's mansion.

Luke's dream of a heavyweight championship was paramount, but he was willing to consider lesser contests in other weight divisions. According to the *Dallas Morning News,* Luke received a dispatch from

William Muldoon on March 15, 1890, asking if he would give $2,500 for two finish fights in Fort Worth, one a middleweight between Mike Cleary and Ed Smith. Smith had defeated LaBlanche "The Marine," who gave Jack "Nonpareil" Dempsey his first defeat, so that could be a popular draw. The second was to be a lightweight contest between Louis Baznia, who had killed a man in the ring, and one Daly of St. Louis. The two battles would certainly be "rattling good fights" but Short was "not hunting anything except a battle for the world's championship" in which Sullivan would serve. Rather than turning Muldoon down totally, however, he informed him "that both fights would pay here" and would be glad to have them come to Fort Worth.

The Myers-Hopper fight was not forgotten, but even though the Associated Press had announced it would take place on April 6, nothing was known about it in the sporting circles of Fort Worth. Short had had some correspondence with Myers' backer "some time ago, but not recently."[13]

With all the work involved in trying to arrange the championship fight Luke may have forgotten about his family; there is little evidence that he often made an effort to visit family members. He learned of his father's passing after the burial, and now his brother William B. Short passed, by an accident, not through gunfire. William B. Short was the youngest of the ten Short siblings. He was born October 21, 1867, and was only twenty-two years of age at the time of his death. The tragedy may have been fairly common in the world where the horse was part of everybody's and everyday's doings. The report came from San Angelo and was dated April 1. It stated that he was killed "by his horse falling on him yesterday at the Tankersly ranch" fifty miles west of San Angelo. Short's remains were brought in and buried in the San Angelo City Cemetery.[14] There is some confusion over the date of Will Short's death. The San Angelo report of April 1 stated he was killed by his horse "yesterday," which would mean March 31, and the *Fort Worth*

Daily Gazette item agreed, yet the Texas Death Records, as well as his tombstone, give the date as March 29, 1890.

Further difficulty in determining exactly what happened on the Tankersly Ranch is due to a report from Fort Worth and printed in the *Dallas Morning News* that Luke Short had gone to San Angelo "to attend the funeral of his brother Will, who was killed by a herd of stampeding cattle on the Tankersly ranch."[15] Could the stampeding cattle have caused Will's horse to bolt, which caused him to fall on his rider? Perhaps both reports held a portion of the truth.

Luke arrived back in Fort Worth on April 8. He immediately returned to his prize fight activities and provided a reporter from Dallas with a status report. It was not promising for fight lovers. The proposed Billy Myers-Jack Hopper fight, which was tentatively set to be held in May, had been postponed. While in March he'd told the *Dallas Morning News* that he hadn't heard from the two pugilists for quite some time, now he said he had heard nothing for "a couple of weeks." Both fighters had "several outside engagements," which would delay any fight between them. Apparently he was now involved in this fight, because he told the reporter that the latest communication he had received from Myers' manager was to the effect that the Myers-Hopper fight could not take place until after May 7, and nothing more had been heard since. Luke was still confident that the fight would take place in Fort Worth sometime in May, as all parties concerned preferred Fort Worth. The key statements in this report followed: "Mr. Short is hopeful over the outlook for a meeting between Sullivan and some aspirant for the championship at Fort Worth before the year is over." If Muldoon or Parson Davies "are connected with the affair, Mr. Short thinks Fort Worth will pull the plum."[16]

But even a fight promoter needs a change in the scenery at times, and Luke Short was no exception. John L. Sullivan was in no hurry to defend his title. Luke may have felt he had time on his hands and thus welcomed an invitation from Jake Johnson to accompany him to a breeding farm in Tennessee. The Belle Meade Plantation at Nashville was the preeminent stud farm for thoroughbred race horses. Starting in 1867 the annual sale of yearlings at Belle Meade attracted the most prominent horsemen of the day from across the country. Luke was with Jake Johnson at the twenty-third annual Belle Meade sale, held in Nashville on April 24, 1890. The amount for the horses Jake bought was reported all across the country, including a Montana newspaper that reported "Jake Johnson, who laid out about $20,000 in yearlings in the Belle Meade sale is ambitious to shine on the turf. He is a bookmaker, and hails from Fort Worth."[17]

Following the Belle Meade sale on April 24, Luke and Jake left Nashville and went to Memphis to take in the races. Also in Memphis was Charles M. Wright, a former partner of Luke's, who would be involved in a gunfight with Luke before the year was over. An incident in Memphis was considered by some to be the genesis of the trouble between Short and Wright. What happened in Memphis involved Short, Jake Johnson, Joe Copeland, Charles Wright, and Budd Fagg, and "other sports" in faro games in the Memphis gambling houses. The limit was $50 and $100. The partners won a significant amount of cash, "some thousands of dollars," which was entrusted to Wright. He was designated as the banker, and presumably would place the winnings in the safe where they stayed, the Gayoso Hotel. Wright occupied a room with Fagg and Copeland, but during the night he was robbed of every cent. He wanted his partners to bear an equal share of the loss but they refused, claiming that it was Wright's responsibility to deposit the money in the house safe; as he had not he alone must bear the consequences. The matter was turned over to the local authorities who decided against Charles Wright. Wright was never satisfied with that decision and had "hard words with several of his ex-partners on the subject since that time, particularly with Short."[18]

The trouble between Wright and his ex-partners continued after all had left Memphis. In Fort Worth, Wright decided to avenge his honor on the person of Budd Fagg. There officer Henry C. Towns arrested Wright for carrying a concealed weapon. Fortunately for Fagg, policeman Towns took hold of Wright before the "concealed weapon" was fired. According to the report "Wright and the gun were just about to levy on Budd Fagg when the police interfered."[19]

Luke was certainly aware of these doings but may not have really considered Charles Wright a threat. After all, Luke Short had the reputation as a dangerous man, and at least for now Wright seemed not to have made any further attempts at confronting any of the other sporting men who were with him in Memphis. He probably would have thought twice before confronting Luke with a pistol. For his part, Luke certainly wasn't giving Wright a thought, since he was far more concerned with a telegram he received regarding the possibility of the contest between John L. Sullivan and Joe McAuliffe, a "rising young heavy weight." Short had received the telegram from Billy Madden the night of May 19 asking "what inducements he could hold out for a championship meeting" between the pair. Luke would take the matter under advisement, and his many friends "believe that with good training he could beat either Sullivan or [Peter] Jackson." Billy Muldoon was consulted, and according to the Associated Press, he "would back Ed Smith against any fighter in the world, except Sullivan, Jackson, and McAuliffe." This statement, assuming it true, put McAuliffe "in the first class by the highest pugilistic authority." Fort Worth was confident that since Peter Jackson would not accept a challenge from McAuliffe, then Sullivan would agree to "a finish fight if the proper inducements are held out." If the "full particulars" were furnished to Madden, and "if there is a reasonable probability of a meeting, he [Short] will offer an inducement which will in all likelihood bring the match to this city."[20]

Promotion plans and thoroughbreds did not occupy Luke's time totally. Hattie now had some family in the Fort Worth area. Her mother and two of her brothers had moved from Kansas and were living nearby. Luke's mother-in-law, Cynthia Allen Buck, had been born in Texas and also had family living in the vicinity. The Short name always was newsworthy. "Miss Mattie Allen, a cousin to Mrs. Luke Short and a kin to Ethan Allen of revolutionary fame," read one item, "is visiting at Mr. Short's residence."[21]

Meanwhile, Luke had decided to expand his ringside activities to include wrestling. It is perhaps difficult to envision the notorious Luke Short holding the stakes on a wrestling match, but such was the case. The pair were Major Will Willie and Captain Tom Shields and they were scheduled to "test their athletic abilities" on Monday night, June 9, at the opera house in a Greco-Roman wrestling match. The prize was $500.[22]

Five hundred dollars must have seemed a paltry sum for Luke Short. In an effort to finally stage a championship fight at Fort Worth, Luke wired the *National Police Gazette* with a new offer. He informed Richard K. Fox that he would offer a purse of $10,000 for a finish fight between John L. Sullivan and Joe McAuliffe "for the Police Gazette championship belt." This fight would take place in October near Fort Worth. Short guaranteed "fair play and protection to satisfaction of both parties."[23] For Joe McAuliffe and his manager Billy Madden, it was a deal they could not refuse.

Billy Madden did accept the proposition but what of Sullivan? It was believed that he would "hold back until he can get a bigger purse." The disadvantage was that McAuliffe was a young fighter, "with not an exceeding amount of prestige" and if Sullivan decided to fight he would have to be satisfied with the $10,000 purse. But if McAuliffe could get an additional $10,000 then Sullivan might be more interested. Short had intended that the match take place during the Dallas fair, "at a point of easy access, possibly somewhere between Dallas and Fort Worth or maybe near Midlothian," a community about thirty miles southwest of Dallas in Ellis County. It was too early to be concerned about the "selecting of the battle grounds yet" as much other work remained to be done. Friends of Sullivan could report that their champion was not "lushing," or drinking and was "at least in fine condition to go into training." But Sullivan's financial condition was reported to be "squally" and that fact would "necessarily drive him to a match very soon." Another factor that could delay the hoped-for match between Sullivan and McAuliffe was that McAuliffe was to leave for England in a few days to fight Frank

"Paddy" Slavin. The results of that match could determine much. If McAuliffe won, then Sullivan would have to face him or else "give up his laurels." If McAuliffe lost then he would never face Sullivan. The Dallas report concluded that there was movement for the match and "it is confidently believed here that sometime during next October, within fifty miles of Fort Worth, the prize ring championship of the world will again be settled."[24]

A week following these concerns Luke and Hattie were in Saratoga Springs, New York, to take in the races. He was a guest of E. M. Lawrence, residing at No. 150 Church Street.[25] Saratoga Springs is located close to the Vermont border in upstate New York. Abundant mineral waters caused it to be developed as a spa in the mid-nineteenth century. Several large hotels were built, including the Grand Union Hotel, which in its day was the largest hotel in the world. Horse racing, which began in 1863, added to its appeal for gamblers such as Luke Short because of the betting. Gambling was wide open in Saratoga Springs at the time Luke visited there. Most of the gambling establishments were located along the shores of Saratoga Lake.

After leaving Saratoga Springs, Luke and Hattie briefly stopped at Hot Springs, Arkansas, and then visited friends in what is now Oklahoma. They returned to Fort Worth on July 5, with correspondence waiting relative to prize fighting. There was the distinct possibility that the California Athletic Club would be going out of business, which was great news for Luke, as "the fighting fraternity naturally turns to Texas, where the law, in consideration of a reasonable license, will permit pugilists to pummel each other as hard as they like." The next fights "on deck" were between George "The Marine" LaBlanche and Charles Mitchell, and between the winner of that fight and Jack "Nonpareil" Dempsey. To add interest Dempsey had been "accidently put to sleep" by LaBlanche "several months ago." It was predicted that later in the fall Sullivan would participate in a contest with either McAuliffe, Slavin, or Jackson. Luke Short was confident that one or all of these proposed fights would take place in Texas. He figured LaBlanche and Mitchell would be worth a purse of $5,000. One between Dempsey and LaBlanche would be worth $15,000 and any fight with Sullivan involved would be worth $25,000 or $30,000. "In all probability," assured the *Dallas Morning News*, "he will make a bid for all of these fights as soon as they are matched."[26]

Luke had come a long way in the fighting world in a relatively short period of time. He was taken seriously by fighters, their managers, and sporting men across the country. He was still pushing for a match with the champion, John L. Sullivan. By late July 1890 Luke's favorite candidate to face Sullivan was Jake Kilrain. Luke made an offer to both Sullivan and Kilrain, which won a ringing endorsement from Richard K. Fox of the *National Police Gazette.* Fox wrote that "the offer of Luke Short to put up $20,000 and give the New York banks as security, is a proposition, sporting men claim, both Sullivan and Kilrain should accept, if they are in earnest."[27] Luke's hopes for staging a championship match involving John L. Sullivan would never be realized, however. Sullivan managed to avoid defending his title until 1892 when he finally agreed to face James J. "Gentleman Jim" Corbett. Luke would be at the Sullivan-Corbett fight, but as a spectator.

Luke went to Dallas on August 30, 1890. The following day it was noted that he was in the city visiting his friends.[28] Some of those friends included bookmakers. He was now heavily involved in betting on thoroughbred horse races. One of Jake Johnson's horses, named Bobby Beach, was running on a track in Chicago and Luke placed his bet with a Dallas bookie for that horse to win. The horse came through and Luke won big. The Dallas newspaper did not identify Luke by name, merely identifying him as a "prominent turfman from Fort Worth" who had come to Dallas on August 30 and won nearly $1,500.[29]

Luke was successful in choosing thoroughbred horses, and he continued to pursue the dream of bringing to the Fort Worth area a championship prize fight. As late as September 1890 he was still chasing the dream. Fort Worth's *Gazette* also seemed to hold out hope for that dream, as it reported that it was "within the range of possibility that Fort Worth will be the scene of a great pugilistic encounter between the famous Jack Dempsey and Reddy Gallagher for the middle-weight championship of the continent." Luke Short reportedly had been in correspondence with the backers of both men and within a few days it was expected there would be a purse, which both would accept. The *Gazette* predicted such an event would be "one of the famous ring fights of modern days."[30]

Boxing promotion remained an unattainable goal for Luke Short. He was destined to be remembered for gunfights, rather than prize fights. As the year 1890 drew to a close, the age of the gunfighter was considered by many to be a thing of the past. You couldn't prove it by Luke Short, however, as he was about to experience yet another gunfight.

Chapter 16

Last Gunfight

> "His wounds are enough to kill a common man but Luke may get well."
>
> — *Hutchinson News* (Kansas), January 7, 1891.

The long-simmering feud between Luke Short and Charles Wright that started in Memphis, Tennessee, in April finally reached the boiling point in Fort Worth on December 23, 1890. The difficulty left no men dead, but the results did provide great copy for the newspapers. The *Fort Worth Gazette* reporter exhibited his flair for alliteration with the main headline "Gore Galore." Neither man died although one might think a man wielding a shotgun would prove to be more accurate than a man with a six-gun. It was considered the "most exciting affray" in Fort Worth since the shooting of Jim Courtright, almost four years before.

This gunfight took place at the Bank Saloon and gambling house on Main Street. Wright's shotgun blast wounded Short in his left hip as well as injuring his left hand. The bullet from Luke's pistol shattered Wright's right wrist. Both men were considered "men of desperate nerve" and the gambling fraternity was well aware of the trouble between them. Many also considered it miraculous that no one was killed since the shooting was at such close quarters.

Louis de Mouche, a saloon owner who happened to be in the crowd when the shooting erupted, was an eye witness who had the nerve to remain and see the deadly exchange. He explained what he saw and heard. Gambler de Mouche

> heard a big noise out on the street and ran out to see what [was] the matter. Everybody was running down stairs from the gambling place. I asked what was the matter, and they told me that Luke Short was up there and there was going to be some shooting. Everybody was down stairs at that time and I ran in. At the head of the stairs I met Luke Short with his revolver in his hand. I put my arm around him and tried to pull him out.

De Mouche said, "Come on away, Luke, or you will get hurt." Luke said nothing, just stood still. At that moment de Mouche saw a door about six feet away pulled open "and a hand thrust out with a revolver in it."

> I pulled Luke around quick and the revolver went off. But Luke was as quick as the stranger, for he fired about the same time. That bullet entered the wrist of the stranger. That's all the shooting that was done.

Now the reporter was confused, as he was convinced Luke was shot with buckshot from a shotgun.

> But that can't be for I was standing right near him, and if he was shot with a load of buckshot why was not I?

De Mouche insisted that there were only two shots fired, and as he was "standing right there" he should know of any others.

The reporter attempted to explain the circumstances behind the shooting. Luke Short had arrived in front of the saloon at the foot of the stairs leading to the gambling room. It was about 9:30 p.m. and Charles Wright's gambling house was "running at full blast." There were a few men standing around. When Short arrived, the porter who carried drinks from the saloon to the gambling rooms came downstairs. Short asked the porter what was going on upstairs. "Oh, shootin' a little craps, Mista' Luke" replied the porter. Then Luke said, "Come along back there with me" and pushed the porter ahead of him. The pair entered the gambling room where faro, chuck-a-luck, poker and other games were "under full headway." Short kept the porter in front of him and with his revolver in hand cried out "Skin out of here, every one of you!"

Since the gamblers all knew Luke Short's history, they were not slow to obey his command, and "[i]n the twinkle of an eye" the room was empty except for Luke Short. In their haste to exit the scene the gamblers overturned tables and chairs and broke lamps. Cards and chips and other instruments of gambling were strewn on the floor.

> Luke Short stepped out in the hall, and had only proceeded a half dozen steps when the shooting took place. The first shot was fired by the hand extended from the door, followed instantly by the discharge of Short's pistol, and after a short intermission the shotgun which gave Short his wounds was discharged, crashing through a pane of glass and lodging in the wainscoting on the opposite side of the hall.

Short was wounded. He then went downstairs without assistance, went up Main Street half a block to the corner of Fifteenth, where he was met by friends who called a hack. Luke was driven to Dr. Duringer[1] who attended to his wounds. Officer Ben Bell now met with Short and took his pistol. It was an ivory-handled silver polished revolver with a blue barrel. Every chamber was loaded, suggesting Luke had either a second weapon or else had reloaded it after shooting Wright.

The reporter described Luke's leg wound as "serious, though not at all dangerous. The full charge of buckshot passed through the flesh, making a tunnel. The muscles on the outside were torn out." The wound on his hand could be dangerous with the thumb and third and fourth fingers "torn badly." The thumb was "taken off at the joint." The unusual nature of the wound occurred as his hand was resting on the hip and the same shot caused both wounds.

Mrs. Short, "a young woman of pleasant appearance and quiet deportment" arrived while the surgeon was dressing the wounds and "helped make the ordeal more bearable." Luke remarked that this was not a very appropriate Christmas present for her. Hattie smiled.

After Short had his wounds dressed the reporter hoped for a statement. "I don't want to say much about the shooting," he said. "When the shot went into my hip it rather dazed me, and I did not notice much. I do not know who did the shooting." Not giving up, the reporter asked if he had fired when the hand protruded through the open door. "Somebody pulled me around just in time to see the gun go off. I do not know who held it, or who did the shooting." The reporter must have been disappointed.

Immediately after the shooting, Deputy Marshal Ben Evans arrived at the scene and found Charles Wright in the hall. He was arrested and taken to the office of Dr. Mullin[2] to have the wound dressed as "the flesh was torn badly." After the wound was dressed he was delivered to the county jail.

The reporter investigated the scene of the shooting. On the floor where Luke had stood were "large spots of blood scattered around. The wadding from a shotgun was picked up, and the wainscoting was perforated where the buckshot lodged." The shooter had been hidden in a storeroom. In the center of the room was a stand with a barrel of liquor placed on it with a faucet in it ready for liquor to be drawn out. Other barrels, boxes, and bottles were stored around the room. A shotgun stood against the liquor barrels in the middle of the floor. Although the shotgun was a double barrel, one barrel was empty. Close to it was a revolver, all chambers loaded. This was presumably the revolver of Charles Wright.

At the county jail the reporter interviewed Wright. The "scribe" found him in "a room by himself" and explained why he was there. The reporter noticed the bandaged wrist while Wright said: "I do not want to talk about the affair. I do not know who did the shooting." What about the wrist? "I don't remember exactly. You see, I was a little excited and am not able to state positively. The doctor will tell you about my wound." The reporter must have been disappointed as he was able to get nothing from either of the two wounded men. He then visited with one of Wright's attorneys. The attorney stated that whatever Charles Wright may have done was "purely in self-defense."

The Short-Wright feud perhaps was only part of a larger situation of gamblers of the up-town working against the gamblers of the lower end of the city, or members of the sporting fraternity working against each other to increase their respective business. Two weeks before the shooting, Charles Wright had been indicted on a charge of swindling by a man named Cole. Judge Robert E. Beckham dismissed the charge, stating it was a matter of gambling, and "there could be no swindling as the term as known in law, in the matter." A month before, Wright stood before Justice Ashbel G. McClung requesting to have Short placed under a peace bond, stating that he feared Short would interfere with his business. McClung decided against the application as the grounds were insufficient.

The reporter had obtained little from either of the wounded men, but still had space to fill. He now provided background information on both shootists, providing "something about the men wounded in last night's affray." Short was described as being about thirty-six-years old who had spent the early years of his life in Cooke County where his father owned a ranch. Back in the 1860s "marauding Indians frequently came to the settlements stealing cattle and in some cases killing the settlers. [Luke] saw a good deal of frontier life, and when he grew older he had to do some Indian fighting himself." More specifically Short was in the northwest when the Northern Cheyenne and Sioux took to the warpath, and "on one occasion took important messages to the army operating against the Indians, notifying them that the word had been received at Rosebud agency that the Indians had arranged to ambush the army."

Short's experience in Arizona was touched on, as were his years in Dodge City "where stormy times were witnessed." The Courtright affair was also briefly reviewed, but the reporter concluded that Luke Short was "well known in this city and neighborhood, and is not often mixed up in street brawls."

Wright was described as about forty years of age, although he looked younger. He was described as a "nomad," having been in Fort Worth "off and on for several years." By occupation he was a "successful manager of sporting enterprises" and had "amassed quite a sum of money." His residence was on the South Side. To be safe, the reporter concluded Wright was "not a quarrelsome man by any means, though nobody ever doubted his nerve if occasion demanded its use."

Both Short and Wright were admitted to bail in the amount of $1,000 each. Jake Johnson, Victor Foster, W. H. Ward, and Joe Wheat were sureties for Short. R. L. Carlock and J. T. Powell were sureties for Wright.[3]

Charles Wright may have had a residence on the south side of Fort Worth but it could not compare to that of Luke Short's. By this time in his career Luke had finally decided to give up renting hotel rooms and built a residence of his own on land purchased from Jake Johnson. It was a larger than average home, in a better than average neighborhood, although hardly as imposing as the mansion owned by Jake Johnson. Luke had told the *Gazette* reporter that he did not wish to speak of the gunfight while the doctor was still dressing his wounds, but later he allowed himself to be interviewed. Presumably it was the same reporter on both occasions. The reporter pointed out that both men were "suffering considerable pain." Luke Short gave the interview in his home on the South Side and provided the press his version of events.

"The statements published that this trouble was caused by a rivalry between our gambling houses is all a mistake," stated Luke, "and there is nothing to it. The difference was a personal affair and had nothing to do with Wright's place and mine. We have not been friends for two years, and matters were aggravated when he ran a 'brace' game over the Bank saloon." The reporter did not query as to what a brace game was; presumably he knew that the expression referred to the collusion between the dealer and case keeper in a game of faro for the purpose of swindling players. Luke Short continued:

> I have my home in Fort Worth, and everybody who knows me will say that I have never tolerated anything but square gambling games. I intend to stay here, but I knew full well that if Wright continued as he was doing it would only be a matter of time until public opinion would be against all classes of gaming, and that I would be closed up with the rest. I have assisted to break up two or three places which were being conducted in a crooked manner, and Sheriff [John C.] Richardson will tell you the same thing.

Short further explained, according to the reporter who summarized his comments rather than quoting him word for word, that he saw no one shooting at him. As soon as he was hit he returned fire, and did not know if he had wounded the man with the shotgun or not. He learned later that his shot had broken the man's arm.[4]

From reading the report in the *Gazette* one might believe that Luke was able to be up and about. The fact is that he was bedridden for months. In 1891 a Chicago newspaper published a lengthy profile of Luke. When discussing the gunfight with Wright, the paper reported: "It was supposed at the time that Short was fatally wounded, and his recovery was wholly due to the careful nursing of his wife, who for three months hardly left his bed side."[5] Newspapers all over Texas gave status reports on Luke's recovery, including a Galveston paper on the other end of the state. "Luke Short and Charley Wright, the two men shot in the affray over the Bank saloon, are rapidly improving." Wright reportedly was getting better and would be out in a short time. For Short it was different, as he "was the greatest sufferer in the fight, [and] will be unable to get out for some time, and it may be that the wound in his leg will in a measure permanently cripple him."[6]

Even in Kansas the condition of Luke Short was of concern. The prevailing opinion was that "his wounds are enough to kill a common man but Luke may get well."[7] Luke Short was a man of national interest.

Chapter 17

Chicago

> Luke Short "always declared against unfair sport, and has refused to allow men who would cheat to associate with him."
>
> —*Chicago Daily Inter Ocean*, September 7, 1891

On February 1, 1891, the grand jury of Tarrant County returned numerous indictments but two were of special interest: one against Like Short and one against Charles Wright, both charged with assault with intent to murder. Both men made bonds without trouble in the sum of $1,000.[1] The trial date would be changed more than once and a final decision would not be arrived at until March 1, 1892. In the meantime Luke was starting to feel well enough to pursue his prizefight ambitions.

By mid-February Billie Simms and Sam Berliner, of San Antonio, offered a purse of $15,000 for a finished fight with kid gloves between Bob Fitzsimmons and Jim Hall of Australia. The fight was to "come off" during the San Antonio fair either the last week of October or the first week of November, with Marquis of Queensbury rules to govern. To show their good faith each would deposit $2,000 with Dick Rocha of St. Louis or else Luke Short of Fort Worth, "as soon as the match is made."[2]

On January 14, 1891, Bob Fitzsimmons had knocked out Jack "Nonpareil" Dempsey in the fourteenth round and became the World Middleweight Champion. It was to be the first of three world championships that Fitzsimmons would hold in three different weight divisions. Hall and Fitzsimmons did agree to meet, but not in Texas, and without the participation of Simms, Berliner, or Short. The match between Hall and Fitzsimmons was scheduled to take place in St. Paul, Minnesota, on July 22, 1891. It was prevented, however, by the governor of Minnesota who had the amphitheater surrounded by four companies of National Guardsmen.[3]

Luke Short and his fellow sporting men would bet on some unusual contests, when there was no boxing match or horse race to attract them. Of all of the off-beat things they might wager on, very few were as bizarre as a contest with broadswords on horseback. It may have been serious, or it may have been an agreement between individuals who later came to their senses.

> Articles of agreement have been entered by Captain T.S. Shiel and Peter Erea for a broadsword contest on horseback for $500 a side. Luke Short is a stakeholder. The battle will occur as soon as the men can train. Prize fights with light gloves have been frequent while the authorities winked at this violation of the law, in spirit if not in letter, but we wonder if men will be permitted to go into a broadsword contest without restraint, and in case they engage in this contest and one is slain, what the charges against the slayer will be?[4]

It is difficult to take this account seriously. It seems likely that this was intended as a joke. Whatever it really was, no further mention has been found regarding the "broadsword contest on horseback." It was a different sort of contest involving horses that interested Luke and his fellow sportsmen that spring. On May 21, 1891, Jake Johnson and Luke Short boarded a train for Chicago. This was going to be an extensive stay, as Hattie accompanied Luke on the trip.[5] The racing season was about to begin and Johnson and Short both owned a string of horses that would be running at Washington Park in Chicago. After staying in Kansas City for a few days, Luke and Hattie continued to Chicago.

During his several visits to Chicago, Luke always stayed at the Leland Hotel on Michigan Avenue. The Leland faced what was then called Lake Front Park (now called Grant Park). The upper floors, on the Michigan Avenue side, offered an unobstructed view of Lake Michigan. A reporter of the *Chicago Herald* found Short worth mentioning just as he was checking in. He described Short as a "short, dark-haired man with keen eyes." The clerk told the bell-boy to show the gentleman to room 79, but the "new arrival" advised him "you can get a copper [tip] on that room if it is above the clouds." Luke Short wanted a room "Just off the ocean [Lake Michigan] spray" and that was done. The reporter may have visited with Short or may have merely jotted down some notes from memory of reading about the man. He was called "one of the great characters of Texas" who in "the early days" was "one of the wildest cowboys that ever threw a rope." When the roundups were over, Luke "used to visit some town and enjoy one continual round of pleasure." On one occasion Luke went into a restaurant in Fort Worth and the waiter gave him a glass of milk in which a fly was "treading water." According to the story, Luke did not shoot the waiter, but threw the glass in the air, jerked his six-shooter, and shot the fly. *Shot the fly.*

With so many dangerous encounters with bad men the reporter may have wondered about battle scars. He noted that with the exception of his left thumb he had no scars, yet "he has a half-dozen notches on his stick" which of course was the reporter's creative mind at work as Short did not notch his revolver to keep score of his victims. "He has been in so many battles on the frontier that whenever he throws back his shoulders to-day his coat will fall off. . . . from force of habit."[6] How much of the interview the reporter believed is uncertain.

Luke and Jake Johnson, along with several other sporting men from Fort Worth, had horses running at the Washington Park race track in

Chicago. A reporter caught up with them and provided a profile of some of the members.

> There is a merry party of Texans in the city. It consists of Colonel Robert McCart, a prominent attorney and real estate man; Mr. Wallace Hendricks, another attorney and real estate man, and Messrs. Jake Johnson and Luke Short, owners of twenty-four horses out at Washington Park. They are all from Fort Worth.
>
> Mr. Hendricks was seen at the Palmer [House] yesterday and said: "I am erecting the largest office building in Texas, but it looks very small in comparison with these tall buildings in Chicago. . . . We take great interest in Chicago down our way, and Fort Worth being the World's Fair headquarters for Texas, and also the stock yards headquarters, we are proud to call it the Chicago of Texas. . . . We have raised a subscription of $300,000 for the World's Fair, and hope to increase it to a million."[7]

A syndicate of politically connected bookmakers was about to launch the Garfield Park race track on Chicago's west side, which would compete with the Washington Park track where Luke and Jake raced their horses. Racing at the Garfield Park Club was set to open on July 20 and, according to reports, promised "some good turf sport."[8]

It did not take long for the Texas turfmen to decide on which track to run. Johnson, Short, and the other turfmen moved their string over to Garfield Park as soon as it opened on July 20. He became a regular at Garfield Park and a few months later the *Daily Inter Ocean* contributed a lengthy profile in its issue of September 7, 1891.

The reporter headlined his article by identifying Short as "a Western Product of Modest Mein" and stated that the familiar figure at Garfield Park "forms a story that reads like a romance." He reviewed how courteous Luke was to reporters and how his dexterity with fire-arms was "well-known." By now the story of Luke shooting the fly that had appeared in his glass of milk was worth repeating, and it was, but now after shooting the fly he caught the milk in his glass "and calmly drank it," thus adding a slight twist to the story.[9]

Getting back closer to reality now, the reporter brought up the subject of the race track, and mentioned that Short always had a string of horses at Garfield Park. Short was an "enthusiastic horseman" and "as good a judge of horse flesh" as anyone who lives. Even then there were rumors that there was dishonesty involved in the races at Garfield. Short and Johnson were not parties to any aspect of illegality but the rumors would increase until there were frequent raids by police.[10]

Short's background now became the focus of the interview, as if the reporter needed to explain to the world what made up this man Luke Short. He was "a man whose life has been shaped and fashioned by circumstances"; if he had been born and educated in the "effete East" he probably would have settled down to "some routine business and became an ornament to polite society." But as he was born in the West; his education was on the plains "where the wild cry of the Indian was familiar to his ear. . . . being quick-witted and bright, he has gathered the polish of a man of the world." Short was "said to control the gambling interests of the city" of Fort Worth. He never talked "shop" in Chicago, and if any reference was made to gambling or gamblers in his presence "his face assumes a pained expression that would do credit to a reformer of high degree."

Luke Short certainly did not bring up the subject of the trouble with Charles Wright, but the reporter was aware of it. He now raised the issue of honesty, reminding the readers that Luke "always declared against unfair sport, and has refused to allow men who would cheat to associate with him." Wright was running a gambling house in Fort Worth where "skin" games were played. Short "entered objection" and entered the house to investigate. According to this report, when Short "opened the door the lights were suddenly turned out and Wright shot at him with a double-barreled shotgun loaded with slugs." Even though his left leg was broken and part of his left hand "shot away" Short quickly drew his revolver and fired into the darkness at where he had seen the flash of the shotgun, "seriously wounding his would-be assassin." Short would have died but for the "careful nursing of his wife, who for three months hardly left his side."

Short's personal appearance did not escape the reporter. The man "would not, in one hundred years, attract attention by his personal appearance." He was "a mild-mannered man, and covers, with an air of apparent listlessness, the spirit with which he is filled." Two photographs of Luke were in existence, according to this report: one owned by his wife and the other "by his warm personal friend, W. A. Pinkerton, to whom he presented it a few years ago."[11] One would have preferred the reporter had now discussed Luke's family, but he now provided a few words about a supposed relative of his named Ed Short. This man, supposedly a cousin of Luke's, had been killed in the Oklahoma country by a member of the outlawed Dalton brothers gang, whom he had arrested. Ed Short was a well-known western character for many years, a Deputy United States Marshal enforcing the laws in the Indian Territory. Luke and Ed —"cousins who were warm personal friends" according to the reporter —each admired the other. To conclude his report with a hint of possible further action, he assured his readers that Luke Short would not "enter upon a career of revenge, [but] it would not be healthy for any one of the Dalton gang to come within shooting range of him."[12]

From the amount of press coverage the Chicago newspapers devoted to Luke Short one might be inclined to think reporters followed him around incessantly. The *Chicago Daily Inter Ocean* and the *Chicago Daily Tribune* both provided history with their version of an incident that could have resulted in tragedy if Luke had been armed, as he normally was. It occurred at the Leland Hotel where Luke was staying. The Leland's "rotunda" was described by the *Inter Ocean* reporter as "exceedingly lively and lurid" for almost an hour that evening when the row erupted. Had it not been for the "presence of mind" of the Leland's chief clerk, Ed Kennedy, several participants might have been shot. The row began over "a rather attractive lady," not identified, who was a guest at the Leland and who had legal business with an attorney named Singleton. Other guests, the Quinn brothers, began paying attention to the lady to which lawyer Singleton "evinced a decided objection." About 11 o'clock that evening Singleton and the Quinn brothers were all in Devine's Saloon. Singleton made a remark about the Quinns "trying to cut him out" which "roused the ire of the bookmakers" who now began to pummel him. Singleton was no match for the Quinns and fled to the clerk to complain about how he was being treated. He was "very noisy and directed his conversation to everybody in general."

Standing near the desk was Luke Short whose "mastery of the art of drawing a gun is only equaled by his propensity for coming out ahead in scrimmages." Did Singleton think Short was part of the Quinn brothers' party? Perhaps, for he began to "throw dirt on," or insult, the "inoffensive looking Mr. Short." Short did not have his pistol, but instead gave Singleton a few kicks which knocked him down, and then Short picked him up, "kicked with skill and precision four times, and led to the door, where, after being kicked some more, he was pushed into the frosty night air."

Short, not yet being "content with the fun he already had with the lawyer," went upstairs to get his gun. While he was gone two young men named respectively Strahorn and Porter, got into a row about what they had witnessed with Short and the lawyer Singleton and Strahorn broke his cane over Porter's head. After a lull in the excitement, Luke was seen descending the stairs with pistol in hand. At the same time William F. "Old Hoss" Hoey, the popular comedian, entered the hotel, totally unaware of what had just transpired. By a "strange fatality" Hoey strongly resembled Singleton, "particularly in the cut of the wind-tempters on his face." Short saw Hoey, thought he was Singleton who had returned to face him even though he had been kicked out, and "made a rush" for him. Short was nearly on Hoey, with "staring eyes, was wondering what the whole thing was about," when the quick thinking clerk Ed Kennedy managed to get between Short and Hoey and explained. Short, now armed, apologized to the comedian and not long afterward "a gurgling sound was heard and much-hand-shaking seen." With a few drinks Short had forgotten about lawyer Singleton as he "had the best of it anyway."[13]

The comedian who bore the strong resemblance to lawyer Singleton was William F. Hoey, known far and wide as "Old Hoss." He was born in New York in 1854. He later teamed up with Charles Evans for an act billed as Evans and Hoey. The partners had twin sisters in their act, Helena and Minnie French. Hoey married Helena and Evans married Minnie. The team's greatest success came in 1888 with a comedy called "A Parlor Match," which played for years in theaters all across the country.[14]

The rival of the *Inter Ocean*, the *Chicago Daily Tribune*, also found the incident in the Leland newsworthy but included certain other details. The former headlined its report "Short and His Gun" with a sub-headline which was sure to attract attention: "How a Man's Whiskers Put Him in Danger." The *Tribune* provided additional headlines: "He Is Glad He's Alive" followed with "Lawyer Singleton Meets Quinn Brothers and an 'Unknown'" and an additional headline: "The Latter Proves to be Luke Short, Who Sustains His Reputation." The opening paragraph set the stage for what was to follow:

> A lawyer, an actor, a trio of bookmakers, a salesman and a man from Texas who has a gun with a score of notches on the handle were characters in what strongly resembled a melodrama heightened by touches of comedy which was played in Devine's wine house on Jackson Street and in the office of the Leland Hotel Tuesday night.

James J. Singleton was the lawyer and the victim as well, at press time "confined to his bed . . . on account of his appearance in the play, which, by the way, barely escaped ending in tragedy." The four Quinn brothers, bookmakers, were guests at the Leland. Two of them had crossed the street to Devine's wine room with another bookmaker. Singleton was there with Harry C. Strahorn. A dispute arose between Singleton and the Quinns, a dispute supposedly caused by a remark about the "Western widow" who remained unidentified. The dispute ended with Singleton getting both eyes blackened by the Quinn brothers.

Singleton, with eyes blackened, and Strahorn went to the Leland and complained about what had happened to him, thanks to the actions of the Quinns who were hotel guests. He "demanded" that the Hotel "should repair his shattered dignity and bind up his wounds." Clerk Ed Kennedy began to explain that the Hotel was not responsible for the actions of its guests, Singleton "lost his temper and aimed a blow at a quiet little man standing nearby."

> The little man happened to be Luke Short of Texas, whose mastery of weapons caused him to be treated with respect in the days when Kansas, and particularly Dodge City, were—well, when they were anything but pleasant localities for persons who didn't know how to shoot.

It was fortunate for Singleton that Luke did not have his gun, but in lieu of a pistol he "attacked Singleton with nature's weapons in such a lively fashion that the lawyer beat a retreat." Companion Strahorn did not fare much better as he had "also tackled a Tartar in the person of a dudishly attired little bit of a chap" —Porter —who was "loitering" about the Leland. Porter punished Strahorn severely with his walking stick.[15]

During this excitement Short had hurried to his room to "fix" himself with a pistol. During his absence, which could only have been a few minutes at most, William F. Hoey entered the hotel. Hoey's resemblance to Singleton was "remarkable" and by now as well the Quinn brothers "with reinforcements" had arrived at the Leland.

The Quinn group now saw Hoey and, thinking he was Singleton, cried out: "There he goes; let's give it to him!" Hoey was "strolling toward the café warbling 'They're after me, after me.'" By now clerk Kennedy recognized the comedian's danger. He jumped over the desk and placed himself between Hoey and the "belligerents just in time" as Luke Short now appeared on the scene, with pistol in hand. Did clerk Kennedy manage to calm everyone down before any further action was taken by any of the parties? This is not made clear in either report, but the *Tribune* reported that when Hoey "learned of the danger in which he had been placed by his resemblance to Singleton he shook part of his beard off in terror. Then he purchased the oysters all around." And perhaps all took turns in purchasing drinks in Devine's wine room.[16]

Lawyer Singleton went to an attorney and swore out warrants against the Quinn brothers but did not appear to prosecute them at press time. When Singleton learned of the identity and record "of the little man with whom he came in contact in the hotel he thanked his stars that he was still well enough to be able to care for his bruised features." Perhaps he thought it best to drop the entire matter rather than trying to prosecute the Quinns in court.

The *Inter Ocean* had further fun before dropping mention of the entire affair, stating that the "location chosen by Lawyer Singleton, Harry Strahorn, Mr. Luke Short, of Texas, the Quinn brothers, and others for their dramatic little rencontre . . . is somewhat celebrated for episodes of similar high-flowered character." And the irony continued: "It is, if the expression may be used, a blooded neighborhood. It is the region of nobby hotels, wine-rooms, high-class apartment houses and livery stables, etc., a region, in short, where dashing young gentlemen of quality and fortune at times congregate very thickly."[17]

Chapter 18

Game Over

> The man "well known in sporting circles in the west and southwest, is lying at death's door."
>
> —*Wichita Daily Eagle* [Kansas], August 4, 1893.

Back in Fort Worth, Luke's trial date was coming up for his December 23, 1890, gunfight with Charles M. Wright. Luke's lawyer had managed to get the case continued more than once. On the morning of November 16 the case of *State v. Luke Short* was called for trial but on motion of the defendant was continued until the next term. The press reminded readers that the case had grown out of the "terrible encounter" between Short and Wright, "two gamblers over the Bank saloon, in which shotguns and six-shooters were used." While Luke had been in Chicago, Wright, reportedly, had gone to New York "but was here to-day to testify in case the case went to trial."[1]

While Luke was awaiting his new trial date, Jake Johnson was busy circulating a petition to aid an old friend of his who also happened to be the most famous gunfighter that Texas had produced: John Wesley Hardin. Johnson had received a letter from Hardin who was serving year number fourteen of a twenty-five-year sentence for the murder of a deputy sheriff of Brown County in 1874. Jake Johnson, who had not forgotten his companion on the 1871 cattle trail to Kansas, now was working to obtain signatures on the pardon for Hardin. When enough signatures were obtained Johnson forwarded the document to Gov. James S. Hogg. Hardin's letter, not included in the report unfortunately, requested Johnson to get signatures of "influential business men" and also included a promise that if released he would return to his family "from which he had been separated so long, that he would so long as he lived lead an upright and honorable life." Johnson "at once" began to collect signatures, and "in a short time" had gathered over sixty signatures of "leading citizens" including Judge R. E. Beckham; Judge W. D. Harris; County Attorney O. W. Gillespie; County Clerk John King; District Clerk L. R. Taylor; Sheriff J. C. Richardson; A. M. Carter, Senator 20th District; Captain M. B. Loyd; Col. William Harrison; Capt. E. B. Harrold, cashier First National Bank; Walter M. Maddox, Tarrant County sheriff from 1880-1886; and Ben H. Shipp, Tarrant County Sheriff from 1886-1888.[2]

Despite his long friendship with Jake Johnson, Luke Short's signature wasn't included in the "long list of leading citizens" of Fort Worth. It may have been felt that with Luke's trial just a little more than two weeks away, his signature wouldn't have been a plus for Hardin, or, more likely, Luke may have simply been out of town when the petition was circulated. Luke's trial began on the leap year date of February 29, 1892.

The biggest court news that day took place in the Forty-Eighth District Court of Tarrant County. The press eagerly awaited its opening and expected exciting news with the case of the *State v Luke Short*, charged with shooting Charles Wright with intent to murder. Both sides were ready for trial and the jury was soon selected and sworn in. According to the report published in the *Dallas Morning News* it was seemingly a clear case of Short intending to shoot Wright. According to testimony, Short had gone to the Bank Saloon about 7:00 p.m. and Short ordered Wright's gambling house to be closed. He held a pistol in his hand when he gave this order and those present scattered in all directions. When he began to descend the stairs someone in a side room fired on him with a double-barrel shotgun. The buckshot not only shot off one of his thumbs but also "plowed through his left thigh making a terrible wound." Short returned fire with his six-shooter "which caused *the parties in the side room* to retreat." (Emphasis by authors.) Shortly thereafter Wright was found shot in the right wrist and he was arrested.

Wright testified on the stand and stated that he shot Short because he thought Short intended to kill him. He did not state that anyone else was in the room with him, although it had been the belief that he was not alone. Several others testified and the result was that there were bad feelings between the two men. Allegedly Short had made previous raids on Wright's gambling house with the avowed purpose of preventing him from gambling in Fort Worth. Important for Short, there was "no proof shown that he made an effort to shoot Wright until after he himself was shot by the man concealed in the side room."[3] This was the summation of the first day's testimony.

The trial attracted a large crowd of spectators as well as wide interest in the press. The *Fort Worth Gazette* provided the most descriptive account of the second day's proceedings, and the outcome. Besides being of great interest, it was the "only case of importance" in the Forty-Eighth District Court. There was no need to review the particulars of the case as the *Gazette* had covered it well when it occurred. This report did reiterate the fact that Wright was "conducting games that were crooked and unfair" and after Short ordered the place closed, the room "was soon vacated by all, who made their exit without questioning Short's authority to act." Obviously none of the patrons in Wright's place cared to challenge Luke Short, no matter if he had any authority or not.

The testimony given on this second day of the trial stated that Short had stepped out into the hall to go down the steps across the street, "when a load of buckshot was fired at him from a room in the rear of the gambling rooms, which also opened into the hallway leading to the stairsteps." Exactly where Short stood when fired upon was disputed, but Short returned fire, "the pistol ball entering Wright's right wrist and lodging near the elbow." The case took up most of the morning and early afternoon. Byron G. Johnson and Robert McCart defended Short, "and strong pleas were made in behalf of the defendant." At 3 o'clock in the afternoon Judge Beckham charged the jury who retired from the court room, accompanied by a deputy sheriff. An hour later the jury returned and asked for instructions in case a verdict of aggravated assault was determined, and as well wanted to know who was liable for the costs of the suit. Judge Beckham provided the answers and the jury retired again. A short time later the jury returned with its verdict. Short was found guilty of aggravated assault and a fine of $150 was assessed against him.[4]

For the next several months Luke Short's name did not appear in newspapers in Texas, or any other state. He might have been in Fort Worth attending to his club rooms at the Palais Royal,[5] or watching his string of thoroughbreds run on tracks in any of the various states on the racing circuit. For once Luke Short left no easy-to-follow paper trail. His name finally surfaced in Galveston early in September 1892 when he and several sporting companions were getting ready to attend a series of prize fights in New Orleans. The Texas and Pacific Railroad was providing a special sleeper on the east-bound train "for the accommodation of parties bound for New Orleans and the great trio of pugilistic encounters at the Olympia Club," which included quite a number of Fort Worth citizens. Among those already booked for the excursion were Alderman Ward, James Thrasher, Sam Finch, "Kid" Wilson, Jim Nichols, Nat Kramer, and Luke Short. There was a party of Oklahoma sports headed by Budd Fagg who joined the Fort Worth crowd that evening.[6]

The three fights were to be held the evenings of September 5, 6, and 7. The most important was the one to be held on September 7. It was between John L. Sullivan, who would defend his heavyweight title, and challenger James J. Corbett. Bat Masterson acted as timekeeper for Corbett, who knocked out Sullivan in the twenty-first round. A Dodge City newspaper reported that Luke Short was there, along with Bat Masterson and another member of the 1883 Dodge City Peace Commission: Charles Bassett. The Dodge City reporter noted that among the "most prominent sporting men and patrons of the pugilistic arena by the leading journals of the east" was the name of Bat Masterson, a man who served as sheriff of Ford County "in the old days." The reporter noted the lengthy interview Masterson gave to the *St. Louis Globe-Democrat* in which he expressed great confidence in Corbett winning the fight. Bat claimed he was betting heavily on his favorite, "Gentleman Jim." Bat always bet against Sullivan. "Charlie Bassett and Luke Short are also among the notables in attendance. Bassett bet his money on Sullivan."[7]

One wishes that these three—Short, Masterson, and Bassett—had gone to a photographer and had their image made in memory of the image made in Dodge City almost a decade before. This gathering on September 7, 1892, at the Sullivan-Corbett fight was almost certainly the last time the trio got together. Luke had just one more year and a day to live when the fight was held. Charles Bassett had less than four years to live. By the start of 1893 it had become apparent that something was seriously wrong with Luke Short's health. Doctors determined that he was suffering from one of the kidney diseases that then went under the now obsolete classification of Bright's Disease. These diseases would be described in modern medicine as acute or chronic nephritis. Luke's symptoms would have included high blood pressure and urine of a dark or bloody color. Edema would have contributed to a slight puffiness in his face, which shows up in his final photograph, as well as the accumulation of fluids in his lower legs that made it difficult for Luke to stand for prolonged periods of time. Bright's disease included several other well-known historical figures among its victims.[8]

It was during this desperate period that William H. Harris came back into Luke Short's life. When the two men met in Tombstone in 1881 Harris was already a man of great wealth. Much of Luke's success in business was due to the tutelage of Harris. By 1893 the student had become the master. Despite declining health and a financial panic that rocked the country in 1893, Luke Short had managed to hold onto his considerable wealth, but Harris was not so lucky. He was now flat broke, having lost most of his fortune before the panic of 1893 even began. William H. Harris now needed a job and Luke gave him one at the club rooms at the Palais Royal. Soon Harris was performing, as an employee, the functions that Luke was no longer able to attend to. Harris was in his late forties and was married to a much younger woman about the age of Luke's wife Hattie. The two young women, still in their late twenties, became close companions during this troubled period for their husbands.

One writer claimed that Luke and Hattie attended the World's Columbian Exposition in Chicago, and that Hattie "bought a hardwood wheelchair and pushed him around."[9] Given the fact that Luke and Hattie all but considered Chicago as their second home, this story normally wouldn't be subject to debate. What does make the story questionable is the state of Luke's health when the World's Columbian Exposition opened to the public on May 1, 1893. Perhaps it was possible that he was pushed around some of the 600-acre site by Hattie. Given the crowds they would have encountered, this would have required a heroic effort on both Luke and Hattie's part.[10]

The few remaining newspaper accounts concerning Luke Short during the final months of his life all reference the state of his health. He was in Denver during July 1893, and drew notice from a local newspaper. "Luke Short, a man who ranks with Wyatt Earp, Bat Masterson, Doc Middleton, Doc Holliday and other noted Western man killers, has been stopping in Denver for the past week," the reporter scribbled, placing the name of Short among two recognized law officers, although their work as lawmen was relatively short lived; a man who gained fame as a horse thief, and a one-time dentist turned gunfighter and gambler. Luke would not have been pleased. The reporter continued: "His present abode is 946 South Tenth Street. He came here by the advice of his physicians to get the benefit of the mild climate, as his health has been somewhat poor lately."[11]

The reporter, obviously impressed with the man, continued with a description which in some respects was accurate, but magnified the number of men who had fallen before his six-shooter.

> Nothing in Mr. Short's speech or personal appearance would indicate that he has taken eleven human lives. Outside of a sternly determined look in his eyes, his face wears an expression of kindly non-combativeness. His voice is soft and has a ring of refinement in it not usual to the ordinary border "terror." He is never loud and talks but little, being particularly reticent about his past history. He never refers in any way to the exploits he has performed with his revolver, and when questioned is loath to repeat them. From his dress and general make-up, Luke Short might be set down as a merchant or bank clerk. He wears little jewelry, and dresses plainly in a grey suit, black derby hat and russet shoes. He is 5 feet 8 inches tall [*sic*] and carries his 160 pounds, weight in a body that is alive and symmetrically proportioned.[12]

Ten days later Luke was back in Fort Worth where the status of his health had diminished from "somewhat poor" to the man being moribund. The news item reminded everyone that Luke Short was, "well known in sporting circles in the west and southwest" and now was "lying at death's door" in Fort Worth. He was suffering from a "fatal affection of the liver" and his doctors indicated that "death is only a matter of a short time."[13]

Medical science in 1893 treated cases such as Luke's with blood-letting in an effort to reduce blood pressure. Luke also suffered from what was then called "dropsy," which today would be described as edema due to congestive heart failure. By this time he was also suffering from a variety of other problems. On August 3 he underwent an operation—tapping for the dropsy—and afterward was reported "somewhat worse" than the day before, though much better than before the operation. His condition was considered "very precarious" but chances for his recovery were even, perhaps positive odds for a professional gambler. The physicians considered it possible to overcome the "dropsical affection" but due to "a complication of diseases" his case was "an unusually difficult one for treatment."[14]

While it can't be stated with certainty, today's medical science could probably have prolonged Luke's life with dialysis to treat his condition. In the worst case, he would be on a waiting list for a kidney transplant. In 1893 Luke Short had no such options, but there was one last ditch effort that was made for him.

Luke Short and a number of friends, and with Hattie beside him, took the north-bound Santa Fe train for Geuda Springs, Sumner County, Kansas. The place offered a change of climate as well as "medicinal qualities of the famous waters" which, hopefully, would do him a considerable amount of good and perhaps "prolong his life." Short was feeling considerably better than at any time since the operation, and was in good condition considering the length of the journey.[15] The community of Geuda Springs was over three hundred miles north of Fort Worth. It had long been a stopping place for nomadic Indian tribes as well as later settlers as the springs provided some relief. During the 1880s entrepreneurs bottled the water and shipped it to other places in Kansas and other states. Later a hotel and bath house were erected and drives established around the area which perhaps Luke and Hattie in their carriage enjoyed, although Luke may have spent most of his remaining days inside.[16]

The tedious train trip to Geuda Springs surrounded by friends and the medicinal qualities of the famous waters did not extend the life of Luke Short. He died a few minutes past 8 o'clock in the morning of September 8, 1893, at a hotel called the Gilbert House there in Geuda Springs. The local newspaper provided the briefest of all possible obituaries, saying merely that "Luke Short died at the Gilbert this morning of dropsy. The remains were embalmed by W. A. Repp today and will be shipped this evening to Ft. Worth, Tex. The remains will be accompanied by the wife and two brothers of the deceased."[17]

In contrast, as would be expected, the *Fort Worth Gazette* provided a lengthy obituary, which devoted most of its space to the killing of

Charles Storms, the events of the "Dodge City War" and the killing of Jim Courtright. Then the *Gazette* continued with his final days.

> His death was no surprise, as it had been hourly expected for several weeks past, and only his strong constitution and powerful vitality kept him alive so long. He was confined in his room in this city for several weeks, suffering from a complication of diseases. . . . The dead man was of small stature and had quiet and gentlemanly manners. There was nothing suggestive about him of the desperado, but to the contrary he looked just the opposite. The remains will arrive on the Rock Island Sunday morning and will be taken to Gause's undertaking establishment, the funeral taking place from the chapel at 3 p.m.[18]

The *Dallas Morning News* also detailed Luke's well-known exploits in Tombstone, Dodge City, and Fort Worth but struck a more personal note with its obituary. According to this reporter even though Short had many faults, he also had many virtues. "First of all he possessed a failing, somewhat out of date now, of standing by his friends. No man ever appealed to him for help in vain, and that is much. He bore no malice against any living man." This suggests Luke may have stood by the reporter on some occasion. But that was not all, and the reporter may have actually interviewed the pastor who knew Short, although there is little evidence that Short was a regular church attendee. The pastor, perhaps a Methodist minister, first stated that he was proud to know Luke Short, and that Short "responded generously to every appeal for charity." He continued:

> I have never hesitated to go to him. I have always been successful with him. He makes no professions [of faith]. He is not a hypocrite. But he has a heart easily moved to suffering and affliction. He gives as much as any member of the church and never stops to ask where the money is going.

This was a noteworthy statement concerning the character of Luke Short and how he lived his life. Significantly, the minister noted that Short was not particularly religious. But the homily continued.

> Beyond this he gives as much on the outside, more than he will ever get credit for. He gives it in the right way, too, without ostentation or much ado. Many a widow has been fed and many an orphan clothed in this city through the generosity of this man, who is in the eyes of many an outcast and a stranger. I make no pretense of judging him. I recognize in him the same spark of immortality that animates you or me, working through ways mysterious and incomprehensible to us, but none the less surely and certainly to the consummation of the omnipotent design.

At this point readers of the minister's remarks may have openly wept, as the reference to widows and orphans may have reminded many of someone they knew who had unknowingly been helped by the mysterious stranger who did not inquire as to who was being helped by his gifts of charity. And what did the minister know for sure about Luke Short?

> I only know he has been charitable in deeds and works, and we are told that charity covers a multitude of sins. I only know that whatever his missteps or his belief, and on that score I have no quarrel with any man, Luke Short has given more than any other man in Fort Worth to the glory of him who sends his rain upon the unjust as well as upon the just, and his sunshine upon the tares as well as upon the wheat.

The Dallas reporter continued with a physical description of Short, that he was "a small man" with a body "slender but lithe as an athlete's." His hair was raven black with "not a twinge of gray." Gray eyes looked at you beneath black eyebrows, and they looked "steadily." Those gray eyes "seemed to be looking into you and through you at something beyond." Short was always "scrupulously polite and quiet" and never attracted attention but "when it was drawn to him he always seemed to dislike it." In conversation the man was free from "profanity or vulgarity" and "of late years he has never gone armed." The man had no touch of vanity in him. Of his family, he left a wife "whom he married here some time ago, but no children." He had two brothers in San Angelo.[19]

Just two days before Luke's death, while Hattie sat by his bedside in Kansas, word arrived that her mother had died in Fort Worth. Cynthia Allen Buck was only fifty-four. A Dodge City newspaper printed a September 8, 1893, dispatch from Fort Worth that stated that "two days ago his mother-in-law died and the two funerals will take place here at the same time."[20] Death had already claimed two of Hattie's sisters and her father. Now her mother and her husband had died just forty-eight hours apart. She had suffered an unusual amount of early death in her family, and now found herself a widow at the age of twenty-nine.

The funeral of Luke Short took place on September 10, 1893. The Rock Island train, which brought the family from Kansas, was several hours late, arriving at 9 o'clock. On the train was Hattie Short, who had been constantly with her husband during his last illness, and his brother George W. Short. A number of Short's friends met the train and accompanied the body to George L. Gause's undertaking chapel, where it lay in state until 1:30 p.m. During the day the chapel was constantly filled with friends who came to pay their last respects. The lid of the coffin was removed and the whole body was exposed to view. "It looked as natural as life," commented the *Gazette*, "save for the emaciated and careworn features, which dumbly spoke the pains of his long illness."

At 2:30 the doors were closed to the public and his wife, brother, and sister, Mrs. Belle Patton of Bowie, Texas, were left alone with the remains of Luke Short. A half hour later they were led away and the casket closed. The body was taken to the Mansion Hotel where the procession formed, then to the city cemetery. A line of carriages more than a mile long followed the body of Luke Short to his final resting place. Three carriages preceded the hearse, which contained the pall-bearers: Messrs. J. H. Martindale, T. J. Powell, Bascom Dunn, J. H. Maddox, Major G. C. Hudgins and W. T. Royster. Rev. Dr. W. F. Lloyd of the Methodist

Church provided a "touching and beautiful" service. Then the casket was lowered into the grave, "forever covered from the gaze of men." Many floral designs covered the casket, among them a card with the words: "After life's fitful fever he sleeps well," which was an appropriate tribute from Major and Mrs. W. H. Harris. Another floral wreath was from Nat Kramer; a floral anchor was provided by Mr. and Mrs. James Ellis. Another anchor attracted the attention of all in attendance. It was a "diminutive one, but was no less beautiful for its smallness." This arrangement was made whole from cape jasmines, and between the tips, worked in red flowers were the words "For Uncle Luke, from Florence." The *Gazette* reporter indicated in conclusion: "No one knew from whence it came, but that it came from a young, tender heart, all knew full well."[21]

Luke L. Short's grave is in Oakwood Cemetery in Fort Worth.[22] His grave marker is as unaffected as the man was himself. It is a simple upright stone, with just a hint of a decorative design at the top beneath which is the simplest of inscriptions:

L. L. Short

1854-1893

Epilogue

The Wild West, whose history Luke L. Short had been such a large part of, was nearly a memory by the time he died. Had he lived, he would still have been in his forties at the start of the twentieth century, and would have needed to find a way to reinvent himself. His friend Bat Masterson had managed to make reinvention appear seamless. Bat had transformed himself from a nineteenth-century gambler and lawman into a twentieth-century newspaperman in New York City. Death robbed Luke, along with two of his fellow "Dodge City Peace Commission" members, of any chance at reinventing themselves. None of the three would live long enough to see the new century.

William H. Harris and his young wife remained in Fort Worth following Luke's death. With Luke no longer in charge of the club rooms at the Palais Royal, Harris soon found himself unemployed. During May 1894 Harris moved into the Clifton House in Kansas City. His wife remained in Fort Worth. She finally joined her husband in Kansas City just before Christmas 1894. Harris went missing on February 5, 1895, after leaving his wife at the Clifton House. When he didn't come home that evening, or the following morning, his wife and several concerned friends began looking for him. His body was found in a room at the Midland Hotel. The coroner's jury found that death was due to morphine poisoning. On his body a letter was found from a prominent Kansas politician, addressed to "Dear Harris" and dated April 24, 1894.

> I was glad to receive your letter with the enclosed clipping, and regret to hear you are not fortunate this year. But who is, except

> the sharks and shylocks and brigands who prey on mankind and thrive by the calumnies, misfortunes and sufferings of the rest of the human race? Poor Luke Short! I remember him well. But he paid the penalty which destiny always exacts from those who violate the inexorable laws of human conduct. Quite likely he is better off than here. Thanks for your good wishes, and the same to you and yours.

It was signed, John J. Ingalls.[1]

The *Dallas Morning News* published a lengthy obituary for W. H. Harris, which noted his friendship with Luke Short, comparing the two with Damon and Pythias, "done in crayon, instead of oil. The gambler and the banker, the fearless fighter and the capitalist—surely a stranger combination was never read of, except in the book of life." That "intimacy" continued until Luke's death, a "long, long time after Harris' riches had fled." The *News* reminded those who may have known that in 1893 Harris turned up in Fort Worth when Luke was "on the verge of the grave." He made Harris manager of the Palais Royal, and a few months later Short was dead. Harris was never one to talk about his own exploits, but one Sunday evening, "when Luke Short's body was lying not half a block away, he sat down on a curbstone in Fort Worth and went over his story from beginning to end, the men he had known, the places he had seen and the things he had done. He had sounded all the depths and shoals of life. And when there was nothing more to explore he laid himself down and died."[2]

Charles E. Bassett died on January 5, 1896, at the age of forty-eight in Hot Springs, Arkansas. According to a Kansas newspaper, Bassett, who was "known to the sporting fraternity all over the country, a prominent figure in the frontier days of Kansas, is dead." He was suffering from inflammatory rheumatism, which was considered the immediate cause, "from which he had been a sufferer for several years." [3]

Hattie Beatrice Short remained in Fort Worth for almost four years after Luke's death, and was listed in the 1894 city directory as "Mrs. Luke

Short."[4] A visit that Hattie and her brother made to Wichita, Kansas, during August 1897, was mentioned in the local newspaper, which reported she and her brother, Mr. W. A. Buck of Fort Worth, were at the Manhattan Hotel.[5] No further mention of "Mrs. Luke Short" has been found in Fort Worth records after 1897. A "Miss Hattie Buck" was listed in the 1901 and 1904 Fort Worth city directories, but it seems highly unlikely that this woman was "Mrs. Luke Short."[6] Hattie Beatrice Short has not turned up on any 1900, 1910, 1920, 1930, or 1940 United States Census records, for any state. One possibility is that she flew under the census radar by getting married again, to a person whose name hasn't been learned. The other possibility is that Hattie died prior to 1900. Given the unusual number of early deaths in her family, the second conclusion is not as far-fetched as it might otherwise seem.[7] The *Texas Death Index* lists a "Hattie Short" who died in Cooke County, Texas, on July 29, 1915. On that date Luke Short's widow would have been fifty-one years old, but no age was given for this "Hattie Short" in the *Death Index*.[8] Texas historian Rick Miller located the death certificate for this "Hattie Short" at the Cooke County Clerk's office in Gainesville. It turned out that this particular "Hattie Short" was only seven years old when she died on July 29, 1915.[9]

Budd Fagg died on March 27, 1900, at Mineral Wells, Texas. According to one obituary Fagg was "one of the best known sporting men in the United States for a quarter of a century or more." Fagg was a native of Springfield, Missouri, and was about fifty years of age at his passing. A few years before Fagg's death he was worth many thousands of dollars, but he died penniless, after being sick most of the time during his last two years.[10]

The **White Elephant Saloon** had moved to a new location in 1896. When it closed its doors on February 26, 1901, a Dallas newspaper offered a brief history. It was established by Gabe Burgower, Nathan Bernstein, James A. "Alex" Reddick, and Sam Berliner in 1882 at 310 Main Street. In 1896 it moved to a new location at 606 and 608 Main Street. William

H. Ward, who had been for several years a passenger conductor on the Missouri, Kansas and Texas Railway, bought a third interest and a year later purchased another third. Short had become a partner and the saloon was under the firm name of Ward & Short until 1886, when Short sold out to Ward who became the sole proprietor until the doors were closed.[11] There is no authentic photograph of the White Elephant, either exterior or interior.

Michael Francis "Frank" McLean did live long enough to see the new century, but not by much. His second child had been born in Fort Worth on April 26, 1887. Soon afterward Frank and his family moved to El Paso where two more daughters were born in 1889 and 1891. The McLean family moved to Chicago in the early 1890s. His wife, Elsie Belle McLean, died there on March 8, 1895. With four young daughters to raise, Frank McLean began looking for a new wife. The one he found was named Anna Gribbin and they were married in Chicago on June 2, 1896. The bride was thirty-one and the groom was forty-two. Michael Francis McLean died on May 11, 1902, at the age of forty-eight. At the time of his death he was living at 833 Wilson Avenue in Chicago. A sporting man to the end, his occupation was given as "manager, club rooms" on his death certificate. He was buried on May 14, 1902, at Rose Hill Cemetery in Chicago.

Nat Kramer was a famous sporting man who, unlike Luke Short, never felt the need to carry a gun. Kramer died of a heart attack on August 8, 1905, while seated on the front porch of his home on East Fifth Street in Fort Worth. He was sixty-eight years old. At the time of his death, a Fort Worth newspaper reported that "he was widely known in this city as a philanthropist and one who gave large donations to charity. He maintained at his own expense a burial plot in Oakwood Cemetery where he buried indigent persons." Nat Kramer's final resting place wasn't in Fort Worth, but in Louisville, Kentucky.

Frederick Dilley Glidden was born on November 19, 1908, in Kewanee, Illinois. Glidden won fame writing western novels using the pseudonym "Luke Short." He died on August 18, 1975.

Hetty Brumley Short, Luke's mother, died in San Angelo, Texas, on November 30, 1908, at the age of eighty-five. She had survived her most famous child by more than fifteen years.

Jacob Christopher "Jake" Johnson had been one of the most important people—if not the most important—in Luke Short's life. When Jake died of Bright's Disease on August 29, 1909, the *Fort Worth Star-Telegram* offered this remembrance:

> Jake Johnson, one of the best known old timers of Fort Worth, died after many months' illness at his home, 1520 Hemphill street, Sunday morning. The funeral took place from the family residence Monday morning with interment at Oakwood Cemetery.
>
> Jake Johnson was born in Gonzales county 58 years ago, but came to Fort Worth when quite a young man, starting out in business here as a clerk in a clothing store. In the early nineties he built the finest residence then on the south side and lived in it up to his death. The beautiful location and grounds still attract much attention.
>
> He is survived by a widow and six children: Mrs. H. G. Wilson of Denver; Mrs. George L. McKinstry of Sherman; Miss Mary Johnson and Messrs. Robert, Stuart and Jake Johnson Jr. of Fort Worth.
>
> Jake Johnson was a man noted as a man who never failed to respond to the need of a fellow man in distress and whenever there was a case of some poor human derelict presented to him with a request for financial assistance Jake Johnson never hesitated to distribute liberally.[12]

Young P. Short, Luke's older brother, died at the age of sixty-two in Lawton, Oklahoma, on December 29, 1914. He had married a woman known only as "Etta," with whom he had five children.

Henry Jenkins Short, Luke's youngest brother, died at the age of fifty-seven in Tom Green County, Texas, on February 4, 1917. He had married Della Bouldin (1877-1964), with whom he had two sons.

William Frederick Petillon, one of the Dodge City Peace Commissioners, died in Richmond, California, on October 22, 1917. He was a seventy-one-year-old widower who was survived by his five children.

John L. Sullivan died in Abington, Massachusetts, on February 2, 1918 at the age of fifty-nine. Jake Kilrain served as a pallbearer at Sullivan's funeral.

John Pleasant Short, Luke's oldest brother, died in Gleeson, Cochise County, Arizona, on April 16, 1919. He had married Louisiana "Lou" Brown (1854-1940), with whom he had nine children.

Charles Edward "Parson" Davies died in Bedford County, Virginia, on June 27, 1920, at the age of sixty-eight. His friend Bat Masterson wrote in his *New York Morning Telegraph* column of July 4, 1920: "Parson Davies was the best-known sportsman in the Western Hemisphere. . . . No better pal ever lived than Parson Davies."

Bat Masterson died on October 25, 1921. He was sixty-seven and was seated at his desk at the *New York Morning Telegraph* when he suffered a massive heart attack.

George T. Hinkel, the sheriff of Ford County during the "Dodge City War," died in Fort Lauderdale, Florida, on July 28, 1922. He was seventy-five.

Lawrence Edward "Larry" Deger died on May 16, 1924, at the age of seventy-nine in Houston, Texas. Forty-one years earlier, during the "Dodge City War," Deger weighed more than twice as much as Luke Short—yet he ended up living more than twice as long.

Cornelius N. "Neil" Brown, one of the Dodge City Peace Commissioners, died on March 18, 1926, at Chandler, Oklahoma. Brown died three days before what would have been his eighty-second birthday.

Wyatt Earp died on January 13, 1929, in Los Angeles from cancer. He was eighty years old. He was the last person in the Dodge City Peace Commission photograph to die.

Martha Frances (Short) Mitchell, Luke's older sister, died on August 16, 1929, in San Angelo, Texas, at the age of eighty-two. She had married Benjamin Mitchell with whom she had four children.

Mary Catherine (Short) Parish, Luke's younger sister, died on February 20, 1933, in Greenwood, Texas, at the age of seventy-seven. She had married James M. Parish (1851-1901) with whom she had six children.

George Washington Short, Luke's younger brother, died in Kendall County, Texas, on October 30, 1935, at the age of seventy-five. He had married Sarah Jane Davis (1873-1948) with whom he had six children.

Charles Abram Conkling, the photographer who took the famous "Dodge City Peace Commission" photograph died in Hutchinson, Kansas, on July 31, 1936. He was eighty years old.

Belle Nannie (Short) Patton, Luke's youngest sister, died in Tom Green County, Texas, on October 20, 1947, at the age of eighty-three. She had married Walter Davis Patton (1858-1942) in 1888 with whom she had six children.

Luke's youngest sister had survived into the dawn of the broadcast television era. While there weren't many TV sets, or programs, when she died, that would change in the decade that followed.[13] By the end of the 1950s westerns dominated television programming. Two of the most popular western programs were *The Life and Legend of Wyatt Earp* and a series called *Bat Masterson.* The Earp and Masterson portrayed in these program had little, if anything, in common with the Earp and Masterson who posed with Luke on June 10, 1883, for the Dodge City Peace Commission image. The real Earp and Masterson were already well known to students of Wild West history, but it was television that granted them a much wider "household word" status that endures to this day—even if that status was the result of totally fictional television scripts.

Luke Short inspired no movie or television westerns. Occasionally he might be featured as a supporting character, as he was in an episode of *Bat Masterson*, but not much beyond that.[14] In real life Luke Short had been the reason that the Dodge City Peace Commission photograph was made, but as television turned the focus on Wyatt Earp and Bat Masterson, Luke receded into the background of the historic photograph he inspired.

Despite standing directly behind Wyatt Earp in the Peace Commission photo, Short and Earp would never have the enduring friendship that Luke and Bat Masterson had. Luke's association with Earp came down to Short's brief time in Tombstone, and Wyatt's coming to his aid during the 1883 "Dodge City War." There is no record of Earp and Short getting together after 1883—while Luke would frequently be in Bat Masterson's company, in several states, between 1883 and his death.

Bat and Luke were remarkably similar. Both had come from large families, but as adults neither of them saw much of their siblings. Both had fought Indians in their youth. Both married when they were in their thirties, but neither of them had children. They were both gamblers whose gaming interests went far beyond the green cloth games played in club rooms. Both loved boxing and both would be involved with it until they died. Both were in good shape financially at the time of their deaths, and left enough of an estate for their widows to live in comfort.

For all their similarities there were obvious differences. Luke had been a cowboy who had participated in trail drives to the Kansas railheads. Bat had never worked as a cowboy, and never exhibited any desire to do so. Bat had been a lawman, off and on, from 1877 until 1909.[15] Luke Short wouldn't have been caught dead wearing a badge of any kind. Bat Masterson was a Canadian by birth who had no allegiance to any particular state until the final period of his life when, as a New York City resident he described himself as a "Broadway Guy" —which indeed he was. Luke Short was born in Arkansas and died in Kansas, but always regarded himself as a Texan. In every city or town that he traveled in across the United States the local newspaper would invariably describe him as "Luke Short of Fort Worth."

Both Bat Masterson and Luke Short are remembered as gunfighters. Each had indeed killed men, but even their combined tally was modest when compared to those of such homicidal maniacs as John Wesley Hardin and Bill Longley. The last thing Luke Short would have wanted was to be lumped in with the likes of Hardin and Longley. Luke had been a cowboy, a dispatch rider during the Indian wars, a gambler who ran saloons and club rooms where the dealers worked for him, a prize-fight promoter, and a "turfman" who ran his thoroughbred race horses across the country.

He was, from all accounts, a modest and quiet individual, until provoked. Calling him a "gunfighter" would certainly have provoked him, since that was not the way he saw himself. In his mind he was simply "Luke Short of Fort Worth" —a sporting man of the Wild West.

Appendix A

From the *National Police Gazette*, Saturday, July 21, 1883. This article was illustrated with an engraving of the now famous "Dodge City Peace Commission" image.

Dodge City's Sensation

The Luke Short affair in Dodge City, Kansas, has created much excitement in that section of the country. The main factor in the affair was Luke Short, a Texan [*sic*], well known as one of the most fearless men in the Lone Star State. He fought a duel some years ago at Tombstone, Arizona, with one Storms, the fighter of the "Slopers," who had been imported to kill him.[1] Storms himself, however, was killed in the duel, and Short became the "cock of the walk." His recent troubles in Dodge City grew out of a shooting scrape, in which no one was hurt. He gave bonds in $2,000 for his appearance and was released, but was rearrested on the following day and ordered by an armed mob to leave the city. Attorneys who came to defend him were prohibited by the authorities from stepping off the train.[2]

Thus matters were looking very blue for our friend, when a number of his friends from different sections—chiefly sheriffs and marshals[3]—came to Dodge city to dictate the terms of a treaty on the basis of Luke Short's return to his place of business in Dodge city without danger of future molestation. After some trouble the "peace commissioners," as they have been termed, accomplished the object of their mission, and quiet once more reigns where for several weeks war and rumors of war were the all absorbing topic.

All the members of the commission, whose portraits we publish in a group, are frontiersmen of tried capacity. The following is a brief but eloquent sketch of each of them, reported as sent to us by Henry E. Gryden, the able Dodge City reporter of the Associated Press, and an occasional correspondent of the POLICE GAZETTE.

"Bat Masterson, of whom so much has been written, arrived from the West prepared for any emergency and with a shotgun under his arm, on the next train after Short returned. His record of having killed 26 men and being 27 years of age, is rather exaggerated.[4] He has been sheriff of Ford County, in which Dodge city is located, and has occupied positions as marshal of a number of rough border towns. All of his killings were done in the discharge of his official duties, and he has never been tried for an offense.

"Wyatt Earp, of California, is the celebrity, who about two years ago went on the warpath at Tombstone, Arizona, against a mob of desperadoes who had assassinated his brother, Morgan Earp. In the terrible encounter which ensued he killed not less than eight of the assassins. Wyatt has been Marshal of Dodge city, Kan., and Tombstone, Ariz., and other frontier towns.

"M. F. McLean has an Arizona and Rio Grande record for wiping out Mexican ruffians, and came from Lower California to see that his friend Luke Short could 'stay in town' to attend to his business. He is cool and clear-headed. The great ability which he displayed in managing a fight has obtained for him the sobriquet of 'The General.'[5]

"Charles Bassett was the first sheriff of Ford county, with his headquarters at Dodge city, being twice elected to that office, and succeeded by Bat Masterson. In those days men always went armed, but he astonished the natives by taking post at the court house door when the district court was in session and disarming all persons desiring to enter. Of the small party that attended court he gathered no less than forty-two six-shooters and only killed one man.[6] He is now engaged in business in Kansas city, but came to Dodge to see if his friend Luke Short could take his regular meals without being molested.

"Neal Brown[7] was formerly marshal of Dodge city, and is a wonderful snap shot with both hands at once, with a cool and determined head in a fight. He came from his cattle ranch, forty miles south of here, to look out for Luke Short's interest.

"W. H. Harris is Short's business partner, and acted as manager of the commission.

"W. H. Petillon was secretary of the peace commission, and as such was instrumental in restoring law and order in Dodge city.

"Since their object in view was accomplished, all, with the exception of the two principals, Harris and Short, have left, and peace hovers like a white winged dove over the late turbulent city."

Appendix B

Luke Short Dictation.

This is a transcript, with annotations, of the original handwritten document. The original spelling and punctuation (or lack thereof) has been retained. The original six-page document is dated March 19, 1886, and is preserved in the Hubert Howe Bancroft Texas Dictations, Manuscript P-033, now archived in the Bancroft Library, University of California, Berkeley.

Dictation of Luke L. Short of Fort Worth Texas—taken by Geo. H. Morrison March 19 1886. Born in Arkansas in 1854[1] and left there in 1858 when 4 years of age and with his family moved into Northern Texas and was educated in Texas never going to school after 15 years of age. His father George [*sic*] W. Short[2] was a cattle raiser and cotton buyer, and raised 7 boys and three girls.[3]

In 1869 he started out for himself and engaged—in dealing in stock and speculating in stock & cotton generally up to and including 1873. In 1873 went to Kansas remaining there about a year at Coffeville[4] [*sic*] when he was there was the general condition of affairs that is to be found in frontier countries some lawlessness[.]

From there he returned to Texas and from Texas to the Black Hills in 1876. He remained there but a short time. The state of society in the Black Hills was anything but good. Horse thieves & reckless characters generally abounded.

In 1877 came from Black Hills to Ogallala Nebraska being one of the largest shipping points in the west. The condition of society at this place was in a rude state. The place being infested with a reckless class of society.[5]

In 1878 He went out with the expedition under Col. Thornburg [*sic*] in the Ute war, where Thornburg was massacred[.] [6] this expedition lasted about 6 weeks. The command of Thornburg was six companies and he joined with Col. Carleton who had 7 companies making about 13 companies [in all.] The circumstances of Mr. Short going with this expedition were as follows.

The expedition started out after the Cheyennes [*sic*] and two days after this departure the news came that the Sioux had broken out and He was urged to follow Thornburg And take the position of scout as it was known that he knew the country thoroughly. He was furnished with a fine horse and offered 15.00 per day which he accepted and started out en rout[e] he met two returning soldiers who with others had been left to guard some ambulances and who had been drawn away by the Indians[.] they tried to deter him from going forward telling him awful stories about what the Indians had done etc but he was not to be frightened and continued on overtaking the command at 9 o'clock two days after he left the starting point.

Thornburg was very much delighted to see him as he was really lost his scouts not knowing the country[.] he ordered Mr Short to take a fresh horse and circle the command for signs of Indians which Short declined on the score of having been Worn out from his two days and two nights in the saddle with out rest or sleep. Thornburg said you must go you are getting $15.00 per day etc[.] in reply, Short says I don't care if I was getting $1500.00 per day I can't go to-night.[7] This seemed to please Thornburg who was his fast friend from that time to the day of his death.

In the fall of 1878 he returned to Ogallala Nebraska and in 1879 went to Leadville[.] at this time Leadville was crowded[.] he paid $25.00 a week for a place to sleep[.] There was more money in circulation at that time than the subject of these remarks ever saw before in all his travels. There was a good deal of betting & shooting[.] there were courts of law in operation yet there were men hung for jumping lots for attempting to rob somebody and for such minor offenses[.]

In 1879 There was an election for officers of Leadville and a gambler and candidate for Mayor and Mr Short saw miners peddling tickets and calling out to the voters to come and vote the gambler and miners ticket. This shows the condition of the public mind. During all this time there was no one in distress for money was generally plenty. The New York capitalists were in there with money and the Little Pittsburg[8] and other mines were turning out more carbon ore than was ever turned out of any one place of like size and under like circumstances[.]

In June 1880 [Short] left Leadville and after a short time in Kansas City Mo[9] went to Arizonia [*sic*] and located in Tombstone in November 1880. Remained in Arizona till April 1881 when he went to Dodge City remained there during the summer of 1881 2 & 3.

April 7th 1883 trouble began between Short and the (at that time) Mayor of the [town] Larry Deger who was engaged in rival business to him, in which Short was incarcerated in the jail at Dodge City, Kansas[10] and all his friends were beguiled into the jail and after being disarmed they were then told that Short must leave the city or they would kill him. This he refused to do till he began to fear that the legalized mob would burn the jail down over his head. He finally concluded to walk out of town and leave his business in the hands of his partner who was the vice president of the Bank at that place to wit W. H. Harris.

After leaving the city he consulted with the Governor G. W. Glick who advised him that no such an outrage had ever been perpetrated and advised him to return which he did. He, with Wyatt Urp [*sic*], W. B. Masterson, M. F. McLean, William Tilman [*sic*], Charles Bassett, Neil Brown & W. H. Harris and W. F. Petillon went with him and he maintained his standing against all the plans that were brought to eject him.

Later the Governor was called on for troops but knowing that Short was in the right he told them to form a possee [*sic*] and protect themselves. Finally a settlement was had and Short sent his armed posse and matters moved along harmoniously. He now has a suit against Dodge City for $20,000 growing out of this with the prospect of winning it. June 1st

1883 saw the trouble ended.[11] I will send you [Hubert Howe Bancroft] scraps of newspaper clippings by which this can be verified showing the condition of society in this new country which in a few years will contain cultural and wealthy people some of whom have taken part in the transaction here spoken of.

In the fall of 1883 Short disposed of his business and moved to San Antonio and in a short time moved to Fort Worth, and established himself in business. Has 600 head of cattle, but pays little attention to [them].

Appendix C

From the *National Police Gazette*, March 15, 1890.

A Western Scout

Luke L. Short, the Famed Indian Fighter and Sporting Man.

A History of His Life

The Police Gazette furnishes its readers an excellent portrait of Luke L. Short, well known throughout the Southwest as well as in the chief cities of the East. His career has been an exciting and varied one and a brief history of his life will prove interesting.

Luke L. Short went to Texas in 1858, when four years old, having been born Jan. 22, 1854.[1] His parents settled in Gainesville in Cooke County, then a small trading post. The country was then full of Indians —Apaches, Kiowas and Comanches, all of the most warlike character. Young Short was early inured to hardships and twice, when a mere boy, saw his father severely wounded by marauding Indians. J. W. Short, his father, purchased a large block of land lying on Elm Fork of the Trinity River, in Cooke County, and went into the cattle business. Soon after he moved to the adjoining county of Montague.

In 1867 the Indians made a terrible raid on the settlers and committed many atrocities, among which Luke relates a particular case, which deeply impressed itself on the young Texan. A family consisting of a mother and four girls was captured, and the mother and the three older girls [were] parceled out to the three tribes. The baby girl was brained in sight of a few settlers, who were intrenched [*sic*] within a stockade.

In 1862 Luke saw the first encounter with Indians, and it never left his mind. His father had gone out some distance from the house, when he was attacked by Indians. An elder brother went to the father's assistance, but found that the bullets in the pouch which [he] carried did not fit his rifle. The father had been wounded twice in the head with arrows and severely lanced in the back. When young Short reached him with the rifle and explained that the bullets did not fit, he took the rifle and told him to go to the house for the other gun. Feinting at the savages with the useless rifle, he stood them off.

Luke stood in the yard when his brother rode up and called for the other rifle. The nervy little fellow ran into the house and finding he could not lift the rifle dragged it out and got it to his brother. His father came up about this time bleeding from a number of wounds and Luke was so horrified that he started to run into the house, but seeing his mother run to his father's assistance he went also. The elder brother coming at this time, drove the pursuing Indians away.

In 1869 Luke took part in his first Indian fight, when the red skins burned houses, killed women and children and devastated the country. After this he was in over thirty Indian engagements and became noted as a splendid shot, cool and nervy man, and brave to a fault. From 1869 to 1875 Luke was engaged in the cattle business and made several drives to Kansas, which in those days, was quite a desperate undertaking, both Indians and cowboys being pretty wild.

In 1875 Mr. Short left Texas and in 1876 went to the Black Hills, at which time the gold fever was at its height. From 1875 to 1877 he was delivering cattle to the Sioux on contract. In 1878 the Northern Cheyennes broke loose from Fort Reno in the Indian Territory, and passing back to Dakota they murdered many people in Kansas on their Way. Col. Thornberg [*sic*] was in command of a force of five hundred men in pursuit of the Cheyennes, when word was received at Gen. Crook's headquarters, at Omaha, from the Rosebud Agency, that the Sioux were coming down 7,000 strong from the North on Thornberg, and that he would be massacred.

This news was telegraphed to Ogallala and the commander there instructed to send a courier to Thornberg at once with dispatches notifying him of his danger. No one in the entire country knew the trail but Luke Short, and the United States Government made a contract with him to go to Thornberg. At 2 o'clock in the morning Luke started and at 9 o'clock the next night, after riding over 200 miles, horse and rider arrived almost dead. Luke delivered his important messages to Col. Thornberg, who had no idea of his danger, and thus saved the lives of the 500 men.

Short remained with Col. Thornberg until the last Cheyenne had been captured and carried back to the reservation. A few months later Col Thornberg and five companies of U.S. cavalry were massacred by the Utes in a canyon leading into Milk River, in Utah [*sic*]. This was in June [*sic*], 1879.[2] At the time of the massacre Luke Short was in Leadville, having gone there from Dakota.

In 1880 Short went to Tombstone, Ariz., at which place there was great excitement over wonderful silver and gold discoveries, millions of dollars being taken out of the mines. In 1881 Mr. Short moved to Dodge City, Kansas, and became part owner of the Dodge City *Democrat*.[3] From there he went to Kansas City and after living there a short time in 1884 went to Fort Worth and has resided there since that time. Mr. Short is an authority on sporting matters and a great lover of a fine horse. One of the noted sons of the famous Longfellow, who has made a fine record on many courses, bears the name of Luke Short in honor of the subject of this sketch.

Mr. Short is quiet, unassuming and bears a high reputation for integrity and fair dealing. His offer of $30,000 to Sullivan and Jackson to fight at or near Fort Worth is a bona-fide one, and he offers these distinguished pugilists the best of New York references that money is in [the] bank and that he means what he says.

Endnotes

Notes to Introduction

1. Bat Masterson, writing in *Human Life*, Vol. 5, No. 1, April 1907. References to *Human Life* are from *Famous Gunfighters of the Western Frontier* by W. B. Masterson, edited and annotated by Jack DeMattos (Monroe, Washington: Weatherford Press, 1982.)

2. A. G. Arkwright, *New York Sun*, July 25, 1897.

3. The 1880 Lyon County, Kansas Federal Census shows the Buck family. Head of household "Oscer" was identified as a 44-year-old carpenter. His wife Cyntha was forty and keeping house. Their seven children ranged in age from twenty-year-old Harvey, farming, to three-year-old Josephine. Hattie was then sixteen and gave as occupation as House Keeper. Their residence was shown as Emporia City. 210B.

4. Luke Short, quoted in the *Dallas Morning News*, September 9, 1893.

Notes to Chapter 1

1. William R. Cox, *Luke Short and His Era: A Biography of One of the Old West's Most Famous Gamblers* (Garden City, NY: Doubleday & Co., 1961), 9.

2. In the interest of full disclosure, it should be stated that one of the authors of this book, Jack DeMattos, did it twice. The first occasion was in his "Gunfighters of the Real West" series, focusing on Short. *Real West*, December, 1982, 26. The second occasion, also in 1982, happened with the publication of his annotated and illustrated edition of Bat Masterson's *Famous Gun Fighters of the Western Frontier*. The Mississippi reference appears on page 65 of that book.

3. On June 15, 1980, author DeMattos was in Tombstone, Arizona, working on a photo feature for *Real West* when he met the seventy-one-year-old man who claimed to be Luke L. Short's grandson. They spent a few hours together, during which time he related the story of his life. According to him, he was born in Tombstone on March 24, 1909. He said his father had been an Arizona Ranger, who was one of two children born to Luke L. Short and his wife. Supposedly, Luke's wife was named Marie Bimbo Berger. Unfortunately, DeMattos wasn't the only person taken in by "Luke Lamar Short II." In his 1991 book *Hell's Half Acre: The Life and Legend of a Red Light District* (page 309 note 66) Richard F. Selcer stated that "Luke Short III, the grandson of the famous gambler, was still alive until recently. He was born Charles William Borger in Tombstone on March 24, 1909." The only thing the 1980 DeMattos meeting with "Luke Lamar Short II" and the 1991 Selcer account of "Luke Short III" – he hadn't added to his Roman numerals when first met—had in common was a birth date of March 24, 1909. There was also the similarity between Berger and Borger which finally raised the red flag that he missed back in 1980. More than thirty years after meeting "Luke Lamar Short II," DeMattos finally learned his real identity. Charles William Berger was his real name. He was, as he claimed, born on March 24, 1909—but in Baltimore, not Tombstone. His parents were John and Margaret Berger, who were in no way related to Luke L. Short. Berger died, under his own name, at the Veteran's Administration Medical Center in Tucson, on December 22, 1987. He was seventy-eight-years-old and was survived by his wife and "seven sons and seven daughters," according to the belated obituary published in the *Tombstone Epitaph* on January 15, 1988.

4. Wayne Short, *Luke Short: A Biography of One of the Old West's Most Colorful Gamblers and Gunfighters* (Tombstone, AZ: Devil's Thumb Press, 1996).

5. On page 193 note 1 of his biography Cox wrote: "The family anecdotes in this chapter were furnished me by the great grandson of Henry Short, who was Luke Short's younger brother. Henry was born in Arkansas

in 1856 [*sic*], proving that Luke was ushered into life while the family was still dwelling in Mississippi. Actually, the Shorts did not begin in Arkansas, but pushed on into Texas after pausing for the birth of Henry." There are a lot of errors contained within the brief space of three sentences. Wayne Short was the grandson, not the great grandson, of Henry Short who was born in 1859, not 1856. The Mississippi stuff is all nonsense, which Cox made worse by stating on page 193 that "it has been assumed that Luke Short was born in Arkansas. According to the family Bible, still extant, this is untrue." Not surprisingly, Cox did not offer any details on what information the "extant" Bible supposedly contained.

6. During his final five years, Luke L. Short formed a close friendship with Richard K. Fox (1846-1922), the editor and proprietor of *The National Police Gazette.* That publication ran a profile of Luke in the issue of March 15, 1890. The article that gave "A History of His Life" stated that Luke was born on January 22, 1854. This article was published while Short was still alive. The information it contained was undoubtedly provided to Fox by Luke Short himself.

7. Of interest is the fact that Luke Short, whose reputation placed him among the Wild West's top gamblers and gunfighters, was a first cousin of one of the members of the notorious Rube Burrow gang of train robbers. Hetty Brumley's brother, James C. Brumley, was the father of Marion Henderson Brumley who joined the Burrow gang in the 1880s. He never gained notoriety as did Luke Short, who probably would have shunned any association with his cousin.

8. 1850 Polk County, Arkansas Federal Census. The Short family members were identified as George W. [*sic*], 35, born in Tennessee; Hetta [*sic*], 23, born in Tennessee; Martha F., three years old, born in Arkansas, and John P., one year old, born in Arkansas. Despite some incorrect ages and spellings of proper names, there is no doubt these people are Luke's parents and siblings.

9. Short family members according to the Montague County census included Josiah, 47 and born in Tennessee; Hetty, 33 and born in Georgia

[*sic*]; Martha, 12; John P., 11; Josiah, 10; Young, eight, Luke, six; Mary, age four; and Henry, two. The birth state for Hetty was incorrect, as she was born in Tennessee. All the children were born in Arkansas.

10. 1870 Federal Census for Grayson County, Texas, shows the family members as J. W., age 57 and his wife Hetty, age 44, both born in Tennessee. The children listed were Josiah, 19; Lucy [?] 17; Luke, 16; Mary, 13; Henry, 11. These children are shown to be Arkansas born. The remaining children, George, seven; Belle, five; and William, three, were born in Texas.

11. "Luke Short Dictation—March 19, 1886." Hubert Howe Bancroft Texas Dictation—Manuscript P-033, Bancroft Library, University of California-Berkeley.

12. The words "which Luke relates" should dispel any doubts about Luke Short being the source of the information contained in the *National Police Gazette* article.

13. *National Police Gazette*, March 15, 1890.

14. "Luke Short Dictation," March 19, 1886.

15. *National Police Gazette*, March 15, 1890.

16. *Dallas Morning News*, September 9, 1893.

17. John Wesley Hardin, *The Life of John Wesley Hardin as Written by Himself*, 43. Reprint by University of Oklahoma Press, with an introduction by Robert G. McCubbin, 1961 edition.

18. *Dallas Morning News*, September 9, 1893.

19. *Chicago Inter Ocean*, September 7, 1891.

20. William Patrick Hackney was born in Van Buren County, Iowa, on December 24, 1842. He married Caroline "Callie" Vanderventer in 1868. He settled in Kansas in 1870, but moved to Winfield, Kansas, in 1874. Hackney was an attorney and served in the Kansas state legislature and as mayor of Winfield in 1887. He died in Los Angeles on July 28, 1926.

21. *Chicago Inter Ocean*, September 7, 1891.

22. "Luke Short Dictation," March 19, 1886. Colonel James A. Coffey started an Indian trading post on what became Coffeyville, Kansas, in 1869. The settlement was named Coffeyville when the railroad arrived in 1871. Incorporated in 1872, the original charter was voided and the city was reincorporated in March 1873.

Notes to Chapter 2

1. "Luke Short Dictation" March 19, 1886.

2. There is no doubt that Llewellyn had the subject of this book in mind when he made his claim in 1884. The truthfulness of his claim is another matter.

3. William Henry Harrison Llewellyn is described as a "beardless stripling" while Luke Short is portrayed as "the toughest kind of tough man." Llewellyn was born on September 9, 1851. Short was born more than two years and four months later on January 22, 1854. Llewellyn was a six-foot man weighing in the neighborhood of 200 pounds, while Short stood no more than five feet six inches and weighed in at about 140 pounds. During the Spanish-American War Llewellyn served with the Rough Riders as captain of Troop G. He died on June 11, 1927, and is buried in the Masonic Cemetery in Las Cruces, New Mexico. Further information on Llewellyn is found in Corey Recko's *Murder on the White Sands: The Disappearance of Albert and Henry Fountain* (Denton: University of North Texas Press, 2007).

4. Llewellyn continued to burnish his image by giving this story to newspapers for years. As late as May 17, 1889, a Las Cruces, New Mexico, newspaper, the *Mesilla Valley Democratic*, published a similar account in which Llewellyn was described as a "mere boy" and "a beardless boy."

5. Millard Fillmore Leech was born in Tionesta, Pennsylvania, on November 24, 1850. He married Emily A. Goslin, with whom he had six

children born between 1879 and 1892. Leech died in Boulder, Colorado, on May 1, 1904, at the age of fifty-three.

6. *New York World*, February 23, 1895. Leech supposedly explained this exploit only when Luke Short was safely dead.

7. The entire Big Springs episode is exhaustively discussed in *Sam Bass and Gang* by Rick Miller (Austin: State House Press, 1999).

8. W. B. Masterson. "Luke Short" in the "Famous Gun Fighters of the Western Frontier" series, first published in *Human Life* April 1907, Vol. 5, No. 1.

9. Masterson obviously meant the Red Cloud agency, located in northwestern Nebraska, just south of the South Dakota line.

10. "Pine Top" was slang, primarily used in southern states, to describe any cheap, illicit whiskey. It is one of the accepted nicknames for Moonshine, along with "Rot Gut" and "Red Eye." The first recorded use of the term "Pine Top" dates from 1858.

11. The *Human Life* story has been condensed for our purposes. Interestingly the story has been accepted by some writers as factual and in giving us their version have greatly expanded the tale into something which Masterson would not have recognized. Considering Bat's initial version was probably fiction, no purpose can be served here by discussing those later expanded versions by other authors.

12. "Reports of Persons and Articles Employed and Hired at Sidney Barracks, Nebraska During the Month of October, 1878," Old Military Records Division, National Archives.

13. "Luke Short Dictation," March 19, 1886.

14. On September 10, 1878, a group of Northern Cheyenne led by Little Wolf, Dull Knife, Wild Hog and Left Hand bolted from the Darlington reservation in what is now central Oklahoma. It was estimated that 345 Cheyenne escaped. Between September 30 and October 3, 1878, several

small parties of Cheyenne attacked settlers in northwest Kansas. Some forty men and boys were killed and an estimated twenty-five women and girls were raped.

15. *National Police Gazette*, March 15, 1890.

16. Short's service, or at least his salary, concluded on October 20, 1878. Dull Knife's band surrendered at Chadron Creek, Nebraska, on October 23, 1878. If Short did stick around for a few more days, there is no record of his being paid for that service.

17. Thornburgh was born on December 26, 1843, in New Market, Jefferson County, Tennessee. His life may have been short but he gained national recognition in the manner of his death. Killed by Ute Indians led by Chief Jack, after his initial burial he was reburied in Arlington National Cemetery. His wife, years later, was buried beside him. The town of Thornburgh in Keokuk County, Iowa, was named in his honor and memory.

18. *Fort Worth Gazette*, September 9, 1893.

19. Sitting Bull and his band fled to Canada during May 1877, where they remained for the next four years. Hunger finally forced them to return to the United States. On July 19, 1881, Sitting Bull and 186 of his followers surrendered at Fort Buford in present-day North Dakota. By the time of that surrender, Luke Short's service as a scout was nearly three years in his past.

Notes to Chapter 3

1. "Luke Short Dictation," March 19, 1886.

2. On May 3, 1878 the "Little Pittsburg" mine revealed massive silver lodes, starting the Colorado silver boom. Horace Tabor (1830-1899) used his partial ownership of the "Little Pittsburg" to invest in other holdings. He eventually sold his interest for one million dollars. When Luke arrived in 1879 the Leadville mines had already produced ore valued

at $11,000,000. Leadville then had 667 business establishments and the district boasted a population of 30,000 people.

3. "Luke Short Dictation," March 19, 1886.

4. *Dallas Morning News*, September 9, 1893.

5. Masterson, *Human Life*, April 1907.

6. Ibid.

7. Stewart H. Holbrook, "Little Luke Short," *American Mercury*, December 1940. Stewart Hall Holbrook (1893-1964) was a self-proclaimed "low-brow historian" and we see no reason to challenge his assessment. In the full text of Holbrook's version of the Leadville incident, Bat's 1907 "game of faro" became Holbrook's 1940 "game of stud." Bat's "bad man" suffered a bullet wound that "passed through his cheek but, luckily, did not kill him." Holbrook's Brown "was shot between the eyes." Inventing Luke Short history was a theme Holbrook would continue, *ad nauseam*, throughout his career. It continued with his ridiculous—and seemingly impossible to eradicate—observation: "They called him 'The Undertaker's Friend' because he shot 'em where it didn't show." Apparently Luke lost the friendship of at least one mortician when he decided to shoot Holbrook's "Brown" between the eyes.

8. Cox, *Luke Short and His Era*, 41-42. William R. Cox (1901-1988) was primarily a mystery and western novelist, who wrote under at least six known pseudonyms for the pulp and paperback market.

9. Denis McLoughlin, *Wild and Woolly: The Encyclopedia of the Old West*, 467. McLoughlin (1918-2002) was a well-known British illustrator. His version of the Leadville incident borrows heavily from Holbrook's 1940 account. For an unknown reason McLoughlin now identifies the victim as Isaac Brown, not satisfied with the "bad man" of Masterson, or the simple "Brown" of Holbrook and Cox. The Cox weapon, a Colt, now had become a Derringer.

10. C. W. Shores, "The Story of Jim Clark, a City Marshall [*sic*] Who Stood in With Criminals," Unidentified Denver newspaper clipping, but dated January 7, 1928, from the collection of the Western History Department, Denver Public Library. Cyrus Wells Shores was born in Lyons, Michigan, on November 11, 1844. He is noted for being the lawman who captured Al Packer, the "Colorado Cannibal." Shores served as a railroad detective, deputy U.S. marshal and as chief of police for Salt Lake City. Shores died on October 12, 1934, and is buried in Gunnison, Colorado.

11. Jim Clark was born about 1841 in Clay County, Missouri. There has been a minor controversy over his real name: Was it Clark or Cummings? Thanks to the research of Robert K. DeArment the controversy should end: he was born James Clark, but at the death of his father his mother remarried to a man named Cummings. His name of course did not change. He was alleged to have been one of Quantrill's raiders as well as a member of the notorious James-Younger gang. He turned up in Leadville during the boom and went to work as a miner. He became marshal of Telluride, Colorado, in 1887. There were already rumors that he operated on both sides of the law. The town council fired Clark and replaced him with another man. Clark did not take his dismissal well and began threatening council members. Around midnight on August 5, 1895, Clark was walking down Telluride's main street when he was shot and killed from ambush. It was rumored that a council member had ordered the assassination. See also "A Formidable Fighting Man, Jim Clark Served as Marshal of Telluride, Colorado" by Robert K. DeArment in *Wild West*, April 2014, 18-19.

12. Chaffee County, Colorado U.S. Census, enumerated June 1, 1880 by W. W. Orrick, 3.

13. "Luke Short Dictation" March 19, 1886.

14. *Kansas City Star*, October 7, 1880.

15. Ibid., October 11, 1880.

16. "Luke Short Dictation" March 19, 1886.

17. Cox, *Luke Short and His Era*, 59.

18. Schoenberger, *The Gunfighters*, 136.

19. William H. Harris was born in Reading, Pennsylvania on July 11, 1845. During the Civil War, he served in the 5th, 128th, and 195th Infantry regiments. In 1876 Harris had moved to Dodge City, where he formed a partnership with Chalk Beeson. The firm of Beeson & Harris purchased the Billiard Hall Saloon and opened it under a new name—the Saratoga Saloon. This was the first of two saloons they owned named after then popular eastern resorts. The second was the Long Branch Saloon—named after the then fashionable seaside resort of Long Branch, New Jersey—which they purchased on March 1, 1878.

20. At 5 feet 8 inches Masterson hardly towered over the 5 foot 6-inch Luke Short. For some reason, Bat's height was rarely mentioned in the hundreds, if not thousands, of newspaper items that appeared in his lifetime. In Luke's case, it was a rarity when his height wasn't mentioned. Bat and Luke were born only 56 days apart. Both were 27 years of age at the time of their first meeting in February 1881. Neither had yet achieved anything like the nationwide celebrity that each would know in just a few years.

21. *Tombstone Epitaph*, July 22, 1880.

22. http://en.wikipedia.org/wiki/Faro_(card_game)

23. *The Private Journal of George W. Parsons*, 128. Published in 1972 by the *Tombstone Epitaph*. George Whitwell Parsons was born in Washington, D.C., on August 26, 1850. He studied law but became disillusioned with it, then went to work in a bank in Los Angeles. Parsons moved to Tombstone in 1880 and remained in town until 1887. He served as one of Wyatt Earp's pall bearers in 1929. Parsons died on January 5, 1933, in Los Angeles, at the age of 82.

24. Masterson, *Human Life*, April 1907.

25. Here Bat is stretching the truth a little bit. We have only his word that he and Storms were "very close friends—as much as Short and I were." We cannot claim knowledge of how well Bat may have known Storms, but it is certain that he first met Luke Short only a matter of days before the Storms killing.

26. Masterson, *Human Life*, April 1907.

27. *Arizona Weekly Citizen* (Tucson), February 27, 1881.

28. *Leadville Democrat*, March 2, 1881.

29. *Arizona Weekly Citizen*, March 6, 1881. This was a reprint of an item that appeared in the *Tombstone Nugget* a few days earlier, exact date unknown, due to missing issues of this time period.

30. Criminal Register of Arizona: *The Territory of Arizona vs. Luke Short for Murder.* T. J. Drum for the Territory, W. J. Hunsaker for the Defendant. Papers filed from Justice's Court on May 2, 1881. "Discharged from custody of Examination for Murder. Ignored by Grand Jury."

31. *Arizona Weekly Citizen*, May 15, 1881. This was a reprint of an item from a Nevada newspaper, the *Virginia City Chronicle*, which quoted a "gentleman writing from Tucson."

32. *Rocky Mountain News* (Denver), June 12, 1887.

33. *Leadville Carbonate Chronicle*, June 20, 1887.

34. *Cincinnati Enquirer*, March 5, 1887.

35. *Leadville Daily Herald*, March 21, 1882.

36. The reference here is undoubtedly to Luke Short. The "Pueblo man" description does not necessarily mean that Short was living in Pueblo at the time of the race. He was, by his own account, a resident of Dodge City when the race took place. The most probable explanation is that Luke had gone to Pueblo to gamble at a time of year when things were quiet in Dodge. He most likely went from Pueblo, as part of a small group, to attend the race in Salida. According to the March 19, 1882, *Leadville*

Daily Herald "the men flocked by the hundreds into the streets, and with the exception of the few who came up from Pueblo, the decision was unanimous that Campbell won the race."

37. *Leadville Daily Herald*, April 27, 1882.

38. *Fort Wayne Daily News*, May 2, 1882.

Notes to Chapter 4

1. *Dodge City Times*, August 2, 1882. The "Mr. Fred Wenie" mentioned was Frederick Thomas M. Wenie (pronounced *When-ee*), who was born in New York State in 1859. The 21-year-old Wenie entered the law offices of Sutton & Colborn as a law student on April 1, 1880. He was admitted to the bar during June 1882 and became Michael W. Sutton's law partner in December 1882, following the departure of Edward F. Colborn. In 1883, Fred Wenie would became one of the two people that Luke Short actually pointed a pistol at during the bloodless "Dodge City War." On May 10, 1887, Wenie married 22-year-old Jessie Anne Clemons who was the niece of Alonzo B. Webster and the sister-in-law of Mike Sutton. Fred Wenie later moved to Kansas City and went into the insurance business. He died in Kansas City on April 15, 1914, at the age of fifty-five.

2. *Dodge City Times*, August 17, 1882. Chalkley McArtor Beeson was born in Salem, Ohio, on April 24, 1848. In 1872 he was a participant, along with such notables as William F. "Buffalo Bill" Cody and Lt. Col. George Armstrong Custer, in the celebrated "Royal Buffalo Hunt" planned by Generals Sherman and Sheridan in honor of the visiting Russian Grand Duke Alexis. He married Ida Gause on July 17, 1876. The newlyweds settled in Dodge City. Shortly after his arrival in Dodge, Beeson formed a partnership with William H. Harris. They purchased the Billiard Hall Saloon, which they renamed the Saratoga Saloon. On March 1, 1878, the firm of Beeson & Harris purchased the Long Branch Saloon. A talented musician, Beeson provided the musical entertainment, while Harris managed the gambling and liquor sales. Over the years, the firm of Beeson

& Harris became a minor conglomerate whose far flung holdings were located as far away as Tombstone, Arizona, and Las Animas, Colorado.

3. Alonzo B. Webster was born in Pembroke, Genesee County, New York in 1844. By the time the Civil War broke out, Webster was living in Michigan. He enlisted in Company M of the Michigan 7th Cavalry on June 22, 1863. He later transferred to Company C of the Michigan 1st Cavalry and was mustered out on March 10, 1866. Webster moved to Hays City, Kansas, in 1867. During July 1869, while Webster was working in the Hays City post office, two men named Joe Weiss and Samuel Strawhun attempted to attack him. Webster drew a pistol and shot and killed Weiss. Strawhun fled, only to be killed by Wild Bill Hickok, in an unrelated encounter on September 27, 1869. Webster married Amanda Jane Colborn, the sister of Edward F. Colborn, at Hays City on March 29, 1872. Webster was elected mayor of Dodge City on April 4, 1881. He had defeated James H. Kelley, who had been serving as mayor since 1877. Twelve days after being elected Webster was with his business partner, Orlando A. "Brick" Bond, in their Old House Saloon, when the sound of gunshots was heard coming from outside, in the direction of the Santa Fe tracks. One of the shooters involved in this "Battle of the Plaza" was Bat Masterson. After all the combatants had run out of ammunition, Mayor Webster came out of the Old House Saloon with a shotgun. City Marshal Fred Singer, who was also armed with a shotgun, accompanied Webster. Webster and Singer arrested Bat. At the hearing in police court that afternoon, Masterson was fined $8.00.

4. Lawrence Edward "Larry" Deger was born in Ohio on February 8, 1845. He was appointed city marshal of Dodge during the spring of 1876. The *Ellis County Star* reported on April 6, 1876, that Deger "is the big man of the town [Dodge City], weighing 307 lbs. He wears on the lapel of his coat a badge with the word 'marshal.'" Deger was reappointed city marshal in April 1877. Later that year Deger ran for sheriff of Ford County. Bat Masterson defeated Deger on November 6, 1877, by the slim

margin of three votes. Bat had received 166 votes to Deger's 163. In the 1880 U.S. Federal Census for Dodge City Deger was listed as a "laborer."

5. The first issue of the *Ford County Globe* came out on December 25, 1877. It contained so many mistakes that owners and editors Daniel M. Frost and William N. Murphy reprinted it and dated it January 1, 1878. The *Dodge City Times* began publishing on May 20, 1876. Initially it was run by the Shinn brothers, Walter and Lloyd. By August 1878 ownership of the paper had changed hands, with Nicholas B. Klaine taking control.

6. *Ford County Globe*, May 1, 1883.

7. Ibid.

8. A reference to the governor who had served Kansas from January 13, 1879, to January 8, 1883, thus his name was fresh in everyone's memory. John P. St. John (1833-1916) was born in Indiana but served in the 143rd Illinois Volunteer Infantry in the Union Army during the Civil War. In 1879 he helped created the Kansas Freedmen's Relief Association during the Great Exodus to assist former slaves in Kansas. The town of St. John, Kansas, is named after him.

9. *Ford County Globe*, May 1, 1883.

10. *Dodge City Times*, May 3, 1883.

11. *Kansas City Evening Star*, May 9, 1883. According to his death certificate John Lyman "Jack" Bridges was born in Maine on July 4, 1833. In 1869 he was living in Hays City, Kansas, and serving as a deputy U.S. marshal. On July 8, 1882, Bridges was sworn in as city marshal of Dodge. Thomas Clayton "Tom" Nixon was born in Georgia in 1837. Nixon and his wife were among the earliest settlers in the vicinity of what later became Dodge City. Celebrated as a buffalo hunter, Nixon slew 3,200 buffalo over a thirty-five-day period. After Alonzo B. Webster was elected mayor of Dodge on April 4, 1883 Clark Chipman was sworn in as Nixon's replacement. During this period, Nixon and his partner,

Orlando A. "Brick" Bond purchased the Lady Gay Saloon from James P. Masterson and Alfred J. Peacock.

12. Charles E. Bassett was born in New Bedford, Massachusetts, on October 30, 1847. He was still only 25 years old when the citizens of Ford County, Kansas, chose him as their very first sheriff on June 5, 1873. Bassett was re-elected twice, serving until January 14, 1878. After City Marshal Ed Masterson was killed on April 9, 1878, the Dodge City Council appointed Bassett as his replacement. Bassett resigned as city marshal on November 4, 1879. The city council appointed James Masterson as Bassett's replacement. For the next three years, Bassett concentrated on his gambling career in towns in Colorado, New Mexico, and Texas. By 1883 he had settled in Kansas City, where he was employed as the manager of Webster & Hughes' Marble Hall Saloon.

13. Otto Muller to Luke Short, May 5, 1883, Governor's Correspondence, Archives Division, Kansas State Historical Society, Topeka.

14. George M. Hoover to Luke Short, May 7, 1883, Ibid. George M. Hoover was born in Ontario, Canada, on August 8, 1847. His story—and the story of Dodge itself—really began on June 7, 1872, when Hoover was 24 years old. On what would become the site of Dodge City, Hoover and a fellow Canadian, John G. "Jack" MacDonald, pitched a tent saloon and opened for business. During April 1876, 28-year-old Hoover became the first elected mayor of Dodge City. By 1877 Hoover's rude tent saloon had been replaced by a wholesale liquor store located at 39 Front Street, one door east of the Long Branch Saloon. George M. Hoover represented Ford County in the Kansas state legislature, and served as chairman of the committee handling the cattle quarantine laws. During March 1883, a special session was called to halt an outbreak of hoof-and-mouth disease. Chairman Hoover used his influence to keep Dodge City open in the Texas cattle trade.

15. *Dodge City Times*, May 10, 1883. William Frederick Petillon was born in Syacuse, New York, during January 1846. He later moved to Cleveland, Ohio, where he married Henrietta Jennings on October 21,

1867. The marriage would produce seven children between 1869 and 1886. The family was living in Chicago at the time of the 1870s U.S. Federal Census. By the time of the 1880 census the family was living in Spearville, Ford County, Kansas, where Petillon worked as a barber and got heavily involved in politics as a Democrat. Petillon's initial foray into politics came on November 4, 1879, when he was elected register of deeds for Ford County. He was defeated in his bid for a second term on November 6, 1881. He was appointed clerk of the Ford County District Court (to fill a vacancy) on February 28, 1882. He went on to be elected clerk, in his own right, on November 7, 1882. He was still serving in that capacity when he decided to lend his support to Luke Short.

16. *Topeka Daily Capital*, May 11, 1883. Governor George Washington Glick was born on July 4, 1827, near Greencastle, Ohio. He moved to Atchison, Kansas, in 1859 and opened a law practice. He served in both houses of the Kansas state legislature. Glick became the ninth governor of Kansas, serving from January 8, 1883, until January 12, 1885. He was forced to give up his political career when a throat infection left him all but unable to speak. He continued his law practice as an attorney representing railroad interests. Glick became the first vice president of the Kansas State Historical Society. He died at age eighty-three on April 13, 1911, in Atchison, Kansas.

17. Petition from Luke Short to Gov. George W. Glick, May 10, 1883, Governor's Correspondence, Archives Division, Kansas State Historical Society, Topeka.

18. The proper name is variously spelled but it is properly spelled Hinkel. Francis Hinkel and Catherine Berthold were married in St. Charles County, Missouri, on November 11, 1844. The first of their four children, George T. Hinkel, was born there during November 1846. Hinkel married Annie C. (maiden name unknown) in 1879. They were both listed as residents of Dodge City in the 1880 U.S. Federal Census. They had one son, Dr. John K. Hinkel, who was born on February 9, 1885, and died on December 31, 1910. George T. Hinkel married his second wife, Nellie

Williams (1854-1953) in 1899. George and Nellie were still living in Kinsley, Kansas, as late as the 1910 census. Soon afterward, they relocated to Fort Lauderdale, Florida, where they ran a store. George T. Hinkel died in Fort Lauderdale on July 28, 1922.

19. Sheriff George T. Hinkel to Gov. George W. Glick, telegram May 11, 1883, Governor's Correspondence, Archives Division, Kansas State Historical Society, Topeka.

20. Governor Glick to Sheriff Hinkel, letter of May 12, 1883, Governor's Correspondence, Archives Division, Kansas State Historical Society, Topeka.

21. *Topeka Daily Capital*, May 12, 1883. This is a very abbreviated summary of the Short-Petillon interview, which appeared in print.

22. Citizens of Dodge City to Governor George W. Glick, May 15, 1883, Governor's Correspondence, Archives Division, Kansas State Historical Society, Topeka. The twelve citizens who signed the letter were: Neil Brown, C. M. Davison, Charles Dickerson, Daniel M. Frost, Samuel Galland, William H. Harris, Charles Heinz, James H. Kelley, Henry J. Koch, Otto Mueller, Patrick F. Sughrue, and William M. Tilghman.

23. *Kansas State Journal*, May 15, 1883.

24. *Topeka Daily Capital*, May 16, 1883.

25. Ibid., May 17, 1883.

26. *Dodge City Times*, May 17, 1883.

27. Thomas Moonlight was born in Forfarshire, Scotland, on September 30, 1833. He came to the United States as a young man and served in the Civil War as a captain in the 1st Kansas Volunteer Light Artillery. When the 11th Kansas Volunteer Infantry was formed he was promoted to lieutenant colonel and put in command of the outfit. He was brevetted brigadier general on February 13, 1865. Moonlight married Ellen Elizabeth Murray and they had seven children. From January 8, 1883, to January

22, 1885, Moonlight served as adjutant general of Kansas. Moonlight was appointed governor of the Wyoming Territory on January 5, 1887, and served until April 9, 1889. He later served as United States Minister to Bolivia from 1893 to 1897. Moonlight died in Kansas on February 7, 1899.

28. *Topeka Daily Capital*, May 18, 1883.

29. *Daily Kansas State Journal* (Topeka), May 18, 1883.

30. *Atchison Daily Globe*, May 23, 1883.

Notes to Chapter 5

1. *Topeka Daily Capital*, May 18, 1883.

2. The reference here is clearly to Bat Masterson and his participation in the so-called "Battle of the Plaza" on April 16, 1881. After all the combatants had run out of ammunition, Bat was arrested by Mayor Alonzo B. Webster and City Marshal Frederick Singer. At a hearing that afternoon in police court, Bat was fined $8. Bat and his brother, James Masterson, along with Charles Rowan and Tom O'Brien who, apparently, had also participated in the shooting, were then advised to leave Dodge City and never return.

3. *Topeka Daily Capital*, May 18, 1883.

4. Ibid.

5. Ibid.

6. One wonders how the shootists were unable to hit their target at apparently such close range. Could each have intentionally missed the mark, each intending only to frighten the other?

7. The identity of the man described as being one of Dodge City's "most respectful citizens" has not been uncovered. No details of this incident were published in the local newspapers.

8. Luke Short had not been run out of Tombstone. He remained there for several weeks after the killing of Charlie Storms.

9. John S. "Jack" McCarty died from smallpox at Neil Brown's ranch, 40 miles south of Dodge, on February 25, 1883. According to his obituary in the *Dodge City Times* of March 1, 1883, he "was regarded as the 'expert confidence man' in the fraternity of crooks." The obituary went on to say that McCarty was "well educated" but that "his genius was turned in the wrong direction. He was a man of middle age, and the greater portion of his life was spent in the wild and reckless manner of the outcast. He killed a man, it is said, in Utah and to escape the vengeance of that deed he afterwards followed the life of the rambling bee, gathering honey by seductive means from whatever frail flowers would give up their sweetness."

10. Luke was not arrested "with six other associates." The total, including Luke were six. The other five were Thomas Lane, Lon A. Hyatt, W. B. Bennett, Johnson Gallagher, and the gambler known only as "Dr. Niel."

11. The reference to Petillon's "claim of 160 acres" was not intended as a compliment. President Lincoln had signed the Homestead Act on May 27, 1862. It authorized any citizen to select any surveyed but unclaimed tract of public land up to 160 acres. After five years residence, making prescribed improvements, and paying a modest $14 filing fee, the homesteader could gain title to his 160 acres of land at a price of $1.25 an acre. Since Petillon had come to Kansas toward the end of 1878, he was still a few months away from completing the five-years residence requirement of the Homestead Act.

12. "A Plain Statement," *Topeka Daily Capital*, May 18, 1883.

13. While it is tempting to conclude that the portion of the sentence reading "the responsibility *will not rest* entirely with the Governor" was a typo—there is no way of proving it. Certainly, given the tenor of the final paragraph it is reasonable to think that the words should have read "the responsibility *will rest* entirely with the Governor." The original handwritten letter no longer exists and we have only the published version in the *Topeka Daily Capital* of May 18, 1883, to go by.

14. "A Plain Statement," *Topeka Daily Capital*, May 18, 1883.

15. Michael Westernhouse Sutton was born at Port Jervis, New York, on January 8, 1848. He enlisted in Company B of the New York Sixth Heavy Artillery Regiment on December 26, 1863. Mike gave his age as eighteen, but he was, in fact only fifteen. He saw plenty of action in the final months of the Civil War. He was mustered out of the Army of the Potomac on August 24, 1865. After the war Sutton moved to Warrensburg, Missouri, where he studied law and was admitted to the bar during March 1872. At Warrensburg, Sutton became friends with Nicholas B. Klaine, publisher of the *Warrensburg Standard*. Sutton moved to Dodge City on November 1, 1876, and was appointed county attorney for Ford County. His friend Klaine moved to Dodge City the following year. Mike had received an appointment to the Atchison, Topeka & Santa Fe Railroad's legal staff. He would augment his income working as a AT&SF attorney for the next forty years, and still held his appointment at the time of his death. Michael Sutton married Florence Estella Clemons on October 1, 1879. The groom was thirty-one and the bride was twenty. The ceremony was performed by Mike's friend Probate Judge Nicholas B. Klaine, at the Dodge City residence of the bride's uncle: Alonzo B. Webster. Sutton became a father on July 15, 1880, when his only child, Stuart C. Sutton was born. The new baby was only 23 days old when a horrible carriage accident happened, which would cause the baby to become a hopeless invalid. Riding in the carriage at the time was Mike's wife, her sister Bessie, and Mrs. Nicholas B. Klaine. The horse pulling the carriage became startled and upset the carriage, throwing all of the occupants to the ground, including the baby. None of the women suffered serious injuries, but Mike's son would need constant care for the remainder of his life.

16. *Daily Kansas State Journal*, May 23, 1883.

17. Ibid.

18. Ibid.

19. Henry F. May was a 34-year-old widower, who moved from his home in Decatur, Illinois, to establish the Dodge City Steam Flouring Mills, which opened for business on June 13, 1879. May's business was housed in a 60 by 90-foot building, containing three stories and a basement. May's business could produce 15,000 pounds of flour a day and employed four men. On October 17, 1882, Henry F. May married 21-year-old Elizabeth "Bess" Clemons, the niece of Alonzo B. Webster, and the sister-in-law of Mike Sutton. The wedding ceremony was performed at the Sutton residence.

20. *Daily Kansas State Journal*, May 23, 1883.

21. Mike Sutton resigned as county attorney on February 28, 1882. Thomas S. Jones was appointed to serve out Sutton's term.

22. *Daily Kansas State Journal*, May 23, 1883.

23. Major General Edward R. S. Canby was assassinated on April 11, 1873, during a peace talk with Modoc Indians near Tule Lake in Northern California. Captain Jack, the Modoc leader, attacked Canby, shooting him twice in the head and cutting his throat.

24. *Daily Kansas State Journal*, May 23, 1883.

Notes to Chapter 6

1. *Caldwell Journal*, May 24, 1883.

2. *Dodge City Times*, May 24, 1883.

3. *Ford County Globe*, June 5, 1883.

4. Sheriff George T. Hinkel to Governor George W. Glick, May 31, 1883, Governor's Correspondence, Archives Division, Kansas State Historical Society, Topeka.

5. *Kinsley Graphic*, June 7, 1883.

6. *Ford County Globe*, June 5, 1883.

7. *Leavenworth Times* (Kansas), June 5, 1883.

8. Masterson's letter appeared in the *Kansas State Journal*, June 9, 1883.

9. Adj. Gen. Thomas Moonlight to Sheriff George T. Hinkel, June 4, 1883, Governor's Correspondence, Archives Division, Kansas State Historical Society, Topeka.

10. *New Orleans Times-Picayune*, June 5, 1883.

11. *Kansas City Evening Star* (Missouri), June 7, 1883.

12. *Topeka Daily Commonwealth*, June 8, 1883.

13. *Atchison Daily Globe*, June 11, 1883. We can only speculate as to what "a basket of chips" referred to. Certainly it wasn't potato chips—or food of any kind. Luke Short, and those who supported him, probably took it as meaning gambling chips. Mayor Deger, and his few remaining supporters, could be forgiven if they interpreted it as meaning buffalo chips.

14. *Ford County Globe*, June 12, 1883. The "screen doors" mentioned in this account do not refer to screen doors used to keep insects out during warm weather. The reference is to a "door shield" that was not transparent, and often featured elaborate designs. Their purpose was to obscure the view from one room to another.

15. On September 8, 1883, Charles A. Conkling purchased a building on Chestnut Street in Dodge City for $275. He opened for business in that more substantial location the following month. Ford County Register of Deeds, Book D, 156.

16. The photo of the "Dodge City Peace Commission" that appears in this book has been reproduced from an original copy of one of those prints, which is in the collection of Robert G. McCubbin. On April 7, 1918, the *Fort Worth Star-Telegram* published a copy of the photo. In the brief write-up beneath the photograph it was stated "in the picture is shown the peace commission of Dodge City in June 1883. It was found last week

in an old desk in Fort Worth." Apparently, the *Fort Worth Star-Telegram* held on to the photo. More than four year later, on June 14, 1922, the paper again ran the photo with a caption that read "Do you remember way back when Dodge City, Kan., was the Western terminus of railroads and the starting point of the westward trail? That was in 1883, and the men shown in the picture above were the 'peace commission' there at that time. The picture was taken June 10, 1883."

17. *Dodge City Times*, June 14, 1883

18. Ibid., August 30, 1883. The famous photograph has been cropped and distorted and one example shows Petillon removed and an image of Bill Tilghman inserted. We could only wish that the Glick Guards had also visited the tent of Mr. Conkling for their image to be preserved.

19. Ibid., August 16, 1883.

20. *Dodge City Times*, August 23, 1883. Robert E. "Bobby" Burns was born on April 6, 1845, in Oswego, New York. He served as probate judge of Dodge City from 1880 to 1884. He later moved to Stillwater, Oklahoma, where he was elected probate judge. He lived in Stillwater until 1917 when he moved to a soldier's home in California. He died on December 13, 1918, and is buried in the Los Angeles National Cemetery.

21. *Barbour County Index* (Medicine Lodge, Kansas) September 14, 1883.

22. *Ford County Globe*, November 20, 1883.

23. *Dodge City Times*, November 22, 1883.

24. *Ford County Globe*, January 1, 1884.

Notes to Chapter 7

1. The "Panther" that supposedly dozed in Fort Worth was an animal that goes by a variety of other names, including puma, cougar, and mountain lion. "Panther City" remains a popular nickname today in Fort Worth, where the police have a panther on their badges. On September

18, 2002 a statue of a sleeping panther, twice life size at eight feet was unveiled on the lawn of the Tarrant County Administration Building in Fort Worth.

2. Fort Worth would experience phenomenal growth during the years that Short was a resident. He first checked the town out in late 1883 when he had made the decision to "get out of Dodge" on his own terms. At that time, Fort Worth had a population of roughly 7,000 people. At the time of Short's death, a decade later, the populace numbered more than 23,000. Today, Fort Worth is the fifth largest city in Texas and the sixteenth largest city in the United States.

3. *Dodge City Democrat,* May 10, 1884.

4. *Dodge City Times,* August 7, 1884.

5. *Wichita Daily Eagle,* August 27, 1884.

6. *Fort Worth Daily Gazette,* August 27, 1884. The jury that found them not guilty consisted of Howard Tully, J. Q. Sinclair, J. L. Tyler, A. Matthews, W. R. Haymaker and W. F. Lake.

7. *Dallas Daily Herald,* August 27, 1884.

8. *Galveston Daily News,* August 27, 1884.

9. *Fort Worth Daily Gazette,* September 28, 1884.

10. Some of the others included Sam Berliner and former "peace commissioner" Michael Francis "Frank" McLean. The smaller shares in the business were constantly changing hands, so it is difficult to determine who these mainly "silent" partners were on a given date.

11. *Fort Worth Daily Gazette,* December 16, 1884.

12. Ibid., December 21, 1884.

13. Ibid., January 16, 1885.

14. Michael Francis McLean was born during April 1854 in Decatur, Marion County, Indiana. He was the youngest of eight children born

to John and Anna McLean. On September 12, 1883, three months after his service as a peace commissioner, McLean married Elsie Belle Polley (1851-1895) in Lawrence, Kansas. She was a divorcee with five children, whose father, Henry M. Beverley (1826-1906) was the business partner of Robert M. Wright in Dodge City. Her first husband, wealthy cattleman Abner Hubbard Polley (1845-1932) won custody of their five children following their divorce, which was the result of Elsie's affair with Frank McLean. Her humiliated parents never spoke to Elsie again. Frank and Elsie McLean had four children together—all girls. The first was Marie Frances McLean who was born in Lawrence, Kansas, on July 18, 1884.

15. *Fort Worth Daily Gazette*, February 21, 1885.

16. Ibid., April 13, 1885.

17. Ibid., May 9, 1885.

18. Ibid., June 29, 1885.

19. Tom Bailey, "King of Cards," *New Magazine for Men*, May 1958, 13-15, 72-74.

20. Charles Coe, with Hugh Walters, *My Life as a Card Shark*, published as a paperback (supposedly) in 1903. No copy of this book is known to exist. There is also no known record showing that it ever did exist.

21. Robert K. DeArment, *Jim Courtright of Fort Worth: His Life and Legend*, 207.

22. *Lawrence Daily Herald Tribune*, August 12, 1885.

23. *Fort Worth Daily Gazette*, October 2, 1885. Interestingly, on the same date the *Dallas Morning News* printed a nearly identical item—except that it stated the payment of the note was for $4,000 rather than $1,000.

Notes to Chapter 8

1. *Fort Worth Daily Gazette*, September 2, 1885.

2. *Dallas Daily Herald*, September 15, 1885.

3. *Dallas Morning News*, November 4, 1885.

4. *Fort Worth Daily Gazette*, December 11, 1885.

5. Ibid., February 14, 1886.

6. *Dallas Morning News*, March 30, 1886.

7. *Fort Worth Daily Gazette*, June 9, 1886.

8. *Kansas City Star*, October 26, 1886.

9. *Dallas Morning News*, November 3, 1886.

10. *Fort Worth Daily Gazette*, November 12, 1886.

11. *Fort Worth Daily Gazette*, November 12, 1886. Short was participating in a harness racing event in which his horse "Tobe" would have raced at a specific gait (a trot or a pace). A two-wheel cart, called a "sulky" would have been attached to Tobe with Luke as the driver. Short most likely would have worn jockey silks.

12. *Dallas Morning News*, November 14, 1886.

13. Ibid., November 16, 1886.

14. *Dallas Daily Herald*, November 18, 1886.

15. *Dallas Morning News*, November 19, 1886.

16. *Dallas Daily Herald*, November 19, 1886.

17. *Dallas Morning News*, December 10, 1886.

18. *Dallas Daily Herald*, December 10, 1886.

Notes to Chapter 9

1. *Dallas Morning News*, January 25, 1887.

2. *Fort Worth Daily Gazette*, January 25, 1887.

3. *Dallas Morning News*, January 30, 1887.

4. *Fort Worth Daily Gazette*, February 8, 1887.

5. Richard F. Selcer, *Hell's Half Acre: The Life and Legend of a Red-Light District*, 185-86 (Fort Worth: TCU Press, 1991).

6. By 1887 Jake Johnson was fabulously wealthy, and was in the process of building the largest mansion then seen in Fort Worth. According to the *Fort Worth Daily Gazette* of January 30, 1887, Johnson "put men at work early this week on an $8,000 residence, which will crown a beautiful height southwest of the hospital."

7. The item regarding the gold watch presented to Courtright by Johnson is from the *Fort Worth Daily Gazette*, January 27, 1884. Jacob Christopher "Jake" Johnson was born on September 27, 1850, in Gonzales County, Texas. On May 8, 1879, he married Nannie Lebur (1858-1934). Nannie and Jake would have six children, three boys and three girls, between 1880 and 1898. Johnson died at his residence at 1529 Hemphill Street in Fort Worth on August 29, 1909, at the age of fifty-eight. His obituary stated that "in the early nineties he built the finest residence on the south side and lived in it up to the time of his death. *Fort Worth Star-Telegram*, August 30, 1909.

8. Much of the false information about Courtright's early years can be traced to the near-fictional writings of Father Stanley Crocchiola who authored many books and pamphlets using the pseudonym of "F. Stanley." The misinformation created by F. Stanley has been debunked by historian Robert K. DeArment. There is no record of Courtright serving either as a drummer or a soldier in the *Official Records of the War of the Rebellion*, nor is there any mention of him in other records in the National Archives. After serious research by historians attempting to verify the claims of F. Stanley one must conclude that Courtright did not serve in either army. Robert K. DeArment, *Jim Courtright of Fort Worth: His Life and Legend*. See chapter one, "The Legend and the Legend Makers," and specifically page 13 (Fort Worth: TCU Press, 2004).

9. DeArment, 114.

10. This brief summary of Courtright's career is based on Richard F. Selcer's chapter in *Fort Worth Characters* (Denton: University of North Texas Press, 2009). For a full-length biographical treatment of Courtright see also Robert K. DeArment's *Jim Courtright of Fort Worth: His Life and Legend.*

11. Tucker's statement is from the *Fort Worth Daily Gazette*, February 9, 1887. This seems like the appropriate place to dispose of one of those legends concerning Luke that can be summed up in three words: It never happened. Bat Masterson claimed, in his April 1907 *Human Life* article on Luke, that he was present at the White Elephant the night Luke killed Courtright. There is no known record of Bat being in Fort Worth that night, although he of course could have been there. Masterson didn't claim any direct involvement beyond being present. The same can't be said for Alfred Henry Lewis who wrote an article called "The King of the Gun-Players: William Barclay Masterson," for the November 1907 issue of *Human Life.* According to Lewis, Masterson "took his six-shooter and begged the privilege of sitting in Mr. Short's cell all night, fearing mob violence . . . It turned out well, however, for the would be lynchers, told by the Sheriff that Mr. Masterson and Mr. Short were together in the jail, and each with a brace of guns, virtuously resolved that the law should take its course, and went home to bed." There never was a lynch mob. Short's only visitors that night were friends, attorneys, and newspaper reporters.

12. *Fort Worth Daily Gazette*, February 9, 1887.

13. Ibid.

14. Ibid.

15. Ibid.

16. *Dallas Morning News*, February 9, 1887.

17. Henry Jenkins Short avoided trouble the rest of his life. He married Della Bouldin (1877-1964) on December 20, 1898, with whom he had two

sons. He was the grandfather of Wayne Short, who published a 1996 "biography" of Luke Short. Henry J. Short died on February 4, 1917.

18. *Fort Worth Daily Gazette*, February 17, 1887.

19. *Dallas Morning News*, February 26, 1887.

20. *Fort Worth Daily Gazette*, March 4, 1887.

Notes to Chapter 10

1. Illinois Marriages 1851-1900, Coles County Court Records, Microfilm # 1301516.

2. 1870 United States Federal Census, Ottumwa, Coffey County, Kansas.

3. 1875 Kansas State Census, Key West, Coffey County, Kansas. Hattie Buck was actually 11 years old when this census was enumerated on March 1, 1875.

4. 1880 United States Federal Census, Emporia, Lyon County, Kansas, 19.

5. 1875 Kansas State Census, Ivy, Lyon County, Kansas.

6. Kansas Marriages 1840-1935. "Lee [*sic*] Short and Hattie Buck 15 March 1887." Indexing batch #M73625-8. GS Film # 1433395. The Church of Latter Day Saints. The credit for finding this elusive document belongs to Dr. Judy Ohmer, who was the significant other of the late Michael Wayne Short, the great-grandnephew of Luke Short. While the marriage record contains errors, there is no doubt the subjects are Luke Short and Hattie Buck. The groom's father was identified as "J. W. Short," which was correct and his mother identified incorrectly as "Bumby" instead of Brumley. Hattie's father was listed only as "Buck" while her mother was identified only as "Allen." Both surnames were correct.

7. *Fort Worth Daily Gazette*, March 25, 1887.

8. *New York Sun*, July 25, 1897.

9. *Fort Worth Daily Gazette*, May 21, 1887.

10. Ibid., June 2, 1887.

11. *Kansas City Times*, June 8, 1887.

12. *Albany Evening Journal* (New York), July 26, 1887.

13. *Fort Worth Daily Gazette*, August 20, 1887.

14. Klaine also started a newspaper in Cimarron at the same time called the *New West Echo*. Klaine sold the New West Hotel in 1902 and ceased publication of his newspaper the same year. Then the New West Hotel became the Cimarron Hotel in 1947, and still retains the name. The Cimarron Hotel was added to the National Register of Historic Places in 1983. It is one of the more beautiful hotels from the Luke Short era remaining, both exterior and interior.

15. A photo of the handwritten register page from the New West Hotel can be viewed at http://en.wikipedia.org/wike/Cimarron_Hotel

Notes to Chapter 11

1. *Fort Worth Daily Gazette*, June 9, 1887.

2. *Dallas Morning News*, July 5, 1887.

3. Ibid., July 6, 1887.

4. *Fort Worth Daily Gazette*, July 14, 1887.

5. *Dallas Morning News*, August 7, 1887.

6. *Fort Worth Daily Gazette*, August 14, 1887.

7. *Dallas Morning News*, October 1, 1887. In the game of Keno, as it was played in 1887, a large globe called a "keno goose" held ninety small ivory balls that were numbered one to ninety. The game was played similar to bingo. Each player bought a card. The first player to get five numbers in a row won the money collected from the sale of the cards after the "keno goose" operator's percentage was subtracted.

8. Ibid., October 3, 1887.

9. *Fort Worth Daily Gazette*, October 5, 1887.

10. Luke's connection to the White Elephant Saloon at this point is difficult to determine. Luke and his future enemy Charles Wright were listed as "proprietors of the gambling house over the White Elephant" in the December 1, 1887, issue of the *Fort Worth Daily Gazette*. Most likely Short and Wright were independent contractors renting space in the White Elephant.

11. *Dallas Morning News*, October 11, 1887.

12. *Fort Worth Daily Gazette*, October 16, 1887.

13. *Dallas Morning News*, November 2, 1887.

14. Ibid., November 5, 1887.

15. *Fort Worth Daily Gazette*, November 11, 1887.

16. Ibid., November 15, 1887.

17. Ibid., December 1, 1887.

18. Ibid., December 2, 1887.

19. Ground had been broken for the Grand Windsor Hotel in Dallas on February 22, 1887. Certain sections had been completed when Luke and Hattie checked in, but the entire hotel was not completed until October 1, 1889.

Notes to Chapter 12

1. Case number 5757—*State of Texas v. Luke Short* "Carrying Pistol," *Reports of Case Argued and Adjusted in the Court of Appeals of Texas*, Vol. 25, Austin Term, 1888, 379-86 (Austin: Hutchings Printing House, 1888).

2. "Giant powder" is a blasting explosive similar to dynamite. It is made with sodium nitrate, nitroglycerin, sulfur and resin, and sometimes kieselguhr.

3. Most likely the detective Thomas was Henry Andrew "Heck" Thomas who had participated in the hunt for desperado Sam Bass during the 1870s. He gained national fame in the 1890s as a deputy marshal working for Judge Isaac C. Parker's court out of Fort Smith, Arkansas. At the time of Short's arrest Thomas was in charge of a business termed the Fort Worth Detective Association.

4. Joseph P. Littlejohn and Thomas P. Martin were owners of the Littlejohn & Martin Insurance Agency located at 513 Main Street in Fort Worth.

5. Since there is no paper trail that would confirm that Luke Short had paid $1000 for an interest in the White Elephant, there is only Ward's testimony to confirm the transaction. Ward goes out of his way to say that no one except he and Short knew about the transaction, raising the suspicion that Ward may have invented the story in order to legitimize Short's carrying a pistol at the White Elephant.

6. Beyond this letter, no other documentation has surfaced showing that Luke Short had ever pistol-whipped a prostitute. This letter seems to indicate that Short was drunk at the time of the alleged incident. This was the second time that an allusion was made to Short having a drinking problem. The first reference was the testimony of S. F. Maddox, who claimed that Short was "crazy drunk" at the time of his December 12, 1887, arrest.

7. This is the convoluted sentence as it appears in the transcript, suggesting that parts of the testimony were lost or garbled. The intent was to suggest that Luke and Hattie could only socialize with "gamblers and whoars" because the "respectable people" or Fort Worth would not have anything to do with them. There is also the accusation of Hattie Short being Luke's "so called wife," which suggests that she wasn't far removed from the "whoars" mentioned in the latter.

8. It is unfortunate that the date of this second letter to Luke Short is not given. The text of this second missive almost comes under the

heading of "a barking dog never bites." The second letter starts off by stating that Short is "certain to be killed" and concludes by stating that "you will get letters regular."

9. Luke had left Fort Worth for Hot Springs on March 24, 1887, and returned on May 22. He left the city again on June 1, 1887, and returned on August 19, 1887.

10. The opinion was delivered May 2, 1888. The appeal was prepared by Byron G. Johnson and N. W. Stedman for the appellant and W. L. Davidson, Assistant Attorney General for the State.

Notes to Chapter 13

1. That one quarter of those in attendance were women is from the *New York Times.* The maiden name of Mrs. Johnson was Nannie Eliner Georgianna Lebur. She was born on October 22, 1859, in Illinois. She married Jake Johnson on May 8, 1879, and they had six children together. At the time of the Futurity Stakes on Coney Island, Nannie would have been 28 and Hattie would have been 24. Nannie Johnson died in Fort Worth on July 14, 1934, at the age of seventy-four.

2. Proctor Knott had been named for Governor J. Proctor Knott (1830-1911) of Kentucky. Until 1956, the Futurity Stakes had a larger purse than the Belmont Stakes.

3. *Dallas Morning News,* September 5, 1888.

4. Ibid., September 9, 1888.

5. May was born in 1854 and died in 1918.

6. Langtry, whose birth name was Emilie Charlotte Le Breton, was born on October 13, 1853, on the Isle of Jersey. She became an internationally acclaimed actress. Due to her exceptional beauty she had a host of admirers, including the Prince of Wales. She married Edward Langtry in 1874 but that marriage ended in divorce, although she continued to use her married name. She became an American citizen in 1887 in order to

obtain that divorce. She enthralled thousands with her acting and her beauty and it was in Texas cities such as Galveston, Houston, Austin, San Antonio, and Fort Worth where she established a "Texas connection." Among other admirers was Judge Roy Bean, the self-styled "Law West of the Pecos" who may have seen her when she appeared in San Antonio. He was so smitten that he named his saloon The Jersey Lilly in her honor, although the pair never met. Langtry died on February 12, 1929. The town of Langtry, Texas is named in her honor. See C. L. Sonnichsen *Roy Bean, Law West of the Pecos* (New York: Macmillan; and repr., Albuquerque: University of New Mexico Press, 1986).

7. Short returned from the Catskills and Adirondacks in New York on August 19, 1887.

8. *Kansas City Times*, October 1, 1887.

9. As late as 1892, Luke would be listed in the city directory as the proprietor of "club rooms at 406 Main" which was the street address of the Palais Royal.

10. *Fort Worth Daily Gazette*, October 21, 1888.

11. Ibid.

12. Dr. J. P. Burts, as identified in the 1880 census record, at this time was about fifty-nine years of age. His name appears in the 1880 Tarrant County census as a physician, born in Texas, and residing in Fort Worth with his wife, three daughters, and mother-in-law. Tarrant County census, 7.

13. *Fort Worth Daily Gazette*, October 29, 1888.

14. Ibid., November 3, 1888.

15. Ibid., November 6, 1888.

16. *Dallas Morning News*, November 18, 1888. The cause of this particular row remains uncertain.

Notes to Chapter 14

1. There are two versions of how Chicago came to be called the "Second City." One states that the reference was to the new city that was built following the Great Chicago Fire of 1871. The other, more familiar version, states that the term described Chicago as the second most populous city in the United States after New York City. The status of Chicago being the "second city" in population ended during the 1960s when it was displaced by Los Angeles.

2. *Chicago Daily Tribune*, July 3, 1889.

3. Charles Edward "Parson" Davies was born in the city of Antrim, Ireland (now in Northern Ireland) on July 7, 1851. His mother died when he was seven years old. Five years later he arrived in New York with his father, Paul Davies. Father and son moved on to Chicago, where Paul became chief clerk for the Pinkerton National Detective Agency. Paul Davies died on December 25, 1867, in Chicago. Orphaned at sixteen, Davies became the ultimate in self-made men. During his career, Davies represented world champion athletes in three sports and every weight class in boxing.

4. *Chicago Daily Inter Ocean*, July 6, 1889.

5. *National Police Gazette*, July 20, 1889.

6. Ibid.

7. *Pittsburgh Dispatch*, July 9, 1889.

8. *Cleveland Plain Dealer*, July 13, 1889, citing an undated article from the *Cincinnati Enquirer*.

9. Ibid.

10. *Arkansas Gazette* (Little Rock), January 26, 1890.

11. Ibid.

Notes to Chapter 15

1. *Dallas Morning News,* October 21, 1889.

2. *Chicago Daily Inter Ocean,* December 18, 1889.

3. *Chicago Daily Tribune,* December 30, 1889.

4. *Pittsburgh Dispatch* (Pennsylvania), January 15, 1890.

5. *Dallas Morning News,* February 7, 1890.

6. Ibid., February 11, 1890.

7. *Galveston Daily News,* February 15, 1890.

8. *Dallas Morning News,* February 15, 1890.

9. *Dallas Weekly Times Herald,* February 22, 1890.

10. *Dallas Morning News,* February 23, 1890.

11. *Rochester Democrat and Chronicle* (New York) March 2, 1890. Charles Watson Mitchell was born on November 24, 1861, in Birmingham, England. He was usually billed as "Charlie" or "Charley" Mitchell. He was in Jake Kilrain's corner on July 8, 1889, when Kilrain fought Sullivan for the title. On January 25, 1894 Mitchell had a title shot of his own against the reigning champion, James L. Corbett. Mitchell was knocked out in the third round. Mitchell died on April 3, 1918.

12. *Dallas Morning News,* March 9, 1890.

13. *Dallas Morning News,* March 16, 1890. William A. Muldoon is considered to be America's first wrestling champion. Born on May 25, 1852, he was the son of Irish immigrants. He served in the Civil War as a drummer boy; later he volunteered for France in the 1870-1871 Franco-Prussian War. Between 1876 and 1881 he served in the New York City Police department. In 1889 Muldoon trained John L. Sullivan for his celebrated 75-round fight against Jake Kilrain. In 1921 he was appointed Chairman of the New York State Athletic Commission. During the same

year he served as one of Bat Masterson's honorary pall bearers, along with Tex Rickard, Damon Runyon and seven others. Muldoon died on June 3, 1933 at the age of eighty-one.

14. *Fort Worth Daily Gazette*, April 2, 1890.

15. *Dallas Morning News*, April 4, 1890.

16. Ibid., April 13, 1890.

17. *Anaconda Standard* (Montana), May 3, 1890. It is not known if Luke Short bought a yearling at the Belle Meade sale, but in less than a year he would have horses racing on tracks in Chicago and New York.

18. *Louisville Courier-Journal* (Kentucky) December 30, 1890.

19. *Fort Worth Daily Gazette*, May 12, 1890.

20. *Dallas Morning News*, May 21, 1890. Billy Madden was born on December 10, 1852 in London, England. He had fought as a welterweight, but is best remembered as a boxing manager. He was credited with discovering John L. Sullivan, whom he managed. During his career he would also manage Charlie Mitchell, Jake Kilrain, and Joe McAuliffe among several others. Madden died on February 22, 1918, at White Plains, New York.

21. *Fort Worth Daily Gazette*, June 2, 1890.

22. *Dallas Morning News*, June 3, 1890.

23. *New York Evening World*, June 6, 1890.

24. *Dallas Morning News*, June 6, 1890.

25. *Daily Saratogian* (Saratoga Springs, New York), June 17, 1890. The 1890 Saratoga Springs City Directory listed Edwin M. Lawrence as a "boarder" at 150 Church Street in a home owned by his mother Caroline W. Lawrence, "widow of Henry." Three other Lawrence women, Edwin's sisters Emma, Lena, and Marian, were also listed as "boarders."

Obviously Hattie had no shortage of women to talk to during her stay at 150 Church Street.

26. *Dallas Morning News*, July 6, 1890.

27. *National Police Gazette*, July 26, 1890.

28. *Dallas Morning News*, August 31, 1890.

29. Ibid., September 1, 1890.

30. *Fort Worth Daily Gazette*, September 8, 1890. John Edward Kelly (1862-1895) was an Irish-born champion boxer, who fought under the name of Jack Dempsey. He stood 5-foot-8-inches tall. His impressive ring career is overshadowed by the career of William Harrison "Jack" Dempsey (1895-1983), the heavyweight champion from 1919 to 1926. Patrick R. "Reddy" Gallagher (1864-1937) was briefly one of Bat Masterson's partners in the Colorado Athletic Association in Denver during April 1899. Gallagher later became a Denver sports writer. He had to dictate his column as he had never learned to read or write.

Notes to Chapter 16

1. Dr. William A. Duringer was born in September 1861 in Illinois, the son of Jacob and Sarah E. Duringer. He died February 18, 1907. Texas Death Certificate #11674. See also Richard Selcer and Kevin Foster's *Written in Blood: The History of Fort Worth's Fallen Lawmen, Vol. 1, 1861-1909.* Denton: University of North Texas Press, 2010.

2. No further information has been located on this Dr. Mullin.

3. The entire description of the shooting affray and its aftermath is from the *Fort Worth Daily Gazette*, December 24, 1890.

4. *Fort Worth Daily Gazette*, December 25, 1890.

5. *Chicago Daily Inter Ocean*, September 7, 1891.

6. *Galveston Daily News*, December 28, 1890.

7. *Hutchinson News* (Kansas), January 7, 1891.

Notes to Chapter 17

1. *Dallas Morning News*, February 1, 1891.

2. *Chicago Daily Inter Ocean*, February 15, 1891.

3. Jim Hall was an alcoholic. On August 23, 1891, he attacked his manager, Charles "Parson" Davies with a bottle in a tavern. Davies retaliated by stabbing Hall in the neck with a small knife. He missed the man's jugular by a quarter of an inch. Jim Hall recovered and continued his ring career.

4. *Galveston Daily News*, February 20, 1891. The *Brenham Weekly Banner* of February 19, 1891, had printed this item of sports news but added their opinion: "If there is no law to prohibit it such a contest the 22th Legislature could do nothing better in the time it would take them to enact one." Brenham, Texas, is the county seat of Washington County and is located some fifty miles east of Austin.

5. *Fort Worth Gazette*, May 22, 1891. The *Gazette* noted that Jake Johnson "and party" had left for Chicago the night before on the Katy. "Katy" was the popular nickname for the Missouri-Texas-Kansas Railroad.

6. *Chicago Herald*, June 3, 1891.

7. *Chicago Daily Inter Ocean*, July 9, 1891.

8. *Chicago Herald*, July 11, 1891.

9. The "Fly Story" was first reported by the *Chicago Herald* on June 3, 1891. That initial version said that the incident happened in a Fort Worth restaurant. This second telling gives the impression that the incident took place in Chicago, although it doesn't actually say so. The story was still being repeated as late as April 7, 1900, when the *Emporia Gazette* of Emporia, Kansas, stated that "some years ago Short was stopping at the Leland Hotel in Chicago. At breakfast a fly lit in his glass of milk,

whereupon he tossed the milk in the air, shot the fly out of it with his .44, caught the fluid again in the glass, drank it, and then quietly resumed his conversation with the reporter to whom he was relating how his eyesight had failed."

10. From the very beginning the honesty of the races held at Garfield Park was questioned. In 1892 the Chicago police raided Garfield Park three times. On September 6, 1892, during the final raid, James Madison Brown, Luke Short's fellow horseman and sometimes business partner, shot two police officers and was himself killed. Following this incident, Chicago's reform mayor, Hempstead Washington, ordered the Garfield Park Race Track closed. For a complete biography of Brown, see *James Madison Brown: Texas Sheriff, Texas Turfman* by Chuck Parsons (Wolfe City, Texas: Henington Publishing Co., 1993).

11. There are at least seven different photographs of Luke Short known to exist at this time. There might be others which will surface in the future. There are also numerous fakes, purporting to be of Short, that do not even have a passing resemblance to the man. William Allen Pinkerton (1846-1923) was also a close friend of Bat Masterson, and published a tribute to Bat at the time of Masterson's death in 1921.

12. Charles Edward "Ed" Short was born in Indiana in 1865. If he was indeed related to Luke Short it was as a very distant "cousin" and certainly not as a first cousin. Ed Short killed a man in Indiana but was found not guilty at his trial. He went to Kansas where he became involved in the "Stevens County War." He married Fannie Culver in Stevens County on September 25, 1887. Only five months later, on February 27, 1888, his bride committed suicide. On August 23, 1891, Deputy Marshal Ed Short was taking his prisoner, Charley Bryant, to Wichita aboard a train when Bryant managed to obtain a pistol. During the ensuing gunfight, Short and Bryant killed each other. Short's body was shipped home to his family in Osgood, Indiana.

13. *Chicago Daily Inter Ocean*, October 29, 1891.

14. William F. "Old Hoss" Hoey died June 29, 1897. An obituary appeared in the *New York Times*, June 30, 1897.

15. Here is an example of why both the reports of the *Chicago Daily Tribune* and the *Chicago Daily Inter Ocean* are discussed here, and we are fortunate that the files of both have been preserved. The *Inter Ocean* article states that "Strahorn broke his cane over Porter's head" while the *Tribune* versions stated that Porter "punished Strahorn very severely with his walking stick."

16. In the *Inter Ocean* version, William F. "Old Hoss" Hoey is confronted by Luke Short alone. The *Tribune* suggests the real threat was from the Quinn brothers, described as "belligerents," who had also brought along "reinforcements." One wonders what else the Quinn brothers needed to do to the hapless attorney and why they needed those reinforcements to do it. In the *Tribune* version, Short appears at the same "moment" as the Quinn brothers and their reinforcements. Short would have represented the most serious threat, because of his pistol, but hardly the only threat.

17. *Chicago Daily Inter Ocean*, November 1, 1891.

Notes to Chapter 18

1. *Dallas Morning News*, November 17, 1891.

2. *Fort Worth Gazette*, February 11, 1892. The original petitions for the pardon of John Wesley Hardin are archived in the Texas State Archives, Austin. Some signatures are too faded to be read while others are simply illegible.

3. *Dallas Morning News*, March 1, 1892.

4. Ibid.

5. The 1892 Fort Worth City Directory listed Luke Short as the proprietor of "club rooms, over 406 Main." The address of the Palais Royal was 406 Main Street.

6. *Galveston Daily News*, September 4, 1892.

7. *Dodge City Globe-Republican*, September 9, 1892.

8. Among them were President Chester A. Arthur; poet Emily Dickinson; "Hanging Judge" Isaac C. Parker; illustrator Howard Pyle; Alice Hathaway Lee Roosevelt, the first wife of Theodore Roosevelt; Bram Stoker, the author of *Dracula,* Ellen Wilson, the first wife of Woodrow Wilson, and Luke's close friend Jake Johnson.

9. Wayne Short, *Luke Short: A Biography of One of the Old West's Most Colorful Gamblers and Gunfighters*, 235-36.

10. Between the opening on May 1 and October 30, 1893, when it closed, the World's Columbian Exposition had an estimated 27,300,000 visitors.

11. *Denver Republican*, July 24, 1893.

12. Ibid.

13. *Wichita Daily Eagle* (Kansas), August 4, 1893.

14. *Fort Worth Gazette*, August 4, 1893.

15. Ibid., August 23, 1893.

16. Frank W. Blackman, ed., *Kansas: A Cyclopedia of State History, Embracing Events, Institutions, Industries, Counties, Cities, Towns, Prominent Persons, Etc.* (Chicago: Standard Publishing Co., 1912), 748.

17. *Geuda Springs Herald* (Kansas), September 8, 1893.

18. *Fort Worth Gazette*, September 9, 1893.

19. *Dallas Morning News*, September 9, 1893.

20. The September 8 dispatch from Fort Worth concerning the death of Luke Short's mother-in-law was published by the *Dodge City Globe-Republican* on September 22, 1893, in a somewhat belated obituary.

21. *Fort Worth Gazette*, September 11, 1893.

22. For those who may wish to visit Short's grave the location is as follows. From the cemetery office go to the second drive and turn left.

The grave is about halfway to the next drive and on the right. The grave is in Block 20, Lot 17, Space 3. Luke's parents, J. W. and Hettie, are buried in the cemetery at Ben Ficklin, a ghost town near San Angelo, Texas. Jim Courtright, Luke Short's most famous shooting victim, is also buried in Oakwood Cemetery. His grave is in Block 27, Lot 11-1/2, Space 1. His grave is about 200 feet from that of Luke Short. James A. Browning, *Violence Was No Stranger: A Guide to the Gravesites of Famous Westerners* (Short, 229) and (Courtright, 59).

Notes to Epilogue

1. John James Ingalls (1833-1909) served as a United States Senator from Kansas from March 4, 1873 until March 4, 1891. Ingalls was elected President pro tempore of the Senate in 1887. The State of Kansas donated a statue of Ingalls to the U.S. Capitol's National Statuary Hall Collection in 1905.

2. *Dallas Morning News*, February 10, 1895.

3. *Kansas City Star*, January 7, 1896.

4. 1894 *Fort Worth City Directory*, 297.

5. *Wichita Daily Eagle* (Kansas), August 19, 1897.

6. There would have been no reason for Hattie Short to resume her maiden name in Fort Worth where she had been known as the wife of Luke Short from 1887 to 1897. The "Miss Hattie Buck" in the 1901 and 1904 city directories is nothing more than a person with a similar name, it is believed.

7. As has been noted, Hattie had two sisters who both died as young women, along with her father, who died in his forties, and mother, who died in her early fifties. In addition to these four, Josephine E. Buck, the youngest of the eight Buck children, died on December 11, 1902, at the age of twenty-four. William A. Buck, Hattie's younger brother, was only thirty-nine when he died on May 4, 1911. Hattie's older brother, Harvey

Joseph Buck, was the only member of his family to reach a comparative old age, at least when measured by the standards of the Buck family. Harvey was sixty-four years old when he died on December 24, 1924.

8. *Texas Death Index*, 1903-2000, Certificate # 14712, for Hattie Short.

9. Rick Miller e-mail to DeMattos, July 17, 2012.

10. *San Antonio Daily Express*, March 28, 1900.

11. *Dallas Morning News*, February 26, 1901.

12. *Fort Worth Star-Telegram*, August 30, 1909.

13. There were less than fifty television sets in the United States when the Kraft Television Theater made its debut on May 7, 1947. Luke's sister was still living at the time of that initial broadcast.

14. *Bat Masterson* was a half-hour black and white television series that ran from October 8, 1958, until June 1, 1961. Gene Barry (1919-2009) played the title role. The series ran for three seasons. An episode called "The Pied Piper of Dodge City" (Season 2, episode 13) was broadcast on January 7, 1960, and featured actor Donald "Red" Barry (1912-1980) as Luke Short. The episode ended with Gene Barry, Don Barry, and other actors posing for the television version of the Dodge City Peace Commission photo.

15. Bat's service as a lawman began during July 1877 when he was hired to serve as Sheriff Charles E. Bassett's "Under Sheriff." Bat was elected sheriff of Ford County, Kansas, on November 6, 1877. Masterson was also appointed a Deputy United States Marshal on January 18, 1879. He later moved to Trinidad, Colorado, and became city marshal there on April 17, 1882. Bat ran for another term and was defeated by a lopsided vote of 637 to 248. Over the years But would pin on a deputy's badge for short-term assignments in various Colorado locations. After moving to New York City Bat was appointed a Deputy U.S. Marshal for the Southern District of New York by President Theodore Roosevelt. The appointment

was a sinecure, but Bat drew down his $2,000 per annum paycheck from March 28, 1905, until August 1, 1909.

Notes to Appendix 1

1. Other than this account written by Harry E. Gryden, there is no evidence that Storms had "been imported to kill" Luke Short.

2. The only attorney who was prevented from stepping off the train during the Dodge City troubles was Nelson "Net" Adams.

3. Of the eight men of the Dodge City Peace Commission only four—Masterson, Bassett, Earp and Brown—are known to have worn a badge at various times.

4. As is well-known, Bat's victims never made it to double-digits. When the Peace Commission photo was made on June 10, 1883, Bat Masterson was twenty-nine, not twenty-seven.

5. Based upon the available evidence, Michael Francis "Frank" McLean (1854-1902) was just a typical "sporting man," with little to distinguish himself from the hundreds of other Wild West gamblers of 1883. No evidence has been found for McLean "wiping out Mexican ruffians," as Harry E. Gryden claimed. The closest McLean ever got to Mexico was a brief residence in El Paso, which was several years after Gryden wrote this account. There is no evidence of his being involved in shooting scrapes in any of the places he is known to have lived (Indiana, Kansas, Texas, and finally Illinois). He seems to have been a somewhat colorless individual whose only claim to fame was being one of the men in the Dodge City Peace Commission photograph.

6. No evidence has been found that would support Gryden's claim that Bassett "killed one man."

7. Cornelius N. Brown (1844-1926) always spelled his name "Neil." Newspapers, and other records, frequently spelled it "Neal" as Gryden did in this article.

Notes to Appendix 2

1. Luke L. Short was born on January 22, 1854, in Polk County, Arkansas, not on February 19, 1854 in Laurel, Mississippi, as some previous accounts state.

2. Luke's father was Josiah Washington Short (February 2, 1812–February 8, 1890).

3. The ten children were Martha Francis Short (1847 - ?), John Pleasant Short (1848-1919), Josiah Short (1851-1935), Young P. Short (1852-1914), Luke L. Short (1854-1893), Mary Catherine Short (1856-1933), Henry Jenkins Short (1859-1917), George Washington Short (1860-1935), Belle Nannie Short (1864-1947) and William B. Short (1867-1890).

4. Col. James A. Coffey started an Indian trading post on what became Coffeyville, Kansas, in 1869. The settlement was named Coffeyville when the railroad arrived in 1871. Incorporated in 1872, the original charter was voided and the city was reincorporated in March 1873.

5. Millard Fillmore Leech (1850-1904) claimed that Luke Short was a member of this "reckless class of society." In an interview in the *New York World* (February 23, 1895), Leech claimed that he arrested Luke Short in Ogallala during July 1876. Back in Nebraska, the *Omaha World Herald* (February 25, 1895) characterized the interview as a "fairy tale by Leech."

6. Major Thomas Tipton Thornburgh was born on December 26, 1843, in New Market, Tennessee. While leading a command of cavalry to rescue settlers under attack by Utes, Major Thornburgh and thirteen of his soldiers were ambushed and massacred on September 29, 1879. This incident happened at Milk Creek, near present-day Craig, Colorado.

7. Between October 6-8, 1878, Luke Short was employed as a dispatch courier at a salary of $10 per day. Short carried dispatches from Ogallala to Major Thomas Thornburgh (1843-1879) of the Fourth Infantry, who was in the field. Short was paid $30 for his service. From October 9-20, 1878 Luke served as a civilian scout for Thornburgh. He enlisted at

Sidney, Nebraska, at a rate of $100 per month. He only got to serve for twelve days and was paid $40 for his service.

8. On May 1, 1878, the "Little Pittsburg" mine revealed massive silver lodes, starting the Colorado silver boom. Horace Tabor (1830-1899) used his partial ownership of the Little Pittsburg to invest in other holdings. He eventually sold his interest for one million dollars.

9. On October 11, 1880, Luke Short was released from jail in Kansas City, where he had been held for six days. Short was charged with trying to swindle a Texan named John Jones out of $280 in a three card *monte* game.

10. Short was placed in jail, along with five others, on April 30, 1883.

11. The trouble didn't end until June 7, 1883.

Notes to Appendix 3

1. We agree with the statement of the *National Police Gazette* that Short was born January 22, 1854, in Polk County, Arkansas. It is significant that this article was published while Short was still alive. While it never actually says so in the article, it would seem likely that the biographical information came from Luke Short himself.

2. Major Thomas Tipton Thornburgh was born on December 26, 1843, in New Market, Tennessee. While leading a command of cavalry to rescue settlers under attack by Utes, Major Thornburgh and 13 of his soldiers —not five companies—were ambushed and massacred on September 29, 1879. The incident happened at Milk Creek, near present-day Craig, Colorado.

3. This account is the only known reference that Luke Short "became part owner of the Dodge City *Democrat.*" If so, he would have had to have been the most silent of "silent partners." Short and William H. Harris sold the Long Branch on November 19, 1883. Shortly afterward, Luke and Bat Masterson went to Fort Worth. Luke returned from Fort Worth in December and went to Kansas City. On December 28, 1883,

Luke Short and Charles E. Bassett returned to Dodge City for a visit. The *Ford County Globe* of January 1, 1884, reported that the pair had "returned to the city last Friday looking well, and show that they have been kindly treated by their friends in the east. They will remain here until after the holidays." On December 29, 1883, the day after Short and Bassett arrived in Dodge, the *Dodge City Democrat* published its very first issue. Initially William Frederick Petillon served as a company director and business manager of the paper. Petillon soon became editor of the *Democrat*, serving in that capacity until 1905.

Bibliography

Books

Cox, William R. *Luke Short and His Era: A Biography of One of the Old West's Most Famous Gamblers.* Garden City, NY: Doubleday & Company, 1961.

Cunningham, Eugene. *Triggernometry: A Gallery of Gunfighters.* Caldwell, ID: The Caxton Printers, 1941.

DeArment, Robert K. *Bat Masterson: The Man and the Legend.* Norman: University of Oklahoma Press, 1979.

———. *Knights of the Green Cloth: The Saga of Frontier Gamblers.* Norman: University of Oklahoma Press, 1982.

———. *Jim Courtright of Fort Worth: His Life and Legend.* Fort Worth: Texas Christian University Press, 2004.

DeMattos, Jack. *Mysterious Gunfighter: The Story of Dave Mather.* College Station, TX: Creative Publishing Company, 1992.

Dodge, Fred. *Under Cover for Wells Fargo: The Unvarnished Recollections of Fred Dodge.* Edited by Carolyn Lake. Boston: Houghton Mifflin Company, 1969.

Dunn, Mark T. *Chicago's Greatest Sportsman: Charles E. "Parson" Davies.* Create Space Independent Publisher. An Amazon Company, 2011.

Dykstra, Robert R. *The Cattle Towns: A Social History of the Kansas Cattle Trading Centers, 1867 to 1885.* New York: Alfred A. Knopf, 1971.

Faulk, Odie B. *Dodge City: The Most Western Town of All.* New York: Oxford University Press, 1977.

———. *Tombstone: Myth and Reality.* New York: Oxford University Press, 1972.

Griffith, T. D. *Outlaw Tales of Nebraska.* Guilford, CT: Globe Pequot Press, 2010.

Haywood, C. Robert. *Cowtown Lawyers: Dodge City and Its Attorneys, 1876-1886.* Norman: University of Oklahoma Press, 1988.

———. *Merchant Prince of Dodge City: The Life and Times of Robert M. Wright.* Norman: University of Oklahoma Press, 1998.

Hutton, Harold. *Doc Middleton: Life and Legends of the Notorious Plains Outlaw.* Chicago: The Swallow Press, 1974.

Knight, Oliver. *Fort Worth: Outpost on the Trinity.* Norman: University of Oklahoma Press, 1953.

Lake, Stuart N. *Wyatt Earp: Frontier Marshal.* Boston: Houghton Mifflin Company, 1931.

Lamar, Howard R., ed. *The Reader's Encyclopedia of the American West.* New York: Thomas Y. Crowell Company, 1977.

Masterson, W. B. (Bat). *Famous Gun Fighters of the Western Frontier.* Annotated and illustrated by Jack DeMattos. Monroe, WA: Weatherford Press, 1982.

Miller, Nyle H., and Joseph W. Snell. *Why the West Was Wild.* Topeka: Kansas State Historical Society, 1963.

O'Connor, Richard. *Bat Masterson: The Biography of One of the West's Most Famous Gunfighters and Marshals.* Garden City, NY: Doubleday & Company, Inc., 1957.

Parsons, Chuck. *James Madison Brown: Texas Sheriff, Texas Turfman.* Wolfe City, TX: Henington Publishing Co., 1993.

Parsons, George W. *The Private Journal of George W. Parsons.* Tombstone, AZ: Tombstone Epitaph, 1972.

Roberts, Gary L. *Doc Holliday: The Life and Legend.* Hoboken, NJ: John Wiley & Sons, 2006.

Rosa, Joseph G. *The Gunfighter: Man or Myth?* Norman: University of Oklahoma Press, 1969.

———. *Age of the Gunfighter.* London: Salamander Books Limited, 1993.

———, and Waldo E. Koop. *Rowdy Joe Lowe: Gambler with a Gun.* Norman: University of Oklahoma Press, 1989.

Schoenberger, Dale T. *The Gunfighters.* Caldwell, ID: The Caxton Printers, Ltd., 1976.

Selcer, Richard F. *Hell's Half Acre: The Life and Legend of a Red Light District.* Fort Worth: Texas Christian University Press, 1991.

———. *Fort Worth Characters.* Denton: University of North Texas Press, 2009.

———, ed. *Legendary Watering Holes: The Saloons That Made Texas Famous.* College Station: Texas A&M University Press, 2004.

Shillingberg, William B. *Tombstone, A.T., a History of Early Mining, Milling and Mayhem.* Spokane: The Arthur H. Clark Company, 1999.

———. *Dodge City: The Early Years, 1872-1886.* Norman, OK: The Arthur H. Clark Company, 2009.

Short, Wayne. *Luke Short: A Biography of One of the Old West's Most Colorful Gamblers and Gunfighters.* Tombstone, AZ: Devil's Thumb Press, 1996.

Sprague, Marshall. *Massacre: The Tragedy at White River.* Boston: Little, Brown and Company, 1957.

Tefertiller, Casey. *Wyatt Earp: The Life Behind the Legend.* New York: John Wiley & Sons, 1997.

Vestal, Stanley. *Dodge City: Queen of the Cowtowns.* New York: Harper & Brothers, 1952.

Wright, Robert M. *Dodge City: The Cowboy Capital.* Wichita, KS: Wichita Eagle Press, 1913.

Young, Fredric R. *Dodge City: Up Through a Century in Story and Pictures.* Dodge City, KS: Boot Hill Museum, 1972

———. *The Delectable Burg: An Irreverent History of Dodge City—1872 to 1886.* Newton, KS: Mennonite Press, 2009

Articles

Cox, William R. "Backgrounds of Famous Western Badmen: Luke Short." *True West Magazine.* October 1961.

DeArment, R. K. "A Formidable Fighting Man, Jim Clark Served as Marshal of Telluride, Colorado." *Wild West Magazine* 26, no. 6 (April 2014).

DeMattos, Jack. "Gunfighters of the Real West: Luke Short." *Real West Magazine*, No. 188, December 1982.

———. "The Dodge City Peace Commission Revealed." *Wild West History Association Journal* 6, no. 2 (April 2013).

Holbrook, Stewart H. "Luke Short, He-Man, Expert at Dodging Bullets." *The Portland Oregonian*, November 13, 1932.

———. "Little Luke Short." *The American Mercury Magazine*, December 1940.

Masterson, W. B. (Bat). "Famous Gun Fighters of the Western Frontier: Luke Short." *Human Life Magazine* 5, no. 1 (April 1907).

Palmquist, Bob. "'Snuffing Out a Gambler'—Short vs. Storms." *Wild West Magazine*, October 2004.

Ryall, William. "The Luck of Luke." *True Western Adventures Magazine*, April 1960.

Short, Wayne. "Luke Short in Fort Worth." NOLA *Quarterly* 22, no. 1 (January-March 1998).

Wagner, Lewis. "Jack L. Bridges—Kansas Lawman." NOLA *Quarterly* 29, no. 3 (July-September 2005).

Walker, Wayne T. "Killer in Fancy Pants." *True West Magazine*, October 1956.

Newspapers

Albany (New York) Evening Journal: July 26, 1887

Anaconda (Montana) Standard: May 3, 1890, Sept. 23, 1893

Atchison (Kansas) Daily Globe: June 5 and 11, 1883

Austin Weekly Statesman: May 3 and 10, 1888

Caldwell (Kansas) Journal: May 24, 1883

Castle Rock (Colorado) Journal: May 3, 1882

Chicago Daily Tribune: July 3, 1889, Dec. 30, 1889, Oct. 29, 1891, Sept. 9, 1893

Chicago Daily Inter Ocean: July 6, 1889, Dec. 17, 1889, Feb. 15, 1891, June 9, 1891, Sept. 7, 1891, Oct. 29, 1891, Nov. 1, 1891, Sept. 10, 1893

Chicago Herald: June 3, 1891, July 11, 1891

Cincinnati Enquirer: March 5, 1887

Cleveland Plain Dealer: July 13, 1889

Dallas Daily Herald: Aug. 27, 1884, Sept. 15, 1885, Nov. 18 and 19, 1886, Dec. 10, 1886

Dallas Morning News: Feb. 11, 1886, March 30, 1886, Aug. 8, 1886, Sept. 8, 1886, Nov. 3, 14, 16, 17 and 19, 1886, Dec. 10 and 31, 1886, Jan. 25 and 30, 1887, Feb. 8, 10, 13, 17, and 26, 1887, March 2, 1887, July 5, 6, and 10, 1887, Aug. 7 and 20, 1887, Sept. 2, 4, 6, 7, and 25, 1887, Sept. 2, 4, 6, 7, and 25, 1887, Oct. 1, 3, and 12, 1887, Nov. 2 and 5, 1887, Dec. 3, 1887, Jan. 6, 1888, March 8, 1888, April 22, 1888, May 5, 1888, Sept. 5, 1888, Oct. 29, 1888, Nov. 18, 1888, Feb. 7, 11, 15 and 23, 1890, March 9 and 16, 1890, April 4, 8 and 13, 1890, May 21, 1890, June 3, 10, 11 and 13, 1890, July 6, 1890, Aug. 31, 1890, Sept. 1 and 18, 1890, Dec. 24, 25 and 28, 1890, Jan. 14 and 27, 1891, Feb. 1 and 5, 1891, Nov. 17, 1891, March 2, 1892, Sept. 9, 1893, Feb. 10, 1895

Dallas Weekly Times Herald: Feb. 22, 1890, July 5, 1890

Denver Republican: July 24, 1893

Denver Rocky Mountain News: June 12, 1887

Denver Times: May 16, 1883

Dodge City Democrat: Dec. 29, 1883, May 10, 1884

Dodge City Ford County Globe: Feb. 6, 1883, May 1 and 22, 1883, June 5 and 12, 1883, Nov. 20, 1883, Jan. 1, 1884

Dodge City Globe-Republican: Sept. 9, 1892

Dodge City Times: August 3, 1882, March 1, 1883, May 3, 10, 17 and 24, 1883, June 14, 1883, Aug. 16 and 23, 1883, Nov. 22, 1883, March 20, 1884, June 5, 1884, Aug. 7, 1884

Emporia (Kansas) Gazette: April 7, 1900

Emporia (Kansas) Weekly News: June 14, 1883

Fort Wayne Daily News: May 2, 1882

Fort Worth Daily Gazette: Jan. 27, 1884, Sept. 28, 1884, Oct. 9, 1884, Dec. 16, 1884, Dec. 21, 1884, Jan. 16, 1885, Feb. 21, 1885, April 13, 1885, May 9, 1885, June 29, 1885, Aug. 29, 1885, Sept. 2, 1885, Oct. 2, 1885, Nov. 4, 1885, Dec. 11, 1885, Feb. 14, 1886, May 15, 1886, June 9, 1886, Oct. 30, 1886, Nov. 11 and 12, 1886, Jan. 25 and 30, 1887, Feb. 9, 10, 17, 25 and 27, 1887, March 4 and 25, 1887, April 29, 1887, May 21, 1887, June 2 and 9, 1887, July 14, 1887, Aug. 14 and 20, 1887, Oct. 16, 1887, Nov. 11 and 15, 1887, Dec. 1 and 2, 1887, Jan. 3, 1888, Oct. 21 and 29, 1888, Nov. 3 and 6, 1888, Jan. 3 and 5, 1889, July 3, 1889, Aug. 17, 1889, Sept. 12, 1889, April 2, 1890, May 12 and 22, 1890, June 2, 3, 8 and 10, 1890, Aug. 1, 1890, Sept. 8, 1890, Nov. 7, 1890, Dec. 24 and 25, 1890

Fort Worth Gazette: May 22, 1891, June 30, 1891, July 21, 1891, Oct. 27, 1891, Nov. 4, 17 and 23, 1891, Dec. 1, 1891, March 2, 1892, Aug. 4 and 23, 1893, Sept. 11 and 15, 1893

Fort Worth Star-Telegram: Aug. 9, 1905, Aug. 30, 1909

Galveston Daily News: May 3, 1888, Dec. 18, 1889, Dec. 28, 1890, Feb. 20, 1891, Sept. 4, 1892

Geuda Springs (Kansas) Herald: Sept. 8, 1893

Hutchison (Kansas) News: Jan. 7, 1891

Idaho Falls (Idaho) Times: Nov. 26, 1891

Kansas City Evening Star: May 9, 1883, June 7, 1883

Kansas City Journal: May 15, 1883

Kansas City Star: Oct. 5, 7 and 11, 1880, Nov. 24, 1880, Oct. 26, 1886

Kansas City Times: June 8, 1887, Oct. 1, 1887

Kinsley (Kansas) Graphic: June 7, 1883

Las Cruces (New Mexico) Mesilla Valley Democrat: May 17, 1889

Lawrence (Kansas) Daily Herald Tribune: Aug. 12, 1885

Lawrence (Kansas) Journal World: Aug. 8, 1884

Lawrence (Kansas) Western Recorder: Nov. 30, 1883

Leadville (Colorado) Carbonate Chronicle: June 20, 1887

Leadville (Colorado) Daily Herald: March 21, 1882, April 27, 1882

Leadville (Colorado) Democrat: March 2, 1881

Leavenworth (Kansas) Times: June 5, 1883

Lima (Ohio) News: Feb. 25, 1891

Little Rock (Arkansas) Gazette: Jan. 26, 1890

Louisville (Kentucky) Courier-Journal: Dec. 30, 1890, July 17, 1892, July 26, 1893

Macon (Georgia) Telegraph: Sept. 14, 1893

Medicine Lodge (Kansas) Barbour County Index: Sept. 14, 1883

National Police Gazette: April 15, 1882, July 21, 1883, March 15, 1890, July 26, 1890

New Orleans Times-Picayune: June 5, 1883, May 29, 1890

New York Daily People: Dec. 8, 1901

New York Evening World: Jan. 13, 1890, June 6, 1890

New York Times: Dec. 25, 1890

New York World: March 25, 1894, Feb. 23, 1895

Omaha Daily Bee: Sept. 12, 1893

Omaha World Herald: Feb. 25, 1895

Pittsburgh (Pennsylvania) Dispatch: July 9, 1889, Jan. 15, 1890

Portland Oregonian: Nov. 23, 1884.

Rochester (New York) Democrat and Chronicle: March 2, 1890

Sacramento (California) Daily Record-Union: Feb. 28, 1881

San Antonio Light: April 2, 1885

San Francisco Morning Call: June 6, 1890

Saratoga Springs (New York) Daily Saratogian: June 17, 1890

Springfield Daily Illinois State Register: June 21, 1891

St. Paul (Minnesota) Daily Globe: Feb. 25, 1891

Topeka Daily Capital: May 11, 12, 16, 17 and 18, 1883

Topeka Daily Commonwealth: May 3, 4, 12, 18 and 20, 1883, June 5 and 8, 1883

Topeka Daily Kansas State Journal: May 18 and 23, 1883, June 9, 1883

Tombstone Epitaph: July 22, 1880, September 13, 1893, Jan. 15, 1988

Tucson Arizona Weekly Citizen: Feb. 27, 1881, March 6, 1881, May 15, 1881

Wichita (Kansas) Daily Eagle: August 27, 1884, August 4, 1893

Census Records

1860 United States Federal Census—Montague, Texas (August 22, 1860).

1870 United States Federal Census—Precinct 3, Grayson, Texas (November 8, 1870).

1870 United States Federal Census—Ottumwa, Coffey, Kansas (June 15, 1870).

1875 Kansas State Census—Key West, Coffey, Kansas (March 1, 1875).

1880 United States Federal Census—Buena Vista, Chaffee, Colorado (June 1, 1880).

1880 United States Federal Census—Emporia, Lyon, Kansas (June 11, 1880).

District Court Records

(Ford County, Kansas District Court)

Case No. 521 – *State of Kansas v. Luke Short*, Criminal Appearance Docket A. Ms. Box 808. Manuscript Department, Kansas State Historical Society.

(Tarrant County, Texas District Court)

Case No. 5757—*State of Texas v. Luke Short* "Carrying Pistol." Short was found guilty on January 6, 1888. Short filed an appeal. The conviction was reversed and remanded by the Texas Court of Appeals on May 2, 1888. "Luke Short v. State, 25 Tex. Ct. App. 379, 8 S.W. 281 (1888)."

Case No. 6199—*State of Texas v. Luke Short* "Assault with intent to murder" (Charles Wright). Filed on Jan. 31, 1891. Short was found guilty on March 1, 1892, and was fined $150. Short filed an appeal, which was dismissed on October 23, 1893, following Short's death.

Miscellanea

Records of the War Department, Office of the Quartermaster General. "Report of Persons and Articles Employed and Hired at Sidney Barracks, Nebraska during the Month of October, 1878." *Luke Short B5* (Oct. 6–Oct. 8, 1878) and *Luke Short B6* (Oct. 9 –Oct. 20, 1878). Old Military Division, National Archives.

"Luke Short Dictation, March 19, 1886" (6 handwritten pages) Hubert Howe Bancroft Texas Dictations, Manuscript P-033, Bancroft Library, University of California, Berkeley.

"Kansas Marriages, 1840-1935, Lee [*sic*] Short and Hattie Buck 15 March 1887."

Indexing Batch Number M73625-8. GS Film Number 1433395. Genealogical records of The Church of Latter-Day Saints.

Index